Summary Judgment and Other Preclusive Devices

Recent Titles from Quorum Books

Summary Judgment and Other Preclusive Devices

WARREN FREEDMAN

Q

QUORUM BOOKS

New York · Westport, Connecticut · London

Library of Congress Cataloging-in-Publication Data

Freedman, Warren.
Summary judgment and other preclusive devices / Warren Freedman.
p. cm.
Includes index.
ISBN 0–89930–377–3 (lib. bdg. : alk. paper)
1. Summary proceedings—United States. 2. Summary proceedings—New York (State) 3. Summary proceedings—Connecticut. I. Title.
KF8999.F74 1989
347.73′077—dc19
[347.30777] 88–37481

British Library Cataloguing in Publication Data is available.

Library of Congress Catalog Card Number: 88–37481
ISBN: 0–89930–377–3

First published in 1989 by Quorum Books

Greenwood Press, Inc.
88 Post Road West, Westport, Connecticut 06881

Printed in the United States of America

The paper used in this book complies with the Permanent Paper Standard issued by the National Information Standards Organization (Z39.48–1984).

10 9 8 7 6 5 4 3 2 1

Contents

Preface

Summary Judgment and Other Preclusive Devices may seem at first to be a slightly misleading title, but upon review it will become clear that the thrust of this book is simply how to bring litigation quietly and quickly to an end. This book delineates many of the devices that tend to preclude the need for prolonged time and effort in trying a case. As used here, the term *preclusion* is definitely not similar to the common law pleading of precludi non, which stated that the plaintiff is not barred or precluded by anything set forth in his or her pleading. In modern-day vernacular preclusion means that the party must move along and head for the destination where the dispute can be resolved.

Summary judgment is a popular preclusive device that saves time and effort. Other such devices include adjudication without trial, the accelerated judgment, the declaratory judgment, and the well-known provisional remedies of attachment, injunction, receivership, and notice of pendency. On the more procedural side are requests for admission to shorten the time span before resolution of the dispute; interpleader and intervention are procedural devices that parties frequently utilize to advance their position toward resolution of the controversy. Release-dismissal and settlement agreements have roles to play as do the preclusive doctrines of res judicata and collateral estoppel, which can stop the action "on a dime." Bifurcation is an experimental procedure to hasten the trial on both liability and on damages. The summary jury trial is a new technique, and court sanctions are available (and more popular than ever before) to see that the case does not bog down on trivialities. All in all, my conclusions are on the side of progress and are favored by bench and bar, so this useful book should prove to be a boon for one and all.

Acknowledgments

The "salt mines" where the research was performed—the Pace University School of Law in White Plains, New York, and the University of Connecticut School of Law in Hartford, Connecticut—must be accorded their due respect as the workplaces where the author received countless courtesies and generous attention.

Without the interest of my loving wife, Esther Freedman, this book might not have been completed. Her understanding and patience were essential.

As a member of the bar in the states of New York and Connecticut (I also serve as a State Trial Referee in Connecticut), I must apologize for the preponderance of New York and Connecticut decisions; but then these two states are at the forefront of the issues delineated hereinafter, with highly respected courts and judicial administration.

1

Introduction

Summary judgment and other preclusive devices are designed to shorten the time framework of litigation by curbing vexatious litigation and by promoting the expeditious resolution of disputes.[1] In brief, if one party can show that there is no "genuine issue of material fact" in the lawsuit, that party is entitled to judgment as a matter of law.[2] The prime example of the summary judgment rule is found in Rule 56(c) of the Federal Rules of Civil Procedure, which states that summary judgment shall be granted where the "pleadings, depositions, answers to interrogatories, and admissions on file, together with affidavits, if any, show that there is no genuine issue as to any material fact and that the moving party is entitled to a judgment as a matter of law." Rule 56(c) is consonant with the overall purpose of the Federal Rules of Civil Procedure "to secure the just, speedy and inexpensive determination of every action."[3] The obvious thrust here is to obviate the need for a trial where no fact issues exist, but since Rule 56 was adopted in 1938, there has not been the expected preclusive reform. U.S. District Judge William W. Schwarzer of the Northern District of California, as recently as 1984, has opined: "Summary judgment is plagued by confusion and uncertainty. It suffers from misuse by those lawyers who insist on making a motion in face of obvious fact issues; from neglect by others who, fearful of judicial hostility to the procedure, refrain from moving even where summary judgment would be appropriate; and from the failure of trial and appellate courts to define clearly what is a genuine issue of material fact."[4]

The U.S. Supreme Court has in recent years given its blessing to the summary judgment device in three significant cases, to wit: *Matsushita Electric Industrial Co. v. Zenith Radio Corp.*,[5] *Celotex Corp. v. Catrett*,[6] and *Anderson v. Liberty Lobby, Inc.*[7] In the *Matsushita* case the petitioners were 21 Japanese corporations that manufactured and/or sold consumer electronic products, and the respondents were American corporations that manufactured and/or sold television sets. The American respondents had in 1974 brought suit alleging that the Japanese corporations had for over 21 years illegally conspired to drive the American respondents from the U.S. market by engaging in a scheme to fix and maintain artificially high prices for television sets sold by petitioners in Japan, and at the same time to fix and maintain low prices for television sets exported to and sold in the United States. The federal district court, finding no conspiracy in restraint of trade, granted the Japanese petitioners' motion for summary judgment, but the Third U.S. Court of Appeals reversed, holding that a reasonable fact finder could determine that there was such a conspiracy.[8] The highest court, however, ruled that the federal appellate court did not apply proper standards in evaluating the lower court's decision to grant respondent's motion for summary judgment. To survive the Japanese petitioners' motion for a summary judgment, the American respondents must establish that there is a genuine issue of material fact as to whether petitioners entered into an illegal conspiracy that caused the American respondents to suffer a cognizable injury. If the factual context renders respondent's claims implausible—that is, if the claims make no economic sense—respondents must offer more persuasive evidence to support their claims than would otherwise be necessary. To survive a motion for a summary judgment, a plaintiff seeking damages must present evidence that "tends to exclude the possibility" that the alleged conspirators acted independently or that the inference of a conspiracy in restraint of trade is reasonable in light of the competing inferences of independent action or of collusive action that could not have harmed respondents.[9] The four dissenting opinions proclaimed that "the Court's opinion today, far from identifying reversible error, only muddies the waters. In the first place, the Court makes confusing and inconsistent statements about the appropriate standards for granting summary judgment. Second, the Court makes a number of assumptions that invade the factfinder's province. Third, the court faults the Third Circuit for nonexistent errors and remands the case although it is plain that respondent's evidence raises genuine issues of material fact."[10]

In the *Celotex* case the plaintiff alleged that her husband's death was caused by exposure to asbestos products manufactured and distributed by 15 defendant corporations. The federal district court granted the defendants' motion for summary judgment because the plaintiff had produced no evidence supporting her claim that her husband had been exposed to defendants' products.[11] The District of Columbia Court of Appeals reversed, holding that the defendant Celotex's summary judgment motion was "fatally defective" in that Celotex had attacked the sufficiency of plaintiff's evidence without making an "effort to adduce any evidence, in the form of affidavits or otherwise, to support its motion."[12] The U.S. Supreme Court reversed by a 5–4 vote, basing its holding on Rule 56(c) of the Federal Rules of Civil Procedure, and addressed the issue of the burden to produce evidence that is placed on moving and nonmoving parties. When a nonmoving party that will bear the burden of proof at trial fails to establish the existence of an element essential to its case, "there can be 'no genuine issue as to any material fact' " because such a failure of proof "necessarily renders all other facts immaterial." When the nonmoving party with the burden of proof has not supported its case, the moving party need only inform the trial court of the basis for its motion and identify those portions of the materials before the court that the moving party believes demonstrate the absence of a genuine issue of material fact. The moving party is not required to support its claim with affidavits negating the elements of the opponent's cause of action.[13] But the party opposing the summary judgment motion must be given an opportunity to prove its case. Rule 56(f) gives the trial court the discretion to deny a premature motion for summary judgment or to order a continuance if the nonmoving party has not had an opportunity to make full discovery. The nonmoving party may avoid summary judgment by producing evidence in a form that would not be admissible at trial.[14] Thus, the *Celotex* case outlined and clarified the shifting burdens of proof that govern all motions for summary judgment under Rule 56 of the Federal Rules of Civil Procedures.

The third U.S. Supreme Court case, *Anderson v. Liberty Lobby, Inc.*, ruled that courts should consider summary judgment motions in light of heightened proof standards that would be applicable at trial.[15] This ruling is likely to increase the frequency with which courts grant summary judgment. This libel case involved a district court's summary judgment for defendants on the ground that the plaintiffs could not prove by clear and convincing evidence that the defendants had acted with malice, as required by *New York Times v. Sullivan.*[16] The federal appellate court reversed in part, holding that the preliminary nature of the summary judgment inquiry made it inappropriate for the trial court to consider the clear and convincing proof standard. Again, the U.S. Supreme Court reversed, and held that courts must consider the standards of proof applicable to each issue at trial, to wit: summary judgment is appropriate whenever resolution of the only facts at issue would not affect the outcome of the suit; and summary judgment must be denied "if the dispute about a material fact is genuine." To escape summary judgment the nonmoving party cannot merely assert that the jury reasonably could disbelieve the defendant's testimony but must set forth facts demonstrating the existence of a genuine issue for trial.[17] The *Anderson* case circumvents the need to characterize questions as factual or legal by focusing the summary judgment inquiry on the determination of whether disputed issues must be resolved by a jury.[18] The highest court ruled that the standard for granting summary judgment "mirrors the standard for a directed verdict under Federal Rules of Civil Procedure 50(a)," and that "the substantive law identified which facts are material."[19]

As a result of the above recent pronouncements by the U.S. Supreme Court, there has been a greatly expanded use of the summary judgment procedure. For example, in *Meiri v. Dacon*[20] the Second U.S. Court of Appeals upheld the summary judgment in favor of the Immigration and Naturalization Service against the plaintiff who alleged that she was discharged from her clerk-stenographer position because of her religion: "To allow a party to defeat a motion for summary judgment by offering purely conclusory allegations of discrimination, absent any concrete particulars, would necessitate a trial in all Title VI cases. Given the ease with which these suits may be brought and the energy and expense required to defend such actions, we believe the trial judge properly granted summary judgment."[21] In *Argus, Inc. v. Eastman Kodak Co.* summary judgment was approved where the plaintiffs could not prove a causal nexus between their alleged economic injury and the defendant's alleged anticompetitive activities.[22] And in *Knight v. United States Fire Insurance Co.* the federal appellate court observed that "some litigants are reluctant to make full use of the summary judgment process because of their perception that this court is unsympathetic to such motions and frequently reverses grants of summary judgment. Whatever may have been the accuracy of this view in years gone by, it is decidedly inaccurate at the present time."[23] However, in complex antitrust litigation "summary judgment is particularly disfavored and the standard for granting summary judgment is strict."[24]

In the state of New York a motion under Section 3211 of Civil Practice Law and Rules (CPL & R) for dismissal of the pleading can and frequently does result in an order for summary judgment under Section 3212 of CPL & R. However, the New York Court of Appeals in *Rovello v. Orofino Realty Co.* had held that, absent some conscious conversion of the dismissal motion to the summary judgment motion, affidavits and other evidence submitted with the prior motion could not be considered in the latter motion.[25] Chief Judge Wachtler, in his dissent in this 1976 case, simply stated that the majority decision emasculated Section 3211 so that it amounted to an old common law demurrer.[26] Most recently, in *Four Seasons Hotels v. Vinnick* a letter agreement was the subject of adjudication: plaintiffs had written a letter and delivered it to defendants who had signed it, but defendants later claimed that the letter was not an enforceable contract.[27] Defendants thereupon moved to dismiss the complaint under Section 3211(a)(7), and plaintiffs cross-moved for partial summary judgment under Section 3212. The court ruled that the cross-motion and accompanying papers "were clearly designated as a motion for summary judgment and defendants' opposition papers showed that defendants were fully apprised of same."

An interesting question naturally arises, how far can courts go in requiring litigants to participate in nonbinding summary jury trials? In the leading case of *Strandell v. Jackson County*,[28] the Seventh U.S. Court of Appeals ruled that federal district courts cannot do so; that is, they cannot promote summary jury trials for unwilling participants.[29] In this case Strandell, a college student, was found dead in a county jail following his arrest; the federal district court ordered an attorney representing the parents of the deceased to participate in a summary trial because the parties' settlement positions were so diverse and the court trial calendar was very full. The attorney refused, claiming that the summary trial process would force him to disclose privileged information and would unnecessarily force the parents to relive their son's death. The attorney was held in contempt of court and fined $500. [It should be noted that during discovery plaintiffs had obtained statements from 21 witnesses whose identity had been disclosed by the defendants; after discovery closed, the defendants moved to compel the statements but plaintiffs resisted on the work-product privilege, and the federal trial court agreed with plaintiffs.] The issue concerned the "legality of compelled participation," according to the federal appellate court, which then ruled that neither Rule 16(c)(7) nor (11) could be read as authorizing a mandatory summary jury trial![30] While these rules were intended to foster settlement through the use of "extrajudicial procedures," they were "not intended to require that an unwilling litigant be sidetracked from the normal course of litigation."[31]

In all fairness to the federal trial court, it had relied on a resolution adopted in 1984 by the Judicial Conference of the United States endorsing summary jury trials in its original draft "with the voluntary consent of the parties," which phrase was omitted in the final draft.[32] Also, Rule 16 does generally give the federal district court "the power to order the litigants to engage in a process which will enhance the possibility of fruitful negotiations."[33] And the Speedy Trial Act[34] does set time limits for commencing trials in criminal cases,[35] which mandate would provide authority for ordering the summary jury trial.

The Seventh U.S. Court, in vacating the contempt judgment against the attorney, stated: "While the pre-trial conference of Rule 16 was intended to foster settlement through the use of extrajudicial procedures, it was not intended to require that an unwilling litigant be sidetracked. . . . A crowded docket does not permit the court to avoid adjudication of cases properly within its congressionally-mandated jurisdiction." The federal appellate court also found that mandatory participation in summary jury trial "would seriously affect the well-established rules concerning discovery and work product privilege."[36] The noble experiment of summary jury trials must find other alternatives.

It would perhaps be remiss not to mention in passing still another aspect of preclusion, although it does not take the form of a device: it is the class suit, which takes many potential plaintiffs into the single lawsuit and thereby precludes a multiplicity of actions. The class suit was an invention of the court of chancery and had its origins as a device to achieve efficiency.[37] The U.S. Circuit Court in Rhode Island in the year 1820 permitted some of the crew of a privateer to sue on behalf of all the crew to recover their share of the prize money resulting from their common effort.[38] The class suit device appeared in the earliest 19th-century codes of the various states; an 1849 amendment to the New York code, for example, authorized litigants to sue or defend on behalf of all persons "when the question is one of a common or general interest to many persons, or when the parties are very numerous and it may be impracticable to bring them all before the court."[39] It was in 1853 that the U.S. Supreme Court in *Smith v. Swormstedt* recognized the class suit; here a dispute arose between 1,500 southerners and 3,800 northerners, all of whom were "traveling and worn-out preachers," who contested the rights of each other to participate in a pension fund established by their common church before it split over the issue of slavery.[40] Sixty-eight years later in *Ben Hur v. Cauble* the highest court utilized the class suit as a device on behalf of an insurance company that sought to fend off numerous suits by numerous policyholders, all contesting the same issue that had been resolved adversely to those policyholders.[41] And in 1940 in the landmark case of *Hansberry v. Lee*[42] the U.S. Supreme Court acknowledged that special treatment was appropriate for the class suit:

> The class suit was an invention of equity to enable it to proceed to a decree in suits where the number of those interested in the subject of the litigation is so great that their joinder as parties in conformity to the usual rules of procedure is impracticable. Courts are not infrequently called upon to proceed with causes in which the number of those interested in the litigation is so great as to make difficult or impossible the joinder of all because some are not within the jurisdiction or because their whereabouts is unknown or where if all were made parties to the suit its continued abatement by the death of some would prevent or unduly delay a decree. In such cases where the interests of those not joined are of the same class as the interest of those who are, and where it is considered that the latter fairly represent the former in the prosecution of the litigation of the issues in which all have a common interest, the court will proceed to a decree.[43]

The Federal Rules of Civil Procedure in 1938 sought to amplify the class suit, for the sake of efficiency, as a means to consolidate the resources of small claimants and enable them to assert claims en masse.[44] Subsequent amendments to Rule 23 enhanced the class suit as a preclusive device.[45]

A further word about the tool of summary judgment: at a time when the civil court systems in nearly all states are hopelessly clogged, every effort should be made to make effective use of the tools at hand to help "unblock" what is impeding justice. As recently as 1986, the U.S. Supreme Court in *Celotex* emphasized that Rule 56 of the Federal Rules of Civil Procedure

> mandates the entry of summary judgment, after adequate time for discovery and upon motion, after a party . . . fails to make a showing sufficient to establish the existence of an element essential to that party's case, and on which that party will bear the burden of proof at trial. . . . In such a situation there can be no genuine issue as to any material fact since a complete failure of proof concerning an essential element of the nonmoving party's case necessarily renders all other facts immaterial. The moving party is entitled to a judgment as a matter of law because the nonmoving party has failed to make a sufficient showing on an essential element of her case with respect to which she has the burden of proof. . . .[46]

It is submitted that the public must regard the court system as one that can and does dispense justice and not simply one that moves cases along a settlement trail. Summary judgment is an adequate tool here.

NOTES

1. See New York Times, Aug. 17, 1987, at D2.
2. See 1 Emanuel's Encyclopedia of American Law (1987) at 189.
3. Rule 1 of Federal Rules of Civil Procedure.
4. See Schwarzer, "Summary Judgment under the Federal Rules," 99 FRD 465 (1984).
5. 106 S. Ct. 1348 (1986).
6. 106 S. Ct. 2548 (1986).
7. 106 S. Ct. 2505 (1986).
8. See Note, NYLJ, Dec. 24, 1987, at 1 et seq.
9. According to the U.S. Supreme Court, "To survive petitioners' motion for summary judgment, 'respondents must establish that there is a genuine issue of material fact as to whether petitioners entered into an illegal conspiracy that caused respondents to suffer a cognizable injury. Fed. Rule Civ. Proc. 56(e);' *First National Bank of Arizona v. Cities Service Co.*, 391 U.S. 253, 288–289 (1968). This showing has two components. First, respondents must show more than a conspiracy in violation of the antitrust laws; they must show an injury to them resulting from the illegal conduct. Respondents charge petitioners with a whole host of conspiracies in restraint of trade. *Supra*, at 7–8. Except for the alleged conspiracy to monopolize the American market through predatory pricing, these alleged conspiracies could not have caused respondents to suffer an 'antitrust injury,' *Brunswick Corp. v. Pueblo Bowl-O-Mat*, 429 U.S., at 489, because they actually tended to benefit respondents. *Supra*, at 7–8. Therefore, unless, in context, evidence of these 'other' conspiracies raises a genuine issue concerning the existence of a predatory pricing conspiracy, that evidence cannot defeat petitioners' summary judgment motion.

Second, the issue of fact must be 'genuine.' Fed. Rule Civ. Proc. 56(c), (e). When the moving party has carried its burden under Rule 56(c) its opponent must do more than simply show that there is some metaphysical doubt as to the material facts. See *DeLuca v. Atlantic Refining Co.*, 176 F.2d 421, 423 (CA2 1949) (L. Hand, J.), cert. denied, 338 U.S. 943 (1950); 10A C. Wright, A. Miller, & M. Kane, Federal Practice and Procedure §2727 (1983); Clark, Special Problems in Drafting and Interpreting Procedural Codes and Rules, 3 Vand. L. Rev. 493, 504–505 (1950). Cf. *Sartor v. Arkansas Natural Gas Corp.*, 321 U.S. 620, 627 (1944). In the language of the Rule, the non-moving party must come forward with 'specific facts showing that there is a *genuine issue for trial*.' Fed. Rule Civ. Proc. 56(e) (emphasis added). See also Advisory Committee Note to 1963 Amendment of Fed. Rule Civ. Proc. 56(e), 28 U.S.C. App., p. 626 (purpose of summary judgment is to 'pierce the pleadings and to assess the proof in order to see whether there is a genuine need for trial'). Where the record taken as a whole could not lead a rational trier of fact to find for the non-moving party, there is no 'genuine issue for trial.' *Cities Service, supra*, at 289.

Respondents argued before the district court that petitioners had failed to carry their initial burden under Rule 56(c) of demonstrating the absence of a genuine issue of material fact. See *Adickes v. S. H. Kress & Co.*, 398 U.S. 144, 157 (1970). Cf. *Catrett v. Johns-Manville Sales Corp.*, 244 U.S. App. D.C. 160, 756 F.2d 181 (1985), cert. granted, 474 U.S.—(1985). That issue was resolved in petitioners' favor, and is not before us.

Rule 56(e) provides, in relevant part: 'When a motion for summary judgment is made and supported as provided in this rule, an adverse party may not rest upon the mere allegations or denials of his pleading, but his response, by affidavits or as otherwise provided in this rule, must set forth specific facts showing that there is a genuine issue for trial. If he does not so respond, summary judgment, if appropriate, shall be entered against him.'

10. The dissenting opinion elaborated as follows: "The Court's initial discussion of summary judgment standards appears consistent with settled doctrine. I agree that '[w]here the record taken as a whole could not lead a rational trier of fact to find for the non-moving party, there is no "genuine issue for trial." ' *Ante*, at 11 (quoting *Cities Service, supra*, at 289). I also agree that '[o]n summary judgment the inferences to be drawn from the underlying facts . . . "must be viewed in the light most favorable to the party opposing the motion." *Ante*, at 12 (quoting *United States v. Diebold, Inc.*, 369 U.S. 654, 655 (1962).' But other language in the Court's opinion suggests a departure from traditional summary judgment doctrine. Thus, the Court gives the following critique of the Third Circuit's opinion: '[T]he Court of Appeals concluded that a reasonable factfinder could find a conspiracy to depress prices in the American market in order to drive out American competitors, which conspiracy was funded by excess profits obtained in the Japanese market. The court apparently did not consider whether it was as plausible to conclude that petitioners' price-cutting behavior was independent and not conspiratorial.' *Ante*, at 6. In a similar vein, the Court summarizes *Monsanto v. Spray-Rite Corp.*, *supra*, as holding that 'courts should not permit factfinders to infer conspiracies when such inferences are implausible . . . ' *Ante*, at 18. Such lanugage suggests that a judge hearing a defendant's motion for summary judgment in an antitrust case should go beyond the traditional summary judgment inquiry and decide for himself whether the weight of the evidence favors the plaintiff. *Cities Service* and *Monsanto* do not stand for any such proposition. Each of those cases simply held that a particular piece of evidence standing alone was insufficiently probative to justify sending a case to the jury. These holdings in no way undermine the doctrine that all evidence must be construed in the light most favorable to the party opposing summary judgment.

If the Court intends to give every judge hearing a motion for summary judgment in an antitrust case the job of determining if the evidence makes the inference of conspiracy more probable than not, it is overturning settled law. If the Court does not intend such a pronouncement, it should refrain from using unnecessarily broad and confusing language.

In *Monsanto*, the Court held that a manufacturer's termination of a price-cutting distributor after receiving a complaint from another distributor is not, *standing alone*, sufficient to create a jury question. 465 U.S., at 763-764. To understand this holding, it is important to realize that under *United States v. Colgate & Co.*, 250 U.S. 300 (1919), it is permissible for a manufacturer to announce retail prices in advance and terminate those who fail to comply, but that under *Dr. Miles Medical Co. v. John D. Park & Sons Co.*, 220 U.S. 373 (1911), it is impermissible for the manufacturer and its distributors to agree on the price at which the distributors will sell the goods. Thus, a manufacturer's termination of a price-cutting distributor after receiving a complaint from another distributor is lawful under *Colgate, unless* the termination is pursuant to a shared understanding between the manufacturer and its distributors respecting enforcement of a resale price maintenance scheme. *Monsanto* holds that to establish liability under *Dr. Miles*, more is needed than evidence of behavior that is consistent with a distributor's exercise of its prerogatives under *Colgate*. Thus, '[t]here must be evidence that tends to exclude the possibility that the manufacturer and nonterminated distributors were acting independently.' 465 U.S., at 764. *Monsanto* does *not* hold that if a terminated dealer produces some further evidence of conspiracy beyond the bare fact of post-complaint termination, the judge hearing a motion for summary judgment should balance all the evidence pointing toward conspiracy against all the evidence pointing toward independent action.''

11. See generally 100 Harv. L. Rev. 100 (1987) at 250–252.
12. 756 F2d 181 (D.C. Cir., 1984) at 184.
13. Supra note 11 at 251; also supra note 6 at 2553.
14. Supra note 6 at 2553–2554.
15. Supra note 7.
16. 376 US 254 (1964).
17. Supra note 7 at 2515.
18. Supra note 11 at 256.
19. Supra note 7 at 2511.
20. 759 F2d 989 (2d Cir., 1985).
21. According to the court, ''The summary judgment rule would be rendered sterile if the mere incantation of intent or state of mind would operate as a talisman to defeat an otherwise valid motion. Indeed, the salutary purposes of summary judgment—avoiding protracted, expensive and harassing trials—apply no less to discrimination cases than to commercial or other areas of litigation.''
22. 801 F2d 38 (2d Cir., 1986).
23. 804 F2d 9 (2d Cir., 1986), cert. den. 107 S. Ct. 1570 (1987).
24. See Hand v. Central Transport, Inc., 779 F2d 8 (6th Cir., 1985) at 10.
25. 40 NY2d 633, 389 NYS2d (1976).
26. Note that the following year the same court decided Guggenheimer v. Ginzburg, 43 NY2d 268, 401 NYS2d 182 (1977).
27. 515 NYS2d 1 (1st Dept., 1987).
28. 838 F2d 884 (7th Cir., 1987).
29. See generally Trial Mag. (May 1988) at 91.
30. Supra note 28 at 887.
31. Id.
32. Supra note 29.
33. Id.
34. 18 USC 3161.
35. See Warren Freedman, The Constitutional Right of a Speedy and Fair Criminal Trial (1988).
36. Supra note 28 at 888.
37. See Brown v. Vermuden, 1 Ch. Cas. 272 (1676).
38. See West v. Randall, 2 Mason 181, 194 (Cir. Ct., R.I., 1820).
39. NY Laws 1849, ch. 438, sec. 119.
40. 57 US 288 (1853).

41. 255 US 356 (1921).

42. 311 US 32 (1940).

43. Id. at 41–42.

44. See Note, 8 U. Chi. L. Rev. 684 (1941).

45. See also 25 Bus. Law. 1259 (1970) and 71 Colum. L. Rev. 1 (1971). Also, see Vasquez v. Superior Court, 484 P2d 964 (Cal., 1971).

46. Supra note 6. Also note Novello, "Summary Judgment: A Tool We Should Use," NYLJ, Feb. 2, 1989, at 3 and 6.

2

The Motion for Summary Judgment

MECHANICS OF THE SUMMARY JUDGMENT

The summary judgment motion was an English procedural innovation of the mid-19th century and was initially restricted to actions on commercial paper, bills of exchange, and promissory notes.[1] It was in 1855 that Parliament enacted legislation to enable the courts to "pierce the pleadings" in order to render prompt decisions without trial against "deadbeats" taking advantage of the law's interminable delays, to the injury of honest creditors.[2] The motion for summary judgment under Rule 56 of the Federal Rules of Civil Procedure was designed to strike sham pleadings and move the proceedings to an early conclusion.[3] Today the courts appear to have taken a liberal view in granting summary judgment where warranted.[4]

Courts will go "behind the pleadings" in deciding summary judgment motions.[5] Illusory pleadings will be scrutinized to ascertain whether there is a genuine issue of material fact. Courts will carefully examine affidavits that are based upon the personal knowledge of the affiant and upon matters that would be admissible at trial by the affiant.[6] Discovery materials will also be routinely viewed.[7] But the opponent to the motion for summary judgment cannot rest on the pleadings, for "the response, by affidavits or as otherwise provided by this rule, must set forth specific facts showing that there is a genuine issue for trial."[8] A mere allegation that the opponent desires to rest his or her case on the credibility of the witnesses is insufficient, standing alone, to preclude summary judgment.[9] Furthermore, the rule of thumb is that the motion for summary judgment must be construed most favorably to the party opposing the motion.[10] If the court decides that affidavits, for example, presented for or against the motion for summary judgment, were made in bad faith or "solely for the purpose of delay," the court may order the party who submitted those affidavits to pay to the other side the costs of presenting opposing affidavits, including attorneys' fees.[11]

In *McKinney v. K-Mart Corp.* an employee sued her employer, alleging that she was damaged by the employer's breach of contract, outrageous conduct, and slander.[12] The federal district court granted summary judgment in favor of the employer, pointing out that plaintiff had failed to produce evidence that would have supported a finding of any of these causes of action. On the outrageous conduct claim the court tersely stated that it was "left with the indelible impression that this is not a case containing facts which can support a theory of outrage."[13]

The liberality of the Federal Rules of Civil Procedure with respect to summary judgment prompted many states to conform to them. But several states limit the procedure, for example, to actions on a liquidated demand arising on a negotiable instrument or commercial contract, permitting summary judgment only in actions against specified persons for certain defaults.[14] Many of these states restricting the use of the summary judgment device have overlooked the noble words of Judge Cardozo in *Richard v. Credit Suisse* more than 80 years ago: "The very object of a motion for summary judgment is to separate what is formal or pretended in denial or averment from what is genuine and substantial, so that only the latter may subject a suitor to the burden of a trial."[15]

One of the better expositions on the administration of summary judgment is found in the California case of *Corwin v. Los Angeles Newspaper Service Bureau:*[16]

> The matter to be determined by the trial court in considering such a motion is whether the defendant (or the plaintiff) has presented any facts which give rise to a triable issue. The court may not pass upon the issue iteself. Summary judgment is proper only if the affidavits in support of the moving party would be sufficient to sustain a judgment in his favor and his opponent does not by affidavit show such facts as may be deemed by the judge hearing the motion sufficient to present a triable issue. The aim of the procedure is to discover, through the media of affidavits, whether the parties possess evidence requiring the weighing procedures of a trial. In examining the sufficiency of affidavits filed in connection with the motion, the affidavits of the moving party are strictly construed and those of his opponent liberally construed, and doubts as to the propriety of granting the motion should be resolved in favor of the party opposing the motion. Such summary procedure is drastic and should be used with caution so that it does not become a substitute for the open trial method of determining facts.

Note that the defendant also may move for summary judgment with or before the filing of his or her answer.[17]

Before the summary judgment motion can be granted the court must find that no questions of fact exist, as more thoroughly discussed by the Fifth U.S. Court of Appeals in *Nunez v. Superior Oil Co.*:[18]

There is no litmus that infallibly distinguishes those issues that are "factual" from those that are "legal" or "mixed." When all those material facts susceptible of objective determination are known, there may be inferences or conclusions to be drawn from them. Many observations that may appear superficially to be factual are the result of inference, viewpoint, and judgment. At ends of the spectrum, it may be relatively easy to separate fact and law, but, as we approach the point where facts and the application of legal rule to them blend, appraising evidentiary facts in terms of their legal consequences and "applying" law to fact become inseparable processes. In some instances where facts may assume infinite variety, legal rules are deliberately stated in a fashion calling for the application of judgment. Thus, in a suit for personal injury from an automobile accident, it might be ascertained, or even stipulated, that the defendant was driving at 50 miles per hour on a certain road at 6:00 p.m. on a rainy January day. The trier of fact must still decide whether this is "negligence." Therefore, the availability of summary judgment depends upon more than an abstract denomination of disputed material issues as "factual" or "legal" or "mixed"; it may turn on whether the application of legal criteria necessarily require judgmental evaluation by the trier of fact, or, to put it another way, whether the trial will require a judge/jury separation of issues.[19]

DENIAL OF MOTION FOR SUMMARY JUDGMENT

The denial of a motion for summary judgment may rest on countless bases, some of which can be delineated in the collection of court decisions set forth hereinafter. For example, in *Tisei v. Town of Ogunquit* the trial court had granted the summary judgment motion of developers who had challenged both the town's temporary moratorium on development and the town's public sewer usage limitations ordinance.[20] But the Maine Supreme Judicial Court reversed, holding that under the Maine statute on summary judgments, the taking of oral testimony on a summary judgment motion is prohibited; the creation of a record through a testimonial hearing is entirely inappropriate. In *Minpeco. S.A. v. Conticommodity Services, Inc.* the federal district court for the Southern District of New York also denied the motion for summary judgment in a civil conspiracy case because the moving party had failed to "present direct or circumstantial evidence that reasonably tends to prove that the defendants had a conscious commitment to a common scheme to achieve an unlawful objective."[21] The court observed that "the economic plausibility of the plaintiff's claims is relevant to a determination whether genuine issues exist for trial; if the claim is one that 'simply makes no economic sense' the plaintiff must come forward with more persuasive evidence to support its claim than would otherwise be necessary." And in *Burke v. New York City Transit Authority* the same federal district court refused to grant a motion for summary judgment to workers (employed by defendant) who challenged the constitutionality of mandatory drug testing for employees. The court pointed out that the current law on that issue was not completely settled and therefore the motion for summary judgment had been premature.[22] In the matter of arbitration between *International Longshoremen's Association v. Delta Steamship Lines, Inc.* the Second U.S.

Court of Appeals observed that "the issue . . . is whether the posture of the case . . . was such that it warranted disposition by summary judgment. After reviewing an unsatisfactory 1,200-page appendix spattered with mutually contradictory and conclusory affidavits, we conclude that it did not. . . . We are not prepared to accept the affidavits submitted by petition-appellee as statements of unassailed and unassailable fact, particularly when they deal with such matters as intentions, understandings, contemplations, ideas, thoughts, and motivations. . . . We hold that inconsistent and contradictory factual allegations in the record create genuine issues which preclude summary disposition."[23]

The New York Apellate Division, First Dept., in *Consolidated Edison Co. v. Jet Asphalt Corp.* ruled that summary judgment was simply not available to the utility:

> A motion for summary judgment may only be granted when there exists no material and triable issues of fact. On such a motion the court's role is limited to one of issue-finding, not issue-determining. Accordingly, it is improper to resolve questions of credibility on a summary judgment motion, unless it clearly appears that the issues are "not genuine, but feigned." . . . The affidavits submitted by defendant in opposition to the motion for summary judgment and on its reargument motion clearly present triable issues of fact as to whether and when defendant knew or reasonably should have known of the underbilling, a factor which determines defendant's liability to pay the underbilling beyond the 1-year limitation period provided by plaintiff's internal rules.[24]

In *Tsakrios v. Toyota Motor Corp.* the plaintiff claimed that he fell while leaving a Toyota automobile because of the defective design of the front seat safety belt.[25] In opposition to defendant's motion for summary judgment, plaintiff submitted an affidavit from his expert who opined that "the safety of the person exiting from the back seat could be increased by a better design than Toyota used, without compromising the safety performance of the front belt system." Defendant called this affidavit to be nothing more than "theoretical speculations" and "unsupported assumptions," but the court disagreed and denied the motion for summary judgment: "Any inquiry into the basis of the expert's opinion, which would necessarily involve essentially technical matters, should be conducted at trial so that he may be examined and cross-examined."

Attorneys' affidavits in favor of or contrary to a motion for summary judgment appear to be unacceptable to many courts, as illustrated by the federal district court in *Motown Productions, Inc. v. Cacomm, Inc.*, where the court stated that "the expert testimony of an attorney as to an ultimate issue of domestic law or as to the legal significance of facts is inadmissible."[26] Also, in *Alexander Co. v. American Lincoln Homes, Inc.*, the same court rejected an attorney's affidavit submitted in opposition to a motion for summary judgment.[27] The affidavit purported to establish a defense of lack of diversity jurisdiction based on a claim that the defendant was a New York corporation. In so ruling against the admissibility of the affidavit, the court pointed out that the affidavit was insufficient because it did not establish on its face that the New York corporation was the party with whom plaintiff had contracted, and that it was "not inherently obvious that this attorney would have personal knowledge of the defendant corporation's possible subsidiaries or practices relating to its business names."[28]

The denial of motion for summary judgment is well illustrated in *Harris v. Manhattan & Bronx Surface Transit Operating Authority*, where the New York court ruled that summary judgment was unavailable in the negligence scenario.[29] At the outset the court observed that "summary judgment should properly be granted in negligence cases *only* in rare instances since often, even if the parties are in agreement as to the underlying facts, the very question of negligence is itself a question for jury determination. . . . The case before us was not such a rare instance." The court thereupon reviewed numerous New York decisions and concluded that "none of the cases . . . concerned the grant of summary judgment prior to the presentation of plaintiff's proof of trial." Accordingly, the court summarized:

> The plaintiff here has done more than to merely characterize the stopping of the bus as sudden and unexpected. She stated in her affidavit that the vehicle was traveling at a very high rate of speed when it came to a sudden, unusual and violent stop. She further alleged that a crowd of people standing behind her was thrown against her by the sudden stop, crushing her against the railing. Thus, she was not the only person on the bus who was affected by the sudden stop. The force of the propulsion of plaintiff into the railing in the vehicle, caused by the movement of the crowd because of the sudden stop, was apparently great enough to crush plaintiff's ribs. In addition, whether or not the bus was permitted to become overcrowded raised another issue with respect to defendant's negligence (see, *Ligon v. International Railway Company*, 269 App. Div. 809).
>
> Accordingly, plaintiff succeeded in raising issues which can not be decided upon the motion for summary judgment, but must await a plenary resolution.
>
> Although defendant attacks the credibility of plaintiff, whether or not her allegations are true is for a jury to decide, not a court upon a summary judgment motion.

The Second U.S. Court of Appeals in *Dolgow v. Anderson* took a dim view of summary judgments by declaring that summary judgment is not allowed if there is the "slightest doubt" of the outcome of the full trial that would be precluded.[30] The summary judgment motion is distinguishable from other motions because it may be supported by information not contained in the pleadings. Other motions essentially assume the facts to be as alleged in the opposing party's pleading; but under a motion for summary judgment, the information outside the pleadings may establish that the undisputed facts are not as the opposing party's pleading alleges. As viewed in *Arnstein v. Porter*[31] by the Second U.S. Court of Appeals, there were issues of fact, that is, copying and improper appropriation of musical compositions:

> We turn first to the *issue of copying*. After listening to the compositions as played in the phonograph recordings submitted by defendant, we find *similarities*; but we hold

that unquestionably, standing alone, they *do not compel the conclusion, or permit the inference, that defendant copied. The similarities, however, are sufficient so that, if there is enough evidence of access to permit the case to go to the jury, the jury may properly infer that the similarities did not result from coincidence.*

Summary judgment was, then, proper if indubitably defendant did not have access to plaintiff's compositions. Plainly that presents an issue of fact. . . . We decide against summary judgment here because we consider it improper in this case. Our decision to that effect will have precedential significance only to the extent that, in any future case, summary judgment is sought when the facts are not beyond the range of actual dispute.[32]

ILLUSTRATIVE CASES

The motion for summary judgment can best be delineated by a review of selected court decisions in several branches of the law. Judge Learned Hand of the Second U.S. Court of Appeals in *Dyer v. MacDougall*, more than thirty-five years ago, granted defendant's motion for summary judgment on these facts: plaintiff alleged that defendant slandered him before two persons, and defendant moved for summary judgment on the basis of affidavits from these two persons who stated therein that they never heard the allegedly slanderous utterances.[33] Defendant argued that since these two persons are the only persons alleged by plaintiff to have heard the slander and since these two persons will testify at trial that they did not hear the alleged slander, defendant's summary judgment motion should be granted. Plaintiff countered with the argument that at trial these two persons will tell the truth only upon cross-examination and admit to hearing the slanderous utterances of defendant. Defendant's argument was essentially that the jury's disbelief of the denials of the two persons is not the kind of evidence that plaintiff must produce to withstand the summary judgment motion. Judge Hand thereupon granted defendant's motion for summary judgment after plaintiff refused an opportunity to depose the two persons. It is difficult to understand why plaintiff did not avail himself of the chance to depose the two persons. Cross-examination on deposition would have enabled plaintiff to perhaps defeat the motion by showing that the two persons were not speaking the whole truth!

Another interesting and illustrative case is *Sarfati v. Wilson Hotel Group, Inc.*, where plaintiff commenced a securities action for conspiracy against defendant and other defendants, and when defendant moved for summary judgment, plaintiff sought a continuance to allow plaintiff to take discovery of the many defendants.[34] The federal district court granted plaintiff's request for continuance since defendant's participation in the conspiracy and the existence of communications between the defendants were clearly relevant to the motion for summary judgment.

In the products liability area there is the significant decision in *Kemp v. Monsanto Co.*, where the defendants, in support of their motion for summary judgment, submitted the affidavit of a physician, who was at the hospital where plaintiff had had her intrauterine device inserted, to the effect that the hospital at that time was not using any IUDs manufactured by defendants.[35] Also submitted was an affidavit of one of its defendants' officers that the particular IUD was not approved for marketing by the Food and Drug Administration in Washington, D.C., until two years after plaintiff had her IUD inserted. Defendant also submitted an affidavit by plaintiff's treating physician who stated that two days after the IUD was removed, plaintiff had informed him that the IUD was not defendant's product. In opposition to the motion, plaintiff offered her own affidavit to the effect that the doctor who removed the IUD told her it was defendant's product. The court ruled that plaintiff's self-serving statement was insufficient to defeat the summary judgment motion because her statement constituted inadmissible hearsay evidence. The statement of plaintiff did not have sufficient circumstantial guarantees of trustworthiness because the statement of her physician was being offered by an interested party, the identity of the physician being unknown, and furthermore there were no witnesses to either the statement itself or to the circumstances surrounding the making of the statement. The Fifth U.S. Court of Appeals in *Viterbo v. Dow Chemical Co.*[36] also affirmed summary judgment in favor of the drug manufacturer because the expert of the plaintiff who allegedly had been exposed to defendant's pesticide "lacked objectivity in that he had diagnosed plaintiff's condition as resulting from exposure to the pesticide based only on the patient's oral history and without the benefit of medical tests. Additionally, plaintiff's expert had no scientific literature to support his position and the test which he performed did not establish a causal link between plaintiff's symptoms and the pesticide."[37] The drug product manufacturer in *Bikowicz v. Neco Pharmacy*, however, was not successful in obtaining summary judgment in its favor; here plaintiff had become addicted to the prescriptive drug over a period of eight years despite the manufacturer's warning that the prescription should not be refilled, a warning that the defendant pharmacy had either ignored or was unaware of.[38] Summary judgment for the drug manufacturer was improper, according to the New York court, because the drug manufacturer is ultimately liable to the patient who uses its product, and therefore a question of fact as to failure to warn exists. The decision of the Fourth U.S. Court of Appeals in *Stanback v. Parke, Davis & Co.*, to the effect that under Virginia law a drug manufacturer's failure to warn plaintiff's physician of the risks associated with the vaccine product does not legally cause plaintiff's injury, opened the door to summary judgment for the drug manufacturer, irrespective of any allegation by plaintiff that the warning was inadequate.[39] Lack of causation is indeed a veritable base for summary judgment in favor of the product manufacturer.[40] Similarly, in *Tri-City Property Management Services, Inc. v. Research Products Corp.*, the Arizona appellate court ruled that since there was no showing that the herbicide manufacturer knew of plaintiff's particular purpose for the herbicide and because defendant's statement that the herbicide would take care of plaintiff's needs was not an express warranty, there was no causal relation that would defeat defendant's motion for summary judgment.[41]

Federal civil rights statutes frequently spell out the bases for summary judgment; for example, under 42 USC 1900, the motion for summary judgment is liberally construed in favor of the plaintiff,[42] although the complaint must still be specifically pleaded.[43] A civil rights complaint should not be dismissed unless it appears to a certainty that the plaintiff would be entitled to no relief under any state of facts that could be proved to support the claim.[44] But bare conclusory allegations that the defendants conspired to deprive the plaintiff of the equal protection of the laws and of his rights and privileges secured by the U.S. Constitution and the laws of the United States, without any support in the facts alleged, cannot protect a complainant under 42 USC 1985(3) from the summary judgment motion.[45] In *Maiorana v. MacDonald* the First U.S. Court of Appeals affirmed the grant of summary judgment in favor of the police-defendants who were accused of acting with gross negligence, bad faith, and using excessive force in killing plaintiff's son while attempting to arrest him.[46] The court held that plaintiff's counter-affidavits did not undercut one defendant's "sworn statement that he saw movement before shooting," and that the affiant reasonably believed in good faith that deadly force was necessary.

The sufficiency of evidence to support the grant of summary judgment in will probate or will contest proceedings was discussed in *Re Estate of Kelly*.[47] Here decedent's nephew filed a petition seeking to have decedent's formal will (prepared by an attorney and leaving all property to him) admitted to probate; at the same time the nephew filed a motion seeking to have a purported handwritten will signed by the decedent subsequently declared invalid. The trial court granted the nephew's motion for summary judgment, but the New Mexico appellate court reversed because there were many genuine material issues of fact concerning the handwritten document, which purported to supplant the formal will.[48]

In a hazardous waste situation,[49] the federal district court in New Jersey in *Township of Gloucester v. Maryland Casualty Co.* entered an order granting defendant insurer partial summary judgment with respect to indemnification of cleanup and closure costs of a hazardous waste site.[50] Defendant's evidence showed that plaintiff had knowledge of the hazardous waste site and its legal liability therefor *prior* to the issuance of the insurance policy. In short, the court proclaimed that "one cannot obtain insurance for a risk that the insured knows has already transpired."

Summary judgment was readily granted in favor of defendant in *Adamowicz v. The Claridge at Park Place, Inc.*, where plaintiff's decedent suffered a cardiac arrest while playing a slot machine in defendant's casino.[51] According to the court, "plaintiffs have failed to prove the existence of any triable issue of fact."[52]

In *Whitfield v. Cohen* summary judgment was granted in favor of the plaintiff in an Employee Retirement Income Security Act (ERISA) action alleging breach of fiduciary duty.[53] The defendant, in seeking to defeat the summary judgment motion, attempted to change his prior sworn testimony in a deposition. But the federal district court noted the disparity in the testimony as amounting to a difference between specific answers and general conclusions concerning defendant's investigation of an investment management company and its principal with which defendant had invested assets. The court found that the deposition contained answers that belied the conclusions set forth in the affidavit opposing summary judgment. Accordingly, the material facts were not in dispute and plaintiff's motion for summary judgment was ordered. But in *First City Federal Savings Bank v. Bhogaonker*, the same court upheld the sufficiency of an attorney's affidavit to defeat the motion for summary judgment.[54]

The U.S. Supreme Court in *Adickes v. S. H. Kress & Co.* pointed out that

> Our own scrutiny of the factual allegations of petitioner's complaint, as well as the material found in the affidavits and depositions presented by Kress to the District Court, however, convinces us that summary judgment was improper here, for we think respondent failed to carry its burden of showing the absence of any genuine issue of fact. . . .
>
> . . . We think that on the basis of this record, it was error to grant summary judgment. As the moving party, respondent had the burden of showing the absence of a genuine issue as to any material fact, and for these purposes the material it lodged must be viewed in the light most favorable to the opposing party. Respondent here did not carry its burden because of its failure to foreclose the possibility that there was a policeman in the Kress store while petitioner was awaiting service, and that this policeman reached an understanding with some Kress employee that petitioner not be served.[55]

A New York judge in *Darcy v. Edward J. Castle Associates* posed the "almost philosophical question": "How summary should a summary proceeding be?"[56] He answered: "It is one which, absent Legislative limitations, cannot be answered with mathematical precision. With greater recognition of due process rights of both parties, causes of action where the facts are solely within the knowledge of the party sued and a liberal attitude toward granting discovery in civil litigation [e.g., to both sides in 'primary residence' suits], modern summary proceedings yield more convoluted, intense pleadings, develop more complex intricate issues . . . last longer in courts, both appellate and trial . . . and evolve into greater time-consuming combat today than was ever previously thought possible. . . . " The court concluded, perhaps with tongue in cheek: "This court has long believed that litigation should be determined "on the merits" whenever possible. Yet the words of American patriot (and second president) John Adams, spoken in 1770 while defending the British soldiers on trial for the Boston Massacre, are appropriate in this regard: "Facts are stubborn things; and whatever may be our wishes, our inclinations, or the dictates of our passions, they cannot alter the state of facts and evidence. This lawsuit was dead long before this motion was brought. Let it now rest. . . . "

NOTES

1. "Before the Hilary Rules of 1834 the English common law system tolerated to a considerable extent the wholly indefensible practice of pleading, for the purpose of delay, pleas which were altogether unfounded in fact, so-called 'sham pleas.' Favorite types of plea used in this end were those of judgment recovered or accord and satisfaction. Certain cases of sham pleas, however, fell outside the toleration. Such were pleas made 'the subject of indecorous justing' or otherwise absurd on their face, as where there was pleaded a judgment recovered in the Court of Piepoudre at Bartholomew's Fair; and these could be treated as nullities without much ado. . . . In this case, if the court had reason to believe that the plea was not interposed in good faith, it would proceed summarily to set it aside on affidavit of its untruth and allow judgment to go forthwith for the plaintiff. There was no real question of interference with the normal trial of facts, for if the plea were actually sham the traditions of the bar naturally forbade any insistence by counsel upon carrying the dishonesty further." Millar, Civil Procedure of the Trial Court in Historical Perspective 237 (1952).

2. See Bauman, "The Evolution of the Summary Judgment Proceeding," 31 Ind L J 329 (1956).

3. *Rule 56. Summary Judgment.*

(a) *For Claimant.* A party seeking to recover upon a claim, counterclaim or cross-claim or to obtain a declaratory judgment may, at any time after the expiration of 20 days from the commencement of the action or after service of a motion for summary judgment by the adverse party, move with or without supporting affidavits for a summary judgment in his favor upon all or any part thereof.

(b) *For Defending Party.* A party against whom a claim, counterclaim or cross-claim is asserted or a declaratory judgment is sought may, at any time, move with or without supporting affidavits for a summary judgment in his favor to all or any part thereof.

(c) *Motion and Proceedings Thereon.* The motion shall be served at least ten days before the time fixed for the hearing. The adverse party prior to the day of hearing may serve opposing affidavits. The judgment sought shall be rendered forthwith if the pleadings, depositions, answers to interrogatories, and admissions on file, together with the affidavits, if any, show that there is no genuine issue as to any material fact and that the moving party is entitled to judgment as a matter of law. A summary judgment, interlocutory in character, may be rendered on the issue of liability alone although there is a genuine issue as to the amount of damages.

4. See New York Times, Aug. 17, 1987, at D2.

5. See 1 Emanuel's Encyclopedia of American Law (1987) at 189 et seq.

6. Rule 56(e) of Federal Rules of Civil Procedure (FRCP).

7. See Warren Freedman, The Tort of Discovery Abuse (1989).

8. Note Rule 56(e) of FRCP.

9. Supra note 5 at 191.

10. Id.

11. Note Rule 56(g) of FRCP. Also see Jacobs, "Supreme Court's 1986 Summary Judgment Trilogy: A Proposed Analytical Model," Def. Couns. J. (Oct. 1987) at 502 et seq.

12. 649 F. Supp. 1217 (SD W. Va., 1986).

13. Supra note 11 for that author's "analytical model" synthesizing the 1986 U.S. Supreme Court cases "into a cohesive procedural tool":

A. Once a party has moved for summary judgment and
   1. has produced evidence proving the absence of, or has directed the court's attention to, the absence of an essential element of the opposing party's case,
   2. for which the opponent will bear the burden of proof at trial,
B. The opponent must:
   1. present admissible evidence,
   2. which would allow a trier of fact to conclude that the opponent can establish a case
   3. which will be able to overcome the ultimate evidentiary standard to be imposed at trial.
C. If the non-moving party's claim is one that is economically implausible, he must present more persuasive evidence than is otherwise required.
D. The motion for summary judgment should be granted if
   1. the non-moving party fails to produce such evidence
   2. after adequate time for discovery. (at 508)

14. See Booth v. Barber Transportation Co., 256 F2d 927 (8th Cir., 1958).
15. 242 NY 346 at 350, and 152 NE 110 at 111 (1926).
16. 484 P2d 953 (Cal., 1971) at 958.
17. See Gifford v. Travelers Protective Assn., 153 F2d 209 (9th Cir., 1946).
18. 572 F2d 1119 (5th Cir., 1978).
19. The court concluded: "If decision is to be reached by the court, and there are no issues of witness credibility, the court may conclude on the basis of the affidavits, depositions, and stipulations before it, that there are no genuine issues of material fact, even though decision may depend on inferences to be drawn from what has been incontrovertibly proved. Under those circumstances, which may be rare, the judge who is also the trier of fact may be warranted in concluding that there was or was not negligence, or that someone acted reasonably or unreasonably, or, as is the case here, that delay under the circumstances proved is justified or unjustified, even if that conclusion is deemed factual or involves a mixed question of fact and law. A trial on the merits would reveal no additional data. Hearing and viewing the witnesses subject to cross-examination would not aid the determination if there are neither issues of credibility nor controversies with respect to the substance of the proposed testimony. The judge, as trier of fact, is in a position to and ought to draw his inferences without resort to the expense of trial. . . .

But, where a jury is called for, the litigants are entitled to have the jury draw those inferences or conclusions that are appropriate grist for juries. Summary judgment 'was not intended to . . . deprive a litigant of, or at all encroach upon, his right to a jury trial. Judges in giving its flexible provisions effect must do so with this essential limitation constantly in mind.' . . .

Juries must consider not only 'questions of fact in dispute, [but] questions of conflicting inferences from undisputed facts.' Buffalo Insurance Co. v. Spach, 5 Cir. 1960, 277 F.2d 529, 531. 'Evidentiary facts, though undisputed, do not always conclusively establish the ultimate fact at issue. When the ultimate fact is to be inferred from evidentiary facts, the choice between permissible inferences is for the trier of facts.' Walker v. U.S. Gypsum Co., 5 Cir. 1959, 270 F.2d 857, 862, cert. denied 1960, 363 U.S. 805, 80 S. Ct. 1240, 4 L.Ed.2d 1148. Of course, if there is 'a *complete absence* of probative facts' to support a particular inference, Planters Manufacturing Co. v. Protection Mut. Ins. Co., 5 Cir. 1967, 380 F.2d 869, 874, cert. denied 1967, 389 U.S. 930,

88 S. Ct. 293, 19 L.Ed.2d 282 (emphasis original), or, if 'the facts and inferences point so strongly and overwhelmingly in favor of one party that the Court believes that reasonable men could not arrive at [but one] verdict,' Boeing v. Shipman, 5 Cir. 1969, 411 F.2d 365, 374, the court may bypass the jury.

Thus, where, as here, the evidentiary facts are not disputed, a court in a non-jury case may grant summary judgment if trial would not enhance its ability to draw inferences and conclusions. But summary judgment is not appropriate if the same case is to be tried to a jury, and the inferences anad conclusions to be drawn are genuinely disputed. To put it in another fashion, whether disputed issues are issues of 'fact' for purposes of Rule 56 depends not only on the state of the evidence and the nature of the issue but hinges also on whether the litigants have a right to a jury determination. . . . ''

20. 491 A2d 564 (Me., 1986).

21. 653 F.Supp. 957 (SDNY, Nov. 17, 1987).

22. 110 FRD 595 (SDNY, Feb. 2, 1988).

23. 832 F2d 754 (2d Cir., Nov. 4, 1987), aff'g 636 F.Supp. 722 (SDNY, 1986).

24. 490 NYS2d 503 (Dec. 10, 1987).

25. 668 F.Supp. 185 (SDNY, Oct. 14, 1987).

26. 668 F.Supp. 285 (SDNY, Sept. 1987).

27. 1987 U.S. Dist. LEXIS 8516 and 11,630 (SDNY, 1987).

28. See Kean v. Iolab Corp., unreported (SDNY, Sept. 2, 1987): ''[t]o obtain relief under Rule 56(f) a party must show by affidavit the reasons that it cannot present facts essential to oppose a motion for summary judgment. When, as here, a plaintiff fails to produce any evidence whatsoever in support of her claim, the Court may properly deny the request for discovery and grant summary judgment against her. . . . A bare assertion that evidence to support a fanciful allegation lies within the exclusive control of the defendants and cannot be obtained through discovery is not sufficient to defeat a motion of summary judgment.''

29. Unreported (New York County, May 15, 1988).

30. 438 F2d (2d Cir., 1970).

31. 154 F2d 464 (2d Cir., 1946).

32. And the court concluded: ''*But in the spirit of that suggestion, we regard it as entirely improper to give any weight to other actions lost by plaintiff. Although, as stated above, the judge in his opinion, except as to one of the previous actions, did not say that he rested his decision on those other suits, the lanugage of his final judgment order indicates that he was probably affected by them. If so, he erred.* Absent the factors which make up res judicata (not present here), *each case must stand on its own bottom, subject, of course, to the doctrine of stare decisis.* Succumbing to the temptation to consider other defeats suffered by a party may lead a court astray; see, e.g. Southern Pacific Co. v. Bogert, 250 U.S. 483, 489, 39 S.Ct. 533, 63 L.Ed. 1099, note 1. *When a particular suit is vexatious, sometimes at its conclusion the court can give some redress to the victorious party. Perhaps the Legislature can and should meet this problem more effectively. But we surely must not do so, as defendant here would have us do, by prejudging the merits of the case before us.*

Modified in part; otherwise reversed and remanded.''

33. 201 F2d 265 (2d Cir., 1952).

34. Unreported (Conn., Oct. 9, 1987).

35. Unreported (SDNY, Dec. 22, 1987).

36. 826 F2d 420 (5th Cir., 1987).

37. Id. at 422.
38. 494 NYS2d 541 (App. Div., 1987).
39. 657 F2d 642 (4th Cir., 1981).
40. Id.
41. 721 P2d 144 (Ariz. App., 1986).
42. See Kauffman v. Moss, 420 F2d 1270 (3d Cir., 1969) cert. den. 400 US 846 (1969).
43. See Abernathy v. Patterson, 295 F2d 452 (5th Cir., 1962), cert. den. 368 US 986 (1962).
44. See York v. Story, 324 F2d 450 (9th Cir., 1964), cert. den. 376 US 939 (1964).
45. See Dunn v. Gazzola, 216 F2d 709 (1st Cir., 1958).
46. 596 F2d 1072 (1st Cir., 1979).
47. 660 P2d 124 (N.M. App., 1986).
48. See generally 53 ALR4th 561.
49. See generally Warren Freedman, Hazardous Waste Liability (1987).
50. 668 F.Supp. 394 (N.J., Aug. 19, 1987).
51. 552 NYS2d 884 (App. Div., 2d Dept., Jan. 6, 1988).
52. The court continued: ''It is well settled that: 'To obtain *summary judgment* it is necessary that the movant establish his cause of action or defense 'sufficiently to warrant the court as a matter of law in directing judgment' in his favor (CPLR 3212, subd. [b]), and he must do so by tender of evidentiary proof in admissible form. On the other hand, to defeat a motion for summary judgment, the opposing party must ''show facts sufficient to require a trial of any issue of fact'' (CPLR 3212, subd. [b]). Normally, if the opponent is to succeed in defeating a motion for summary judgment he, too, must make his showing by producing evidentiary proof in admissible form' (see, Friends of Animals v. Associated Fur Mfrs., 46 N.Y. 2d 1065, 1067).

To this end, mere conclusions, expressions of hope or unsubstantiated allegations or assertions are insufficient (see, Zuckerman v. City of New York, 49 N.Y. 2d 557; Alvord & Swift v. Muller Constr. Co., 46 N.Y. 2d 276).

In the instant case, the order appealed from stated that any application for summary judgment was *premature* in that discovery had not been completed. Our review of the record, however, reveals no indication that the disclosure sought by the plaintiffs will yield any evidence sufficient to defeat the application. . . .

In seeking summary judgment, the appellant submitted the affirmation of one Joseph G. Hayes, a physician, board certified in internal medicine and in cardiology, and Chairman of the Emergency Cardiac Care Committee of the American Heart Association, New York Affiliate, who, after reviewing the videotape and the decedent's hospital record, concluded, with a reasonable degree of medical certainty, that the CPR performed upon the decedent following her heart attack was in accordance with acceptable standards of care and practice. To this end, he stated that 'while the patient ultimately expired, it cannot be related to any failure on the part of those providing cardiopulmonary resuscitation.' According to Dr. Hayes, the presence of a 'normal sinus rhythm' on the electrocardiogram taken at Atlantic City Medical Center 'confirms the effectiveness of the CPR performed in this case.'

In response to the appellant's application for summary judgment, no substantive opposition was interposed by the plaintiffs beyond the conclusory assertions of counsel that 'the plaintiff has shown triable issues of fact.' In order to defeat the appellant's application for summary judgment, it was incumbent upon the plaintiffs to lay bare their proofs, and come forth with admissible evidence to refute the proof submitted by the appellant. At the very least, the plaintiffs had an obligation to show, by way of expert opinion, that there was some negligence in the emergency care rendered by the appellant. No such evidence was proffered, and accordingly, the plaintiffs have failed to meet their burden to defeat the motion. Moreover, under the circumstances of this particular case, it does not appear that the disclosure sought by the plaintiffs will yield facts or information to support any of the legal theories asserted by them.

In any event, even assuming, arguendo, that the plaintiffs had established the existence of a triable issue of fact with respect to whether or not the casino's emergency medical technicians acted in a negligent manner in their performance of CPR on the decedent, we find that the appellant is shielded from liability by virtue of the following provisions of the New Jersey Good Samaritan Statute:

'Any individual, including a person licensed to practice any method of treatment of human ailments . . . or licensed to render services ancillary thereto, who in good faith renders emergency care at the scene of an accident or emergency to the victim or victims thereof, shall not be liable for any civil damages as a result of any acts or omissions by such person in rendering the emergency care' (see, N.J. Statutes, 2A: 62A-1).

In view of our finding that summary judgment should be granted to the appellant, the remaining issues raised on this appeal are rendered academic, and need not be addressed here.''

Note—

Rule 3212. Motion for summary judgment.

(a) *Time; kind of action.* Any party may move for summary judgment in any action after issue has been joined.

(b) *Supporting proof; grounds; relief to either party.* A motion for summary judgment shall be supported by affidavit, by a copy of the pleadings and by other available proof, such as depositions and written admissions. The affidavit shall be by a person having knowledge of the facts; it shall recite all the material facts; and it shall show that there is no defense to the cause of action or that the cause of action or defense has no merit. The motion shall be granted if, upon all the papers and proof submitted, the cause of action or defense shall be established sufficiently to warrant the court as a matter of law in directing judgment in favor of any party. Except as provided in subdivision (c) of this rule the motion shall be denied if any party shall show facts sufficient to require a trial of any issue of fact. If it shall appear that any party other than the moving party is entitled to a summary judgment, the court may grant such judgment without the necessity of a cross-motion.

(c) *Immediate trial.* If it appears that the only triable issues of fact arising on a motion for summary judgment relate to the amount or extent of damages, or if the motion is based on any of the grounds enumerated in subdivision (a) or (b) of rule 3211, the court may, when appropriate for the expeditious disposition of the controversy, order an immediate trial of such issues of fact raised by the motion, before a referee, before the court, or before the court and a jury, whichever may be proper.

(d) [Repealed]

(e) *Partial summary judgment; severance.* In a matrimonial action summary judgment may not be granted in favor of the non-moving party. In any other action summary judgment may be granted as to one or more causes of action, or part thereof, in favor of any one of more parties, to the extent warranted, on such terms as may be just. The court may also direct:

1. that the cause of action as to which summary judgment is granted shall be severed from any remaining cause of action; or

2. that the entry of the summary judgment shall be held in abeyance pending the determination of any remaining cause of action.

(f) *Facts unavailable to opposing party.* Should it appear from affidavits submitted in opposition to the motion that facts essential to justify opposition may exist but cannot then be stated, the court may deny the motion or may order a continuance to permit affidavits to be obtained or disclosure to be had and may make such other order as may be just.

(g) *Limitation of issues of fact for trial.* If a motion for summary judgment is denied or is granted in part, the court, by examining the papers before it and, in the discretion of the court, by interrogating counsel, shall, if practicable, ascertain what facts are not in dispute or are incontrovertible. It shall thereupon make an order specifying such facts and they shall be deemed established for all purposes in the action. The court may make any order as may aid in the disposition of the action.

§3213. Motion for summary judgment in lieu of complaint.

When an action is based upon an instrument for the payment of money only or upon any judgment, the plaintiff may serve with the summons a notice of motion for summary judgment and the supporting papers in lieu of a complaint. The summons served with such motion papers shall require the defendant to submit answering papers on the motion within the time provided in the notice of motion. The minimum time such motion shall be noticed to be heard shall be as provided by subdivision (a) of rule 320 for making an appearance, depending upon the method of service. If the plaintiff sets the hearing date of the motion later than the minimum time therefor, he may require the defendant to serve a copy of his answering papers upon him within such extended period of time, not exceeding ten days, prior to such hearing date. No default judgment may be entered pursuant to subdivision (a) of section 3215 prior to the hearing date of the motion. If the motion is denied, the moving and answering papers shall be deemed the complaint and answer, respectively, unless the court orders otherwise.

53. 682 F.Supp. 188 (SDNY, March 1988).
54. 1988 U.S. Dist. LEXIS 2660 (SDNY, March 1988).
55. 398 US 144 (1970).
56. Unreported (Civil Ct., Jan. 17, 1989).

3

Adjudication without Trial: Common Preclusive Devices

VOLUNTARY DISMISSAL

It should be obvious that by voluntary dismissal of a complaint the plaintiff may be able to adjudicate the dispute without trial. However, if the defendant has served an answer or has moved for a summary judgment, the federal courts may not agree to a voluntary dismissal "without prejudice."[1] The general rule appears to be that only the *first* voluntary dismissal of a claim can be "without prejudice," which means that the plaintiff may bring the suit at a later date.[2] Should a plaintiff have once voluntarily dismissed the claim in either a federal or a state court, the *second* voluntary dismissal will generally operate as an "adjudication on the merits," thus barring the plaintiff from bringing the same claim a *third* time.[3] Once the defendant has answered the complaint or has perhaps moved for summary judgment, the plaintiff may voluntarily dismiss only with the court's consent and approval and on the court's terms and conditions.[4] The court might well order the plaintiff who seeks voluntary dismissal for the second time to pay the court costs of the first action before ruling on the second requested voluntary dismissal.[5]

Some states like New York have simplified procedures for court determination of disputes, for example, by sanctioning actions without pleadings.[6] This simplified procedure is consensual and requires the agreement of all parties, their signatures, and the signatures of their attorneys. It would appear, however, that the voluntary dismissal of a case could not be achieved without the consent and approval of all the parties and their attorneys.[7]

Obviously, the voluntary dismissal obviates the need for a plenary trial, but it should be observed that Rule 41(a) of the Federal Rules of Civil Procedure states that the plaintiff's right to unilateral voluntary dismissal must be exercised "at any time before service by the adverse party of an answer or of a motion for summary judgment, whichever first occurs. . . . " Plaintiff's right of voluntary dismissal is curtailed where defendant has set up a counterclaim or otherwise sought affirmative relief. Interestingly, under Section 581(1) of the California Civil Code the plaintiff may voluntarily dismiss "at any time before the actual commencement of trial."

INVOLUNTARY DISMISSAL

The involuntary dismissal of a case by court order can take place for a myriad of reasons, including (a) failure to prosecute or simply failure of the plaintiff to pursue his or her remedy after a reasonable period of time; (b) disobedience of a court order, such as plaintiff's failure to respect a pretrial procedure or to comply with a discovery order; and (c) plaintiff's failure to assert a valid cause of action or to show that he or she is entitled to relief.[8] Should the court in a nonjury case involuntarily dismiss the claim, the court will normally make findings of fact as if the case has been fully tried and adjudicated. In a jury case the involuntary dismissal is in effect a directed verdict.[9] The point is clear: an involuntary dismissal is "with prejudice" and has the effect of an adjudication on the merits, an adjudication without trial. There are, however, several exceptions to this postulate, to wit: (a) lack of jurisdiction over parties or subject matter or both, or insufficient and improper service of process; (b) improper venue; or (c) failure to join an indispensable party.[10] These exceptions are examined at length in civil procedure textbooks and treatises.[11]

MOTION PRACTICE

There are innumerable state and federal rules of procedure that address motion practice as to particularity of statements and as to amendment or supplement or correction of pleadings, all of which can constitute adjudication without trial. For example, Rule 3024 of New York Civil Practice Law and Rules (CPL& R) delineates the motion to correct pleadings.[12] Vague or ambiguous pleadings and scandalous or prejudicial matter are subject to removal from the pleadings; motions to strike the pleadings or motions for more definite statement may lead to adjudication.[13] Amended and supplemental pleadings are described in Rule 3025 of New York CPL & R,[14] and approval or disapproval of such motions is generally within the discretion of the court.[15] In *Glasser v. Jewish Hospital & Medical Center* the trial court properly granted defendant's motion for leave to amend its answer to assert the defense of statute of limitations; there was no prejudice to plaintiff by the amended pleading, but since there was a delay on the part of the defendant in so moving, the court assessed costs upon defendant's attorney, who would pay the monies to the plaintiff.[16] In New York the plaintiff is generally entitled to serve an amended complaint as a matter of right, without seeking leave of the court, within 20 days after service of defendant's motion to dismiss on jurisdictional grounds.[17] Indeed, Rule 3025 in New York is specific in its direction that leave should be given freely to a party to amend his or her pleading.[18] In an action by a contractor against the City of New York to recover cost overruns on a street repaving contract, the trial court did not abuse its discretion as a matter of law in permitting the city to amend its answer to assert the affirmative defenses of waiver and release, since there must be lateness coupled with significant prejudice to the other side in order to bar amendment.[19]

Rules 3013 and 3014 of New York CPL & R deal with particularity of statements generally and with pleading statements in particular.[20] Again, such rules may result in adjudication before trial, although in most instances courts are liberal in not deciding disputes without evidence of other violations of pleadings.[21] Bills of particulars are described in Rule 3041, and the procedure is detailed in Rule 3042.[22] In a medical malpractice action summary judgment was properly entered in favor of defendants where plaintiff's excuse for failure to comply with a 20-day conditional order of preclusion, entered after plaintiff had failed to furnish defendants with a copy of a bill of particulars, was essentially due to law office failure.[23] Rule 3043 sets forth the necessary particulars that may be required to recover for personal injuries in New York.[24] Verification of the bills of particulars is briefly outlined in Rule 3044.[25]

The motion to dismiss is a preclusive weapon particularly used in civil rights actions, and 42 USC 1479 is one example where the 10th U.S. Court of Appeals was unwilling to grant defendant's motion to dismiss, although the federal district court did dismiss on grounds that the complaint was frivolous.[26] Here the plaintiff brought his civil rights action under 42 USC 1983, claiming that he was beaten while in custody of the county sheriff. The federal appellate court held in *Collins v. Hladky* that crucial fact of whether the sheriff beat or directed the beating of the plaintiff could not be determined solely from conflicting affidavits or in summary judgment–type proceedings.[27] On the other hand, where the complaint alleging violation of civil rights was so verbose, confused, and redundant, in violation of Rule 8(a) of Federal Rules of Civil Procedure, dismissal was deemed warranted.[28] A civil rights action, wherein the inmate of a state correctional institution challenged the constitutionality of internal procedures for screening incoming mail, was not dismissed for failure to exhaust administrative remedies where there was no proof that, considering the inmate's attempt to seek relief within correctional institution, such remedies were neither speedy nor readily available.[29]

NOTES

1. See Rule 41(a)(1) of the Federal Rules of Civil Procedure (FRCP).
2. See 1 Emanuel's Encyclopedia of American Law (1987) at 188 et seq.
3. See Chapter 3 hereinafter on the preclusive effects of res judicata and collateral estoppel; also see Warren Freedman, Res Judicata and Collateral Estoppel (1988).
4. See Rule 41(a)(2) of FRCP.

5. See Rule 41(d) of FRCP.

6. *§3031. Simplified procedure for court determination of disputes—action without pleadings.*

An action may be commenced without the service of a summons, or may be continued after the service of a summons, without pleadings, by the filing of a statement, signed and acknowledged by all the parties or signed by their attorneys, specifying plainly and concisely the claims and defenses between the parties and the relief requested. Signing constitutes a certificate that the issues are genuine, and such filing, together with a note of issue, to be filed at the same time, shall constitute the joinder of issues in the action. The procedure in any action commenced under this section shall constitute "the New York Simplified Procedure for Court Determination of Disputes" and it shall be sufficient so to identify the procedure in any contract or other document referring to it. A submission of a controversy under this procedure shall constitute a waiver by the parties of the right to trial by jury.

Rule 3032. Contents of statement.

The statement required when an action is commenced without summons, or continued after the service of a summons without pleadings, shall set forth plainly and concisely the claims and defenses in dispute between the parties and the relief sought, including the amount of money demanded, if any. With the permission of the court, amended or supplemental statements may be served and filed at any time.

§3033. Contracts to submit; enforcement of submission.

1. Any written contract, otherwise valid under the substantive law, to submit any existing or future controversy to the court pursuant to section 3031 is valid and enforceable and shall be construed as an implied consent of the parties to the jurisdiction of the supreme court of this state to enforce it pursuant to the procedures of rule 3036, and to enter judgment thereon, and shall constitute a waiver by the parties of the right to trial by jury.

2. If the parties to a dispute arising under a contract to submit a controversy to the court under section 3031 are unable to agree on a statement of claims and defenses and relief sought pursuant to that section, the court on motion shall settle the terms of the statement. In deciding the motion the court shall consider and determine any questions as to the existence of the contract or its validity or the failure of any party to perform it. If a substantial issue of fact be raised as to the making of the contract or submission or the failure to comply therewith, the court or judge shall proceed to trial of such issue without a jury, unless either party should demand a jury trial.

7. See Stell Manufacturing Corp. v. Century Industries, Inc., 260 NYS2d 547 (1970), aff. 16 NY2d 1020, 213 NE2d 313 (1970).

8. See Rule 41(b) of FRCP and also Rule 12(b) of FRCP.

9. See the section "Action on Submitted Facts" in Chapter 4.

10. Supra note 2 at 189. Also note Rules 19 and 41(b) of FRCP.

11. Supra note 2 at 1 to 326.

12. *Rule 3024. Motion to correct pleadings.*

(a) *Vague or ambiguous pleadings.* If a pleading is so vague or ambiguous that a party cannot reasonably be required to frame a response he may move for a more definite statement.

(b) *Scandalous or prejudicial matter.* A party may move to strike any scandalous or prejudicial matter unnecessarily inserted in a pleading.

(c) *Time limits; pleading after disposition.* A notice of motion under this rule shall be served within twenty days after service of the challenged pleading. If the motion is denied, the responsive pleading shall be served within ten days after service of notice of entry of the order and, if it is granted, an amended pleading complying with the order shall be served within that time.

13. See People v. Zachary, 381 NYS2d 112 (1975).

14. *Rule 3025. Amended and supplemental pleadings.*

(a) *Amendments without leave.* A party may amend his pleading once without leave of court within twenty days after its service, or at any time before the period for responding to it expires, or within twenty days after service of a pleading responding to it.

(b) *Amendments and supplemental pleadings by leave.* A party may amend his pleading, or supplement it by setting forth additional or subsequent transactions or occurrences, at any time by leave of court or by stipulation of all parties. Leave shall be freely given upon such terms as may be just including the granting of costs and continuances.

(c) *Amendment to conform to the evidence.* The court may permit pleadings to be amended before or after judgment to conform them to the evidence, upon such terms as may be just including the granting of costs and continuances.

(d) *Responses to amended or supplemental pleadings.* Except where otherwise prescribed by law or order of the court, there shall be an answer or reply to an amended or supplemental pleading if an answer or reply is required to the pleading being amended or supplemented. Service of such an answer or reply shall be made within twenty days after service of the amended or supplemental pleading to which it responds.

15. See De Carlo v. Economy Baler Division of American Hoist & Derrick Co., 394 NYS2d 468 (1977).

16. 440 NYS2d 55 (1981).

17. See Badger v. Lehigh Valley Railroad Co., 360 NYS2d 523 (1974).

18. See A. J. Pegno Construction Corp. v. New York, 463 NYS2d 214 (App. Div., 1st Dept., 1983).

19. Edenwald Contracting Co. v. City of New York, 60 NY2d 957, 459 NE2d 164 (1983).

20. *§3013. Particularity of statements generally.*

Statements in a pleading shall be sufficiently particular to give the court and parties notice of the transactions, occurrences, or series of transactions or occurrences, intended to be proved and the material elements of each cause of action or defense.

Rule 3014. Statements.

Every pleading shall consist of plain and concise statements in consecutively numbered paragraphs. Each paragraph shall contain, as far as practicable, a single allegation. Reference to an incorporation of allegations may subsequently be by number. Prior statements in a pleading shall be deemed repeated or adopted subsequently in the same pleading whenever express repetition or adoption is unnecessary for a clear presentation of the subsequent matters. Separate causes of action or defenses shall be separately stated and numbered and may be stated regardless of consistency. Causes of action or defenses may be stated alternatively or hypothetically. A copy of any writing which is attached to a pleading is a part thereof for all purposes.

21. See Ditmar Explosives, Inc., v. A. E. Ottaviano, Inc., 20 NY2d 498, 231 NE2d 756 (1971).

22. *Rule 3042. Procedure for bill of particulars.*

(a) *Notice.* A request for a bill of particulars or a copy of the items of an account shall be made by serving a written notice stating the items concerning which such particulars are desired. If the party upon whom such notice is served is unwilling to give such particulars, in whole or in part, he may move to vacate or modify such notice within ten days after receipt thereof. The notice or supporting papers shall specify clearly the objections and the grounds therefor. If no such motion is made the bill of particulars shall be served within twenty days after the demand therefor, unless the court shall otherwise direct.

(b) *Motion.* Instead of proceeding by demand, the party may move for a bill of particulars, or copy of the items of account in the first instance.

(c) *Preclusion for failure to supply bill.* In the event that a party fails to furnish a bill of particulars, or copy of the items of an account the court, upon notice, may preclude him from giving evidence at the trial of the items of which particulars have not been delivered.

(d) *Preclusion for defective bill.* Where a bill of particulars, or copy of the items of an account, is regarded as defective or insufficient by the party upon whom it is served, the court, upon notice, may make an order of preclusion or directing the service of a further bill. In the absence of special circumstances, a motion for such relief shall be made within ten days after the receipt of the bill claimed to be insufficient.

(e) *Conditional order of preclusion.* A preclusion order may provide that it will be effective unless a proper bill is served within a specified time.

(f) *Affidavits.* Affidavits to be used in support of or in opposition to a motion under this rule may be made by a party or his attorney.

(g) *Amendment.* In any action or proceeding in a court in which a note of issue is required to be filed, a party may amend his bill of particulars once as of course before trial, prior to the filing of a note of issue.

23. See O'Neal v. Pankin, 456 NYS2d 228 (App. Div., 3d Dept., 1982).

24. *Rule 3043. Bill of particulars in personal injury actions.*

(a) *Specified particulars.* In actions to recover for personal injuries the following particulars may be required:

(1) The date and approximate time of day of the occurrence;

(2) Its approximate location;

(3) General statement of the acts or omissions constituting the negligence claimed;

(4) Where notice of a condition is a prerequisite, whether actual or constructive notice is claimed;

(5) If actual notice is claimed, a statement of when and to whom it was given;

(6) Statement of the injuries and description of those claimed to be permanent, and in an action designated in subsection (a) of section five thousand one hundred four of the insurance law, for personal injuries arising out of negligence in the use or operation of a motor vehicle in this state, in what respect plaintiff has sustained a serious injury, as defined in subsection (d) of section five thousand one hundred two of the insurance law, or economic loss greater than basic economic loss, as defined in subsection (a) of section five thousand one hundred two of the insurance law;

(7) Length of time confined to bed and to house;

(8) Length of time incapacitated from employment; and

(9) Total amounts claimed as special damages for physicians' services and medical supplies; loss of earnings, with name and address of the employer; hospital expenses; nurses' services.

(b) *Supplemental bill of particulars without leave.* A party may serve a supplemental bill of particulars with respect to claims of continuing special damages and disabilities without leave of court at any time, but not less than thirty days prior to trial. Provided however that no new cause of action may be alleged or new injury claimed and that the other party shall upon seven days notice, be entitled to newly exercise any and all rights of discovery but only with respect to such continuing special damages and disabilities.

(c) *Discretion of court.* Nothing contained in the foregoing shall be deemed to limit the court in denying in a proper case, any one or more of the foregoing particulars, or in a proper case, in granting other, further or different particulars.

25. *§3044. Verification of bill of particulars.*

If a pleading is verified, a subsequent bill of particulars or a copy of the items of account of that pleading shall also be verified. A bill of particulars of any pleading with respect to a cause of action for negligence shall be verified whether such pleading be verified or not.

26. See Warren Freedman, Frivolous Law Suits and Frivolous Defenses (1987).

27. 603 F2d 824 (10th Cir., 1985).

28. See Corcoran v. Yorty, 347 F2d 222 (9th Cir., 1965), cert. den. 382 US 966 (1966); also 382 US 1002, 384 US 923, and 388 US 925 (1966).

29. See Cofone v. Manson, 409 F. Supp. 1033 (Conn., 1976).

4

Accelerated Judgments: An Overview

There are innumerable preclusive devices under the heading of accelerated judgments, such as motion to dismiss,[1] offer of judgment, judgment by confession, default judgment, voluntary discontinuance, action on submitted facts, and directed verdict and/or judgment notwithstanding the verdict.

OFFER OF JUDGMENT

Rule 68 of the Federal Rules of Civil Procedure provides that, at any time more than 10 days before trial begins, a party defending against a claim or against a counterclaim or cross-claim may serve upon his or her opponent an offer to allow judgment to be taken with costs then accrued.[2] If the opposing party accepts the offer of judgment, judgment is entered in accordance with the terms of the offer; but, if the offer of judgment is rejected, either expressly or as a result of the offeree's failure to accept it in a timely manner, the offeree assumes the risk of incurring the offeror's subsequent costs if the judgment finally obtained is not more favorable than the terms contained in the offer of judgment. Rule 68 is applicable not only where the ultimate judgment is in the complaining party's favor, but on terms less favorable than those offered.[3] Federal Rule 68 has also been adopted by many states, including California, Connecticut, and Michigan.[4]

The U.S. Supreme Court in *Marek v. Chesney* illustrates Rule 68 in action.[5] Here three police officers shot and killed the son of the plaintiff, who sued the police officers in federal court under the federal civil rights statute[6] and also under several Illinois tort laws. The defendants made a timely offer of judgment of $100,000, including accrued costs and attorneys' fees, which plaintiff promptly rejected. Subsequently, plaintiff was awarded $5,000 on the wrongful death claim, $52,000 on the civil rights cause of action, and $3,000 in punitive damages, for a total of only $60,000. Thereupon plaintiff filed a claim for $172,000 in costs and attorneys' fees, an amount that included costs and fees incurred *after* the Rule 68 offer of judgment. The parties agreed that $30,000 was a fair estimate of allowable costs, including attorneys' fees accrued before the offer of judgment. The federal district court agreed with defendants that plaintiff was not entitled to an award of costs and attorneys' fees incurred *after* the time of the offer of judgment.[7] But the Seventh U.S. Court of Appeals reversed, ruling that Congress, in enacting Rule 68, could not have intended to deter good-faith civil rights lawsuits with the prospect of losing the award of attorneys' fees should the ultimate recovery not exceed the judgment offer, no matter how inadequate the offer.[8] The highest court then reversed the federal appellate court, holding that Rule 68 and the civil rights cause of action authorized the inclusion of attorneys' fees in the cost-shifting provision of Rule 68, and that no express congressional intent to the contrary existed. Thus, defendants were not liable for costs and attorneys' fees incurred subsequent to the offer of judgment by defendants.[9]

New York's statutes delineate the tender,[10] the offer to liquidate damages conditionally,[11] and the offer to compromise.[12] The tender statute in New York enables the party to make a deposit of the monies demanded by the other party, and is especially useful in the mortgage scenario. For example, in *362 Washington Street Corp. v. Peninsula National Bank*, the mortgagee, who mailed a check for less than the entire amount of an escrow fund to the mortgagor upon condemnation of the property, failed to make a tender sufficient to stop the running of interest and costs in an action by the mortgagor to recover the entire amount of the escrow.[13] The necessary ingredient of the tender statute is the actual payment of money into court.[14] The offer to liquidate damages conditionally in New York must be a formal tender so as to stop the running of interest.[15] And the offer to compromise (except in a matrimonial action) is also designed to stop the running of interest and accruing costs.[16]

It is obvious that the salutary purpose of Rule 68 of the Federal Rules of Civil Procedure and of the various state statutes is to encourage prompt settlement of disputes and to avoid unnecessarily protracted litigation.[17] The risks of bearing the burden of the offeror's costs after the offer of judgment has been made gives impetus to the rule.[18] The offer of judgment here must be unconditional, must be reasonable as to amount, and certainly must not be ambiguous.[19] The offer of judgment has a binding effect when refused as well as when accepted.[20] It should be observed that whether the offer of judgment is more favorable than the judgment ultimately obtained, the complaining party's post-offer costs are not added to the judgment obtained for purposes of making the comparison.[21] The U.S. Supreme Court in 1985 confirmed that, for purposes of the cost-shifting provisions of Rule 68, costs include attorneys' fees where such fees are within the definition of costs under the relevant substantive law or statute at issue.[22] Where attorneys' fees are not within the definition of costs under the relevant substantive law or statute at issue, the courts have generally held that they are not to be included as costs under Rule 68 of the Federal Rules of Civil Procedure.[23]

In the California decision of *Morin v. ABA Recovery Service, Inc.*, the plaintiff sued in 1980 when the defendant wrongfully repossessed plaintiff's trailer; plaintiff also sought recovery for intentional infliction of emotional distress and other damages.[24] In 1983 plaintiff made an offer of judgment in the sum of $24,000 under the California offer of settlement statute, but defendant rejected that offer. The 1985 trial resulted in a jury verdict of $67,500 for the winning plaintiff, and plaintiff requested statutory prejudgment interest, which was denied. On appeal, the California appellate court agreed with plaintiff that the California statute required an award of interest, but the appellate court could not do so because it could not compute the interest since the verdict did not apportion damages among plaintiff's many damage claims!

JUDGMENT BY CONFESSION

Another adjudication without trial is the judgment by confession, illustrated in Section 3128 of New York CPL & R.[25] In the leading case of *Princeton Bank & Trust Co. v. Berley*, the New York appellate court explained that the confessed judgment statute and its gloss do not require a procrustean dovetailing of detail, since such an overly meticulous reading of the statute would place in doubt all but the most exquisitely composed affidavits; it is sufficient under the New York statute that there appear to be an honest recital of enough detail to permit a check of its genuineness and to simplify an investigation of the underlying facts.[26] Furthermore, errors of detail that are not clearly prejudicial and that are minor, or are balanced by other details that correct them, should not have the devastating effect of invalidating the confessed judgment. While a strict compliance must still be shown with the provisions of the New York statute, the statute is intended to protect creditors of a defendant from judgments entered on confession by collusion, and any alleged deficiency in the statement of confessions is not available to the judgment debtor.[27] The statutory mandate that confession of judgment be entered upon affidavit by defendant "stating concisely the facts out of which the debt arose and showing that the sum confessed is justly due or to become due" is designed for the protection of third persons who might be prejudiced in the event that collusively confessed judgment is entered and not for protection of defendant, according to *Mall Commercial Corp. v. Chrisa Restaurant, Inc.*, a leading case on this particular issue.[28]

DEFAULT JUDGMENT

Adjudication without trial is also evident in the default judgment that arises when a defendant has "failed to appear, plead or proceed to trial of an action reached and called for trial, or when the court orders a dismissal for any other neglect to proceed.''[29] But a default judgment dismissing the complaint upon plaintiff's failure to apear has not been termed an adjudication on the merits, according to the Commissioner of Social Services on behalf of *Truehart v. Hargrove*.[30] Indeed, the default judgment may be collaterally attacked when it is sued upon in the same or another jurisdiction; the victim of the default judgment may make such a collateral attack either upon the first court's jurisdiction over the parties or upon its subject matter jurisdiction.[31] The sufferer of the default judgment may also contend that his or her failure to appear in the first action was the result of fraud by the other party. In *Britton v. Gannon*[32] the defendant successfully avoided an Oklahoma action to enforce a prior Illinois default judgment on the grounds that he had been fraudulently induced to suffer a default judgment by plaintiff's statement that defendant was a necessary defendant but that plaintiff only wanted to recover property and would not pursue a money judgment against him.[33] But a defendant who appeared in the first action without objecting to the jurisdiction of the court hearing the first action, or a defendant who unsuccessfully litigated the jurisdictional issue in the first action, may not collaterally attack that judgment. In *Baldwin v. Iowa State Traveling Men's Assn.* the defendant had made a special appearance in a Missouri court, lost his objection based on jurisdiction of that court, and then declined to file an answer, with the result that a default judgment was entered against him.[34] Plaintiff then brought suit in Iowa on the default judgment entered in Missouri. The U.S. Supreme court ruled that defendant had no right to raise the jurisdictional objection a second time in Iowa. Note that the highest court had earlier in *Chicot County Drainage District v. Baxter State Bank* held that parties to an action may be held to have waived their objection to the fact that the particular court's eventual judgment was made under a federal statute subsequently determined to be unconstitutional, and therefore they were unable to collaterally attack the default judgment.[35]

The New York court in *Doroski v. Mintler* did not lack jurisdiction to enter a default judgment on a promissory note merely because the statute of limitations may have run during the period in which the plaintiffs were attempting to make service of process.[36] In an action to recover legal fees for services rendered, the New York Appellate Division, Second Dept., in *Dinerstein & Lesser, P.C. v. Ambulette Assn. of New York*, unconditionally granted the law firm's motion for a default judgment where defendant previously had been granted relief from its first default in answering the complaint, where defendant had failed to comply with a prior order permitting it to serve a later answer, and where defendant's excuse for the delay had been insufficient in that it amounted to a law office failure.[37] A default judgment was granted against the owner of property on which blasting operations occurred, although the owner had served a notice of appearance and had filed an answer 13 months after service of the complaint upon it; in *Kliman v. Hutchinson Associates* the New York Appellate Division, Second Dept., observed that no meritorious defense had been shown and that the owner's insurance broker had mistakingly forwarded the complaint to the wrong insurer.[38] Similarly, a default was entered against defendants where at trial their attorney appeared before the court not intending to participate in the trial but solely for the purpose of requesting an adjournment.[39]

To open a default judgment the moving party must present a proper legal excuse and make a showing of a meritorious defense.[40] Where the defendant was a resident of New York at the time of the transaction sued upon, the excuse that he was in Brazil and that he was under the impression that service there was ineffectual because he subsequently became a bona fide resident of Brazil, was insufficient to require an opening of the default judgment.[41] In *Fitzgerald v. Patz* the defendant product manufacturer had defaulted in answering the complaint; the evidence revealed that the product manufacturer had been waiting out a decision on its motion for a change of venue after the other defendant had been removed from the case.[42] The New York court vacated the default judgment on these facts.

Where there is "want of prosecution," as delineated in Section 3216 of the New York CPL & R, the default judgment customarily results.[43] In the federal courts, notice of default is significant, particularly where the evidence points to that party-defendant ignoring the proceeding from the very beginning.[44] Failure to comply with Rule 55(b) of the Federal Rules of Civil Procedure, for example, could be a denial of due process of law, rendering the default judgment void and vulnerable to attack under Rule 60(b)(4).[45] In *Winfield Associates, Inc. v. Stonecipher* the defendant did not make any appearance in the proceeding and manifested no interest in the actions of the court.[46] On the board issue of excusable neglect and mistake of counsel, see *Universal Film Exchanges, Inc. v. Lust*.[47]

VOLUNTARY DISCONTINUANCE

Still another preclusive device that results in adjudication without trial is the voluntary discontinuance, as illustrated by New York's Section 3217 of CPL & R.[48] This statute authorizes a discontinuance without an order of the court under certain conditions, and under other conditions upon order of the court and upon terms and conditions as the court deems proper.[49] The right to discontinue is generally discretionary with the court.[50] Where a summons but not a complaint had been served on the defendant husband and the defendant husband had served a demand for a copy of the complaint, the plaintiff wife in *Hutchison v. Hutchison* was deemed entitled to effect voluntary discontinuance of the divorce proceeding.[51] Obviously, voluntary discontinuance is related to the voluntary dismissal of the complaint,[52] but differs only with respect to the particular statute under which the voluntary action takes place.

In the federal courts, it has been held that a motion to dismiss voluntarily is not a motion for summary judgment.[53] In *American Cyanamid Co. v. Mc-*

Ghee[54] the trial judge was upheld in granting a motion for dismissal voluntarily without prejudice even though it was a second dismissal:

> Rule 41(a)(1) is the shortest and surest route to abort a complaint when it is applicable. So long as plaintiff has not been served with his adversary's answer or motion for summary judgment he need do no more than file a *notice* of dismissal with the Clerk. That document itself closes the file. There is nothing the defendant can do to fan the ashes of that action into life and the court has no role to play. This is a matter of right running to the plaintiff and may not be extinguished or circumscribed by adversary or court. There is not even a perfunctory order of court closing the file. Its alpha and omega was the doing of the plaintiff alone. He suffers no impairment beyond his fee for filing. But this quick and ready tool may be used once, and only once, if clear consequences are to be avoided. A second notice of dismissal not only closes the file, it also closes the case with prejudice to the bringing of another.
>
> The reason for this arbitrary limitation, pointed out in numerous decisions, is to prevent unreasonable abuse and harassment.[55]

ACTION ON SUBMITTED FACTS

The action on submitted facts, as evidenced by Section 3222 of the New York CPL & R, is another preclusive device designed to effect adjudication without trial.[56] It is a useful device to resolve, upon stipulated facts, many controversies such as a determination whether a trust may be terminated,[57] or a controversy as to whether the town board or the town assessor had discretion as to whether to assess town property at full or fractional value,[58] or insurance undertakings, although the record submitted must not be patently incomplete or truncated.[59] As pointed out in *Ciunci v. Wella Corp.*, the New York statute calling for an action on submitted facts is not applicable where the record disclosed that the parties did not agree upon what the facts were but merely acknowledged what the witnesses would testify to if such witnesses were called to testify at trial.[60]

DIRECTED VERDICT AND/OR JUDGMENT NOTWITHSTANDING THE VERDICT

The directed verdict takes the case away from the jury and is a thorough preclusive device that adjudicates before trial.[61] The directed verdict determines the outcome of the case as a matter of law. But a verdict may be directed only if the evidence points all one way and is not susceptible to reasonable inferences that would sustain the position of the nonmoving party.[62] In *Butler v. Goldblatt Bros., Inc.* the Seventh U.S. Court of Appeals upheld a directed verdict againt police officers who had arrested plaintiffs primarily on the basis of an informant's word; the informant, an undercover agent for the security department of the defendant store, was not known to be reliable.[63] Accordingly, the court observed that there was no reasonable basis for believing the information to be reliable, "since the police did not undertake an independent investigation to corroborate the details of the accusations." On the other hand, also in a civil rights case, the Fifth U.S. Court of Appeals reversed a judgment notwithstanding the verdict, or judgment n.o.v.(non obstante veredicto),[64] and reinstated a jury verdict against a mayor, chief of police, and others in connection with an apparent politically motivated arrest of the plaintiff. The court found that reasonable persons could conclude that defendants acted with malice against plaintiff: "Reliance on advice of counsel does not serve as an absolute defense to a civil rights action. . . . A jury is entitled to evaluate the testimony about advice of counsel and to make a decision concerning its credibility."[65]

To evaluate the evidence as to whether a directed verdict is proper, the court should look at all the evidence, both favorable and unfavorable, before determining that the court would be duty-bound to set aside the verdict; or the judge should consider only the evidence favorable to the party having the persuasion burden. In *Powers v. Continental Casualty Co.* the Sixth U.S. Court of Appeals applied a strict standard and stated that a directed verdict should not be issued "unless the fact in dispute is established by the undisputed testimony of one or more disinterested witnesses and different minds cannot reasonably draw different conclusions from such testimony."[66] The Second U.S. Court of Appeals in *Simblest v. Maynard* opined that "only the evidence favorable to the plaintiff and the uncontradicted, unimpeached evidence unfavorable to him" should control; if a reasonable person could not find for the plaintiff, a verdict must be directed against him.[67]

Admittedly, a judge who is requested to direct a verdict is in a dilemma.[68] If the judge grants the directed verdict, the appellate court may find that he or she erred, and an entire new trial would become necessary, wasting the time and expense of the judicial system. On the other hand, if a judge denies the request for directed verdict, he or she may be sending a case to the jury that should be decided by him or her as a matter of law, and again the judge risks being overturned on appeal. The dilemma is generally resolved in the federal courts by the judge "reserving judgment" on the motion for directed verdict and submitting the case to the jury. If the jury decides against the moving party, the judge can then evaluate the legal sufficiency of the evidence on a motion for judgment n.o.v., which would result in the entry of judgment for the party who lost the verdict, that is, a finding that the jury verdict had no sufficient legal basis. The use of the judgment n.o.v. avoids the need for a second trial if the appellate court agrees that the evidence was not sufficient to take the case from the jury. Indeed, in the federal courts, a motion for directed verdict is an absolute prerequisite for the making of a motion for judgment n.o.v.[69] In *Marsh v. Illinois Central Railroad Co.*, where the trial judge granted a judgment n.o.v. in favor of the defendant because the evidence was "overwhelmingly against the plaintiff," the federal appellate court reversed: "There was evidence offered by the plaintiff which if believed might authorize a jury to accept this claim.''[70] Accordingly, the judgment n.o.v. was improper, and a new trial must be held. If a party has unsuccessfully moved for a directed verdict and the verdict turns out against it, the party must move for judgment n.o.v. if the appellate court is to have authority to enter judgment in its favor.[71]

NOTES

1. See the section ''Motion Practice'' in Chapter 3; note Rule 3211 of New York Civil Practice Law and Rules (CPL & R):

Rule 3211. Motion to dismiss.

(a) *Motion to dismiss cause of action.* A party may move for judgment dismissing one or more causes of action asserted against him on the ground that:

1. a defense is founded upon documentary evidence; or
2. the court has not jurisdiction of the subject matter of the cause of action; or
3. the party asserting the cause of action has not legal capacity to sue; or
4. there is another action pending between the same parties for the same cause of action in a court of any state or the United States; the court need not dismiss upon this ground but may make such order as justice requires; or
5. the cause of action may not be maintained because of arbitration and award, collateral estoppel, discharge in bankruptcy, infancy or other disability of the moving party, payment, release, res judicata, statute of limitations, or statute of frauds; or
6. with respect to a counterclaim, if may not be properly interposed in the action; or
7. the pleading fails to state a cause of action; or
8. the court has not jurisdiction of the person of the defendant; or
9. the court has not jurisdiction in an action where service was made under section 314 or 315; or
10. the court should not proceed in the absence of a person who should be a party.

(b) *Motion to dismiss defense.* A party may move for judgment dismissing one or more defenses, on the ground that a defense is not stated or has no merit.

(c) *Evidence permitted; immediate trial; motion treated as one for summary judgment.* Upon the hearing of a motion made under subdivision (a) or (b), either party may submit any evidence that could properly be considered on a motion for summary judgment. Whether or not issue has been joined, the court, after adequate notice to the parties, may treat the motion as a motion for summary judgment. The court may, when appropriate for the expeditious disposition of the controversy, order immediate trial of the issues raised on the motion.

(d) *Facts unavailable to opposing party.* Should it appear from affidavits submitted in opposition to a motion made under subdivision (a) or (b) that facts essential to justify opposition may exist but cannot then be stated, the court may deny the motion, allowing the moving party to assert the objection in his responsive pleading, if any, or may order a continuance to permit further affidavits to be obtained or disclosure to be had and may make such other order as may be just.

(e) *Number, time and waiver of objections; motion to plead over.* At any time before service of the responsive pleading is required, a party may move on one or more of the grounds set forth in subdivision (a), and no more than one such motion shall be permitted. Any objection or defense based upon a ground set forth in paragraphs one, three, four, five and six of subdivision (a) is waived unless raised either by such motion or in the responsive pleading. A motion based upon a ground specified in paragraphs two, seven or ten of subdivision (a) may be made at any subsequent time or in a later pleading, if one is permitted. An objection based upon a ground specified in paragraphs eight or nine of subdivision (a) is waived if a party moves on any of the grounds set forth in subdivision (a) without raising such objection or if, having made no objection under subdivision (a), he does not raise such objection in the responsive pleading. Where a motion is made on the ground set forth in paragraph seven of subdivision (a), or on the ground that a defense is not stated, if the opposing party desires leave to plead again in the event the motion is granted, he shall so state in his opposing papers and may set forth evidence that could properly be considered on a motion for summary judgment in support of a new pleading; leave to plead again shall not be granted unless the court is satisfied that the opposing party has good ground to support his cause of action or defense; the court may require the party seeking leave to plead again to submit evidence to justify the granting of such leave.

(f) *Extension of time to plead.* Service of a notice of motion under subdivision (a) or (b) before service of a pleading responsive to the cause of action or defense sought to be dismissed extends the time to serve the pleading until ten days after service of notice of entry of the order.

2. Rule 68 provides: ''At any time more than 10 days before the trial begins, a party defending against a claim may serve upon the adverse party an offer to allow judgment to be taken against the defending party for the money or property or to the effect specified in his offer, with costs then accrued. If within 10 days after the service of the offer the adverse party serves written notice that the offer is accepted, either party may then file the offer and notice of acceptance together with proof of service thereof and thereupon the clerk shall enter judgment. An offer not accepted shall be deemed withdrawn and evidence thereof is not admissible except in a proceeding to determine costs. If the judgment finally obtained by the offeree is not more favorable than the offer, the offeree must pay the costs incurred after the making of the offer. The fact that an offer is made but not accepted does not preclude a subsequent offer. When the liability of one party to another has been determined by verdict or order of judgment, but the amount or extent of the liability remains to be determined by further proceedings, the party adjudged liable may make an offer of judgment, which shall have the same effect as an offer made before trial if it is served within a reasonable time not less than 10 days prior to the commencement of hearings to determine the amount or extent of liability.'' Also see generally Case & Comment (January–February 1987) at 22 et seq.

3. Note Delta Airlines, Inc. v. August, 450 US 346 (1981).

4. See Section 998 of California Code of Civil Procedure; Sections 52–193 to 52–195 of Connecticut General Statutes Annotated, and Rule 2.405 of Michigan Rules of Court.

5. 473 US 1 (1985).

6. 42 USC 1983.

7. 547 F. Supp. 542 (ND Ill., 1982).

8. 720 F2d 474 (7th Cir., 1983).

9. Note generally Def. Couns. J. (April 1988) at 153 et seq.

10. *Rule 3219. Tender.*

At any time not later than ten days before trial, any party against whom a cause of action based upon contract, expressed or implied, is asserted, and against whom a separate judgment may be taken, may, without court order, deposit with the clerk of the court for safekeeping, an amount deemed by him to be sufficient to satisfy the claim asserted against him, and serve upon the claimant a written tender of payment to satisfy such claim. A copy of the written tender shall be filed with the clerk when the money is so deposited. The clerk shall place money so received in the safe or vault of the court to be provided for the safekeeping thereof, there to be kept by him until withdrawal by claimant or return to the depositor or payment thereof to the county treasurer or commissioner of finance of the city of New York, as hereinafter provided. Within ten days after such deposit the claimant may withdraw the amount deposited upon filing a duly acknowledged statement that the withdrawal is in satisfaction of the claim. The clerk shall thereupon enter judgment dismissing the pleading setting forth the claim, without costs.

Where there is no withdrawal within such ten-day period, the amount deposited shall, upon request be repaid to the party who deposited it. If the tender is not accepted and the claimant fails to obtain a more favorable judgment, he shall not recover interest or costs from the time of the offer, but shall pay costs for defending against the claim from that time. A tender shall not be made known to the jury. . . .

11. *Rule 3220. Offer to liquidate damages conditionally.*

At any time not later than ten days before trial, any party against whom a cause of action based upon contract, express or implied, is asserted may serve upon the claimant a written offer to allow judgment to be taken against him for a sum therein specified, with costs then accrued, if the party against whom the claim is asserted fails in his defense. If within ten days thereafter the claimant serves a written notice that he accepts the offer, and damages are awarded to him on the trial, they shall be assessed in the sum specified in the offer. If the offer is not so accepted and the claimant fails to obtain a more favorable judgment, he shall pay the expenses necessarily incurred by the party against whom the claim is asserted, for trying the issue of damages from the time of the offer. The expenses shall be ascertained by the judge or referee before whom the case is tried. An offer under this rule shall not be made known to the jury.

12. *Rule 3221. Offer to compromise.*

Except in a matrimonial action, at any time not later than ten days before trial, any party against whom a claim is asserted, and against whom a separate judgment may be taken, may serve upon the claimant a written offer to allow judgment to be taken against him for a sum or property or to the effect therein specified, with costs then accrued. If within ten days thereafter the claimant serves a written notice that he accepts the offer, either party may file the summons, complaint and offer, with proof of acceptance, and thereupon the clerk shall enter judgment accordingly. If the offer is not accepted and the claimant fails to obtain a more favorable judgment, he shall not recover costs from the time of the offer, but shall pay costs from that time. An offer of judgment shall not be made known to the jury.

13. 279 NYS2d 204 (1971).

14. See Deck v. Chatauqua Colony Patrons' Fire Relief Assn., 343 NYS2d 855 (1974).

15. Supra note 11.

16. See Bache & Co. v. Liberty Mutual Insurance Co., 367 NYS2d 11 (1975).

17. Supra note 2 at 27; also see Staffend v. Lake Central Airlines, Inc., 47 FRD 218 (ND Ohio, 1969).

18. See Waters v. Heublein, Inc., 485 F. Supp. 110 (ND Cal., 1979).

19. Note Boorstein v. New York, 107 FRD 31 (SDNY, 1985).

20. Id.

21. See Marek v. Chesney, 105 S. Ct. 3012 (1985).

22. Id.

23. See Coleman v. McLaren, 92 FRD 754 (ND Ill., 1981) and 98 FRD 638, 572 F. Supp. 178, 631 F. Supp. 749, and 631 F. Supp. 763 (1983).

24. 240 Cal. Rptr. 509 (1987).

25. *§3218. Judgment by confession.*

(a) *Affidavit of defendant.* Except as provided in section thirty-two hundred one, a judgment by confession may be entered, without an action, either for money due or to become due, or to secure the plaintiff against a contingent liability in behalf of the defendant, or both, upon an affidavit executed by the defendant:

1. stating the sum for which judgment may be entered, authorizing the entry of judgment, and stating the county where the defendant resides or if he is a non-resident, the county in which entry is authorized.

2. if the judgment to be confessed is for money due or to become due, stating concisely the facts out of which the debt arose and showing that the sum confessed is justly due or to become due; and

3. if the judgment to be confessed is for the purpose of securing the plaintiff against a contingent liability, stating concisely the facts constituting the liability and showing that the sum confessed does not exceed the amount of the liability.

(b) *Entry of judgment.* At any time within three years after the affidavit is executed, it may be filed with the clerk of the county where the defendant stated in his affidavit that he resided when it was executed or, if the defendant was then a non-resident, with the clerk of the county designated in the affidavit. Thereupon the clerk shall enter a judgment in the supreme court for the sum confessed. He shall tax costs to the amount of fifteen dollars, besides disbursements taxable in an action. The judgment may be docketed and enforced in the same manner and with the same effect as a judgment in an action in the supreme court. No judgment by confession may be entered after the defendant's death.

(c) *Execution where the judgment is not all due.* Where the debt for which the judgment is entered is not all due, execution may be issued only for the sum which has become due. The execution shall be in the form prescribed for an execution upon a judgment for the full amount recovered, except that it shall direct the sheriff to collect only the sum due, stating the amount with interest and the costs of the judgment. Notwithstanding the issuance and collection of such an execution, the judgment shall remain in force as security for the sum or sums to become due after the execution is issued. When further sums become due, further executions may be issued in the same manner.

(d) *Confession by joint debtors.* One or more joint debtors may confess a judgment for a joint debt or to become due. Where all the joint debtors do not unite in the confession, the judgment shall be entered and enforced against only those who confessed it and it is not a bar to an action against the other joint debtors upon the same demand.

26. 394 NYS2d 714 (1977).

27. Giryluk v. Giryluk, 289 NYS2d 458 (1969), affd, 23 NY2d 894, 245 NE2d 818 (1969).

28. 381 NYS2d 391 (1975).

29. See Section 3215 of New York CPL & R as set forth hereinafter:

§3215. Default judgment.

(a) *Default and entry.* When a defendant has failed to appear, plead or proceed to trial of an action reached and called for trial, or when the court orders a dismissal for any other neglect to proceed, the plaintiff may seek a default judgment against him. If the plaintiff's claim is for a sum certain or for a sum which can by computation be made certain, application may be made to the clerk within one year after the default. The clerk, upon submission of the requisite proof, shall enter judgment for the amount demanded in the complaint or stated in the notice served pursuant to subdivision (b) of Rule 305, plus costs and interest. Upon entering a judgment against less than all defendants, the clerk shall also enter an order severing the action as to them. When a plaintiff has failed to proceed to trial of an action reached and called for trial, or when the court orders a dismissal for any other neglect to proceed, the defendant may make application to the clerk within one year after the default and the clerk, upon submission of the requisite proof, shall enter judgment for costs. Where the case is not one in which the clerk can enter judgment, the plaintiff shall apply to the court for judgment.

(b) *Procedure before court.* The court, with or without a jury, may make an assessment or take an account or proof, or may direct a reference. When a reference is directed, the court may direct that the report be returned to it for further action or, except where otherwise prescribed by law, that judgment be entered by the clerk in accordance with the report without any further application. Except in a matrimonial action, no finding of fact in writing shall be necessary to the entry of a judgment on default. The judgment shall not exceed in amount or differ in type from that demanded in the complaint or stated in the notice served pursuant to subdivision (b) of rule 305.

(c) *Default not entered within one year.* If the plaintiff fails to take proceedings for the entry of judgment within one year after the default, the court shall not enter judgment but shall dismiss the complaint as abandoned, without costs, upon its own initiative or on motion, unless sufficient cause is shown why the complaint should not be dismissed. A motion by the defendant under this subdivision does not constitute an appearance in the action.

(d) *Place of application to court.* An application to the court under this section may be made, except where otherwise prescribed by local court rules, by motion at any trial term in which the action is triable or at any special term in which a motion in the action could be made. Any reference shall be had in the county in which the action is triable, unless the court orders otherwise.

(e) *Proof.* On any application for judgment by default, the applicant shall file proof of service of the summons and the complaint, or a summons and notice served pursuant to subdivision (b) of rule 305 or subdivision (a) of rule 316, and proof by affidavit made by the party of the facts constituting the claim, the default and the amount due. Where a verified complaint has been served it may be used as the affidavit of the facts constituting the claim and the amount due; in such case, an affidavit as to the default shall be made by the party or his attorney. When jurisdiction is based on an attachment of property, the affidavit must state that an order of attachment granted in the action has been levied on the property of the defendant, describe the property and state its value. Proof of mailing the notice required by section three hundred eight of the civil practice law and rules shall also be filed where such notice is required.

(f) *Notice.*

1. Notice is not required when the judgment may be entered by the clerk. Except as otherwise provided with respect to specific actions, if application must be made to the court, any defendant who has appeared is entitled to at least five days' notice of the

time and place of the motion, and if more than one year has elapsed since the default any defendant who has not appeared is entitled to the same notice unless the court orders otherwise. The court may also dispense with the requirement of notice when a defendant who has appeared has failed to proceed to trial of an action reached and called for trial.

2. Where an application for judgment must be made to the court, the defendant who has failed to appear may serve on the plaintiff at any time before the motion for judgment is heard a written demand for notice of any reference or assessment by a jury which may be granted on the motion. Such a demand does not constitute an appearance in the action. Thereupon at least five days' notice of the time and place of the reference or assessment by a jury shall be given to the defendant by service on the person whose name is subscribed to the demand, in the manner prescribed for service of papers generally.

(g) *Judgment for excess where counterclaim interposed.* In an action upon a contract where the complaint demands judgment for a sum of money only, if the answer does not deny the plaintiff's claim but sets up a counterclaim demanding an amount less than the plaintiff's claim, the plaintiff upon filing with the clerk an admission of the counterclaim may take judgment for the excess as upon a default.

(h) *Default judgment for failure to comply with stipulation of settlement.*

1. Where, after commencement of an action, a stipulation of settlement is made, providing, in the event of failure to comply with the stipulation, for entry without further notice of a judgment in a specified amount with interest, if any, from a date certain, the clerk shall enter judgment on the stipulation and an affidavit as to the failure to comply with the terms thereof, together with a complaint or a concise statement of the facts on which the claim was based.

2. Where, after commencement of an action, a stipulation of settlement is made, providing, in the event of failure to comply with the stipulation, for entry without further notice of a judgment dismissing the action, the clerk shall enter judgment on the stipulation and an affidavit as to the failure to comply with the terms thereof, together with the pleadings or a concise statement of the facts on which the claim and defense were based.

30. 446 NYS2d 715 (App. Div., 4th Dept., 1981).

31. See 1 Emanuel's Encyclopedia of American Law (1987) at 65–66.

32. 285 P2d 407 (Okla., 1955).

33. Supra note 31 at 65–66.

34. 283 US 522 (1931); also see U.S. v. Cirami, 535 F2d 736 (2d Cir., 1976).

35. 308 US 371 (1940).

36. 374 NYS2d 721 (1975).

37. 451 NYS2d 441 (App. Div., 2d Dept., 1982).

38. 456 NYS2d 809 (App. Div., 2d Dept., 1982).

39. See First National Bank & Trust Co. v. Classic Collateral Corp., 355 NYS2d 504 (1974).

40. See Broadlawn Harbor Assn. v. Aetna Casualty & Surety Co., 457 NYS2d 431 (App. Div., 2d Dept., 1982).

41. See Krebs v. Raborg, 290 NYS2d 380 (1968).

42. 458 NYS2d 599 (App. Div., 1st Dept., 1983).

43. *Rule 3216. Want of prosecution.*

(a) Where a party unreasonably neglects to proceed generally in an action or otherwise delays in the prosecution thereof against any party who may be liable to a separate judgment, or unreasonably fails to serve and file a note of issue, the court, on its own initiative or upon motion, may dismiss the party's pleading on terms. Unless the order specifies otherwise, the dismissal is not on the merits.

(b) No dismissal shall be directed under any portion of subdivision (a) of this rule and no court initiative shall be taken or motion made thereunder unless the following conditions precedent have been complied with:

(1) Issue must have been joined in the action;

(2) One year must have elapsed since the joinder of issue;

(3) The court or party seeking such relief, as the case may be, shall have served a written demand by registered or certified mail requiring the party against whom such relief is sought to resume prosecution of the action and to serve and file a note of issue within ninety days after receipt of such demand, and further stating that the default by the party upon whom such notice is served in complying with such demand within said ninety day period will serve as a basis for a motion by the party serving said demand for dismissal as against him for unreasonably neglecting to proceed.

(c) In the event that the party upon whom is served the demand specified in subdivision (b)(3) of this rule serves and files a note of issue within such ninety day period, the same shall be deemed sufficient compliance with such demand and deligent prosecution of the action; and in such event, no such court initiative shall be taken and no such motion shall be made, and if taken or made, the court initiative or motion to dismiss shall be denied.

(d) After an action has been placed on the calendar by the service and filing of a note of issue, with or without any such demand, provided, however, if such demand has been served, within the said ninety day period, the action may not be dismissed by reason of any neglect, failure or delay in prosection of the action prior to the said service and filing of such note of issue.

(e) In the event that the party upon whom is served the demand specified in subdivision (b)(3) of this rule fails to serve and file a note of issue within such ninety day period, the court may take such initiative or grant such motion unless the said party shows justifiable excuse for the delay and a good and meritorious cause of action.

(f) The provisions of this rule shall not apply to proceedings within rule thirty-four hundred four.

44. See Sonus Corp. v. Matsushita Electric Industrial Co., Ltd., 61 FRD 644 (Mass., 1974).

45. Note Bass v. Hoagland, 172 F3d 205 (5th Cir., 1949).

46. 429 F2d 1087 (10th Cir., 1970).

47. 479 F2d 573 (4th Cir., 1973).

48. *Rule 3217. Voluntary discontinuance.*

(a) *Without an order.* Any party asserting a claim may discontinue it without an order.

1. by serving upon all parties to the action a notice of discontinuance at any time before a responsive pleading is served or within twenty days after service of the pleading asserting the claim, whichever is earlier, and filing the notice with proof of service with the clerk of the court; or

2. by filing with the clerk of the court before the case has been submitted to the court or jury a stipulation in writing signed by the attorneys of record for all parties, provided that no party is an infant, incompetent person for whom a committee has been appointed

or conservatee and no person not a party has an interest in the subject matter of the action.

(b) *By order of court.* Except as provided in subdivision (a), an action shall not be discontinued by a party asserting a claim except upon order of the court and upon terms and conditions, as the court deems proper. After the cause has been submitted to the court or jury to determine the facts the court may not order an action discontinued except upon the stipulation of all parties appearing in the action.

(c) *Effect of discontinuance.* Unless otherwise stated in the notice, stipulation or order of discontinuance, the discontinuance is without prejudice, except that a discontinuance by means of notice operates as an adjudication on the merits if the party has once before discontinued by any method an action based on or including the same cause of action in a court of any state or the United States.

49. See D v. D, 449, 584 (1982).

50. See Glenmark, Inc. v. Carity, 253 NYS2d 481 (1970).

51. 386 NYS2d 897 (1975).

52. See the section ''Voluntary Dismissal'' in Chapter 3.

53. See Kilpatrick v. Texas & Pacific Railroad Co., 166 F2d 788 (2d Cir., 1948). Cf. Tele-Views News Co. v. SRB TV Publishing Co., 28 FRD 303 (ED Pa., 1961).

54. 317 F2d 295 (5th Cir., 1963).

55. On the issue of ''judgment not on the merits,'' note Section 48.1 of Restatement (Second) of Judgments:

§48.1. Judgment for Defendant—Exceptions to the General Rule of Bar

(1) A personal judgment for the defendant, although valid and final, does not bar another action by the plaintiff on the same claim:
  (a) When the judgment is one of dismissal for lack of jurisdiction, for improper venue, or for nonjoinder or misjoinder of parties; or
  (b) When the plaintiff agrees to or elects a nonsuit (or voluntary dismissal) without prejudice or the court directs that the plaintiff be nonsuited (or that the action be otherwise dismissed) without prejudice; or
  (c) When by statute or rule of court the judgment does not operate as a bar to another action on the same claim, or does not so operate unless the court specifies, and no such specification is made.

(2) A valid and final personal judgment for the defendant which rests on the prematurity of the action or on the plaintiff's failure to satisfy a precondition to suit, does not bar another action by the plaintiff instituted after the claim has matured, or the precondition has been satisfied, unless a second action is precluded by operation of the substantive law, or the circumstances are such that it would be manifestly unfair to subject the defendant to such an action.

56. *Rule 3222. Action on submitted facts.*

(a) *Commencement.* An action, except a matrimonial action, may be commenced by filing with the clerk a submission of the controversy, acknowledged by all parties in the form required to entitle a deed to be recorded. The submission shall consist of a case, containing a statement of the facts upon which the controversy depends, and a statement that the controversy is real and that the submission is made in good faith for the purpose of determining the rights of the parties. If made to the supreme court, the submission shall specify the particular county clerk with whom the papers are to be filed.

(b) *Subsequent proceedings.* Subsequent proceedings shall be had according to the civil practice law and rules except that:

1. an order of attachment or a preliminary injunction shall not be granted;
2. the controversy shall be determined on the case alone;
3. if the submission is made to the supreme court, it shall be heard and determined either by the appellate division, or by special term, or, with his consent, by a specified judge or referee, as the parties may stipulate;
4. on such a submission the court, judge or referee may find facts by inference from the facts; and
5. if the statement of facts in the case is not sufficient to enable the court to enter judgment the submission shall be dismissed or the court shall allow the filing of an additional statement.

57. See Robinson v. Marine Midland Trust Co., 323 NYS2d 219 (1973).
58. See McAlevey v. Williams, 344 NYS2d 193 (1983).
59. See Public Service Mutual Insurance Co. v. Fireman's Fund Insurance Co., 422 NYS2d 430 (1979).
60. 271 NYS2d 317 (1971).
61. See Rule 50(a) and (b) of Federal Rules of Civil Procedure (FRCP).
62. See Lumbermens' Mutual Casualty Co. v. Rhodes, 402 F2d 2 (8th Cir., 1968), cert. den. 394 US 965 (1968).
63. 589 F2d 323 (7th Cir., 1978), cert. den. 48 USLW 3213 (1979).
64. See Rule 50(b) of FRCP.
65. See Crowe v. Lucas, 595 F2d 985 (5th Cir., 1979).
66. 301 F2d 386 (8th Cir., 1962).
67. 427 F2d 1 (2d Cir., 1970).
68. Supra note 31 at 208–210.
69. Rule 50(b) of FRCP.
70. 175 F2d 498 (5th Cir., 1949).
71. See Cone v. West Virginia Pulp and Paper Co., 330 US 212 (1947).

5

The Declaratory Judgment

Quia timet relief is the axiomatic way of granting a plaintiff a judicial determination of the legal relationship between the plaintiff and the defendant ''because he (plaintiff) fears'' that plaintiff's out-of-court situation may be prejudiced if plaintiff is forced to act without official advice. The declaratory judgment has a long history in equity. The device is similar in purpose to the equitable remedy of interpleader,[1] by which a person holding property claimed by two or more persons may commence an action against the claimants and compel the claimants to fight out their competing interests or claims among themselves; the stakeholder thereby insures against the possibility that each of the claimants may later sue him or her and perhaps recover against him. The summary judgment device is also similar to the petition, by a trustee or receiver[2] or other fiduciary charged with managing property, for an examination and approval of his or her accounts or for direction as to how to proceed in managing the property, so that those claiming an interest in the property may not later assert claims of mismanagement against the trustee or receiver or fiduciary.[3]

The declaratory judgment device had a late start in judicial history, and during the 19th century there was little development of the ancient quia timet relief. States waited until England had utilized the device before sanctioning the device legislatively.[4] A basic fear was the possibility that the device would open the judicial doors to gratuitous judicial advice.[5] But declaratory judgment today mandates that the applicant or plaintiff show that he or she confronts real, not potential, risk in proceeding with the course of conduct that he or she seeks to follow.[6]

The New York case of *Bunis v. Conway* concerned an adjudication that the book *Tropic of Cancer* by Henry Miller was ''obscene'' within the meaning of Section 1141 of the New York Penal Law.[7] The bookseller brought a declaratory action against the local attorney general in Rochester, who had threatened to prosecute him under the statute. The trial court dismissed the complaint on the ground that "an action for declatory judgment would not lie under the circumstances set forth in the complaint." In reversing, the New York Appellate Division, Fourth Dept., responded:

> An action for a declaratory judgment is the appropriate remedy for the determination of a justiciable controversy, where the plaintiff is in doubt as to his legal rights and wishes to avoid the hazard of taking action in advance of the determination of such rights (James v. Alderton Dock Yards, 256 N.Y. 298, 305, 176 N.E. 401, 403).
>
> It is the settled law that an action for a declaratory judgment will lie "where a constitutional question is involved or the legality or meaning of a statute is in question and no question of fact is involved" (Dun & Bradstreet v. City of New York, 276 N.Y. 198, 206, 11 N.E.2d 728, 732). The remedy of declaratory judgment is available, not only where the validity of a statute is in question, but also where its construction or its application to an undisputed set of facts is in question (New York Foreign Trade Zone Operators, Inc. v. State Liquor Authority, 285 N.Y. 272, 34 N.E.2d 316).
>
> However, as the Court of Appeals noted in the case last cited, the remedy "is not available to restrain the enforcement of a criminal prosecution where the facts are in dispute, or open to different interpretations" (285 N.Y. at p. 276, 34 N.E.2d at p. 319, citing Reed v. Littleton, 275 N.Y. 150, 9 N.E.2d 814). The rationale seems to be that, if the facts upon which the propriety of a criminal prosecution would depend are in dispute, the dispute ought to be resolved by the trier of the facts in the criminal prosecution in accordance with the rules governing criminal cases and that the obtaining of a declaratory judgment as to the facts would improperly interfere with the administration of the criminal law. This reasoning, however, is inapplicable, if the crucial question is one of law, since the question of law will be decided by the court in any event and not by the trier of the facts. Therefore, it has been held that a determination of the question of law in a declaratory judgment action would not "improperly interfere with criminal processes" (New York Foreign Trade Zone Operators, Inc. v. State Liquor Authority, supra 285 N.Y. at p. 277, 34 N.E.2d 319). "Resort to this remedy and also to that of an injunction may be had even with respect to penal statutes and against a public official or public agency whose duty it is to conduct appropriate prosecutions, if the purpose be to avoid irreparable injury and if the sole question is one of law" (De Veau v. Braisted, 5 A.D.2d 603, 606–607, 174 N.Y.S.2d 596, 600, aff'd. 5 N.Y.2d 236, 183 N.Y.S.2d 793, 157 N.E.2d 165, aff'd. 363 U.S. 144, 80 S.Ct. 1146, 4 L.Ed.2d 1109; see also, Herald Publishing Company v. Bill, 142 Conn. 53, 111 A2d 4; Lucky Calendar Co. v. Cohen, 19 N.J. 399, 117 A.2d 487).
>
> The question of whether a particular book is obscene within the meaning of section 1141 of the Penal Law is a question of law, appropriate for decision in a declaratory judgment action, under the rule laid down in the authorities cited. No question of fact is involved, in the sense of a question as to what had factually occurred or what is factually proposed to be done. The content of the book is fixed and immutable. There may be different views as to whether the book comes within the condemnation of section 1141 of the Penal Law but this presents a question of law for ultimate decision by the court, depending upon the court's determination of the meaning, scope and applicability of the statute.

The court concluded:

> If relief by way of a declaratory judgment were not available, the chief of police, the district attorney or other local law enforcement authorities could impose an informal censorship merely by announcing that anyone selling a particular book would be prosecuted. Booksellers are naturally reluctant to incur the risk of criminal prosecution since that entails adverse publicity and physical and mental strain as well as expense, even though the prosecution should ultimately terminate in the dismissal of the charge. They may therefore refrain from selling the book denounced by the authorities and, in that event, no occasion for criminal prosecution ever arises. The mere threat of prosecution may thus have the effect of deterring or suppressing the sale of the book without any judicial determination ever being made as to whether the book is actually obscene. Such a system of informal censorship has been repeatedly condemned as a prior restraint by the action of governmental officials, in violation of the First and Fourteenth Amendments. It has been held that, if the public authorities promulgate a list of "objectionable" books or magazines and threaten to prosecute any person who sells the listed books or magazines, an action for an injunction may be maintained against the publicizing of the list and the making of the threats of prosecution, on the ground that these acts of themselves are a violation of due process (Dearborn Publishing Co. v. Fitzgerald, 6 Cir., 271 F. 479; American Mercury, Inc. v. Chase, 13 F.2d 224; HMH Publishing Co., Inc. v. Garrett, D.C., 151 F.Supp. 903; New American Library of World Literature, Inc. v. Allen, D.C., 114 F.Supp. 823; Bantam Books, Inc. v. Melko, 25 N.J. Super. 292, 96 A.2d 47, modified 14 N.J. 524, 103 A.2d 256; for a parallel case of an injunction against a threat of the revocation of newsdealers' licenses by the Commissioner of Licenses, see Sunshine Book Company v. McCaffrey, 4 A.D.2d 643, 168 N.Y.S.2d 268; but see Bantam Books, Inc. v. Sullivan, 176 A.2d 393 (R.I.), probable jurisdiction noted by the United States Supreme Court June 26, 1962; see note, 110 University of Pennsylvania Law Review 1162 [June, 1962]; note, 33 N.Y.U. Law Review 989, 1007–1008).
>
> The use of declaratory judgment procedure is the most effective method of overcoming any attempt by local government officials to impose extralegal censorship. A bookseller, faced with a threat of prosecution if he sells a book condemned by the authorities, may escape from the dilemma by procuring, in an action for a declaratory judgment, a judicial determination as to the legality of the sale of the book, without first selling the book and incurring the risk of prosecution (see De Veau v. Braisted, supra, 5 A.D.2d 603, 607, 174 N.Y.S.2d 596, 600, aff'd. 5 N.Y.2d 236, 183 N.Y.S.2d 793, 157 N.E.2d 165, aff'd. 363 U.S. 144, 80 S.Ct. 1146, 4 L.Ed.2d 1109).
>
> The entertaining of declaratory judgment actions in obscenity cases thus not only protect the legitimate interests of booksellers but also serves the public interest by preventing the creation of an extra-legal system of censorship by the local police or prosecuting authorities.

"CASE OR CONTROVERSY"

According to Section 3001 of the New York Civil Practice Law & Rules, the trial court "may render a declaratory judgment having the effect of a final judgment as to the rights and other legal relations of the parties to a justiciable controversy, whether or not further relief is or could be claimed. If the court declines to render such a judgment, it shall state its grounds.''[8] Historically, the key phrase was ''justiciable controversy,'' for courts have traditionally refused to permit advisory opinions, and hence there was a need for an actual ''case or controversy'' before a declaratory judgment procedure was possible. In the 1927 case of *Liberty Warehouse Co. v. Grannis*, the matter of declaratory judgment first came before the U.S. Supreme Court in the midst of grave constitutional limitations on federal judicial powers.[9] The highest court indicated in 1927 that the declaratory judgment technique was inconsistent with Article III of the U.S. Constitution. An advisory opinion could only be rendered by a court at the request of some governmental department in response to a constitutional issue framed by that government department. It was not until 1933, in *Nashville, Chicago & St. Louis Railroad Co. v. Wallace*, that the highest court came to see that the declaratory judgment was not necessarily subject to the defects inherent in the advisory opinion.[10] Here the declaratory judgment rendered by a state court was valid as a controversy justiciable under Article III. The next year Congress enacted the Federal Declaratory Judgment Act of 1934,[11] which provided, inter alia, that ''in cases of actual controversy'' (except with respect to federal taxes other than action brought under Section 7428 of the Internal Revenue Code of 1954 or a proceeding under Section 505 or 1146, Title 11), the federal courts may ''declare the rights and other legal relations'' of the parties ''whether or not further relief is or could be sought.'' In the 1937 decision of *Aetna Life Insurance Co. v. Haworth*, the act was adjudged constitutional, but the act was confined to conventional ''case or controversy.''[12] In *Poe v. Ullman* it was held that the federal courts are barred from considering constitutional issues ''prematurely,'' or before the case or controversy is ''ripe''; that is, when the governmental act being challenged has a direct adverse effect upon the person or persons making the challenge.[13] Until that stage of actual effect, there can be no ''case or controversy.'' But a self-executing statute is ''ripe'' for challenge as soon as it is enacted, and the challenger does not have to wait for official action to bring his or her motion for declaratory judgment.[14] The mere fact that a criminal statute, for example, has not been enforced to the stage of prosecution is not alone sufficient to make a ''case or controversy'' within the meaning of the act.[15] Although federal courts generally do not intervene by way of either injunction or declaration in state criminal prosecutions, a federal injunction was granted in *Dombrowski v. Pfister* against a state prosecution that was part of a plan to harass the parties and discourage them and their supporters from vindicating their First Amendment rights.[16] Bad faith and similar unusual circumstances lacking in good faith frequently compel federal courts to respond by declaratory judgment.[17]

THE UNIFORM DECLARATORY JUDGMENTS ACT

The Uniform Declaratory Judgments Act, first proposed in 1922, has been adopted with slight modifications in 41 states.[18] Alaska, California, Connecticut, Hawaii, Kansas, Kentucky, Mississippi, New Hampshire, and New York have not adopted the act, although only Mississippi appears to have no statute authorizing declaratory judgments.[19] The Uniform Act provides that courts shall have the power to declare rights, status, and other legal relationships, whether or not further relief is or could be claimed. The declaration may either be affirmative or negative and has the force and effect of a final judgment or decree.[20]

In the state of New York[21] both Sections 3001 and 3017(b) of the Civil Practice Law & Rules (CPL & R) delineate the declaratory judgment in action. The commencement of the declaratory judgment action does not constitute a bar to a jury trial if the action would otherwise have been triable by a jury as of right.[22] An ordinary qualified voter in a city has standing to seek declaratory judgment relief as to the constitutionality of a local law establishing a two-year residency requirement for eligibility to hold certain city offices.[23] The New York Court of Appeals in *New York Public Interest Research Group, Inc. v. Carey* opined that the fact that a court may be required to determine rights of parties upon the happening of a future event does not mean that the declaratory judgment will be merely advisory; where the future event is an act contemplated by one party, it is assumed that the parties will act according to law and thus, the court's determination today will have immediate and practical effect of influencing their conduct.[24] In *Cullen v. Naples* the court observed that declaratory judgment was the proper remedy to determine whether the driver at the time of the accident was operating the automobile with the owner's implied permission and consent.[25] It should be noted that Section 3017(b) of New York CPL & R requires that the demand for relief "shall state whether further or consequential relief is or could be claimed, and the nature and extent of any such relief which is claimed."[26] And most recently in *Nyland (CFS), Ltd. v. Chemical Bank*,[27] the New York court emphasized that "it is within the discretion of the court to exercise its jurisdiction in a declaratory judgment action."[28]

On the federal level, note *Goya Foods, Inc. v. Tropicana Products Inc.*, where the federal district court for the Southern District of New York declined to exercise jurisdiction under the Federal Declaratory Judgment Act over a complaint seeking a declaration of noninfringement of two trademarks.[29] The court remarked that there was no trademark infringement claim asserted by Tropicana in the administrative proceedings before the Trademark Trial and Appeal Board: "The filing of an opposition in a trademark registration proceeding is not tantamount to a charge of infringement or a warning of a future charge of infringement."

DECLARATORY JUDGMENTS IN INSURANCE DISPUTES

Both the Federal Declaratory Judgment Act and the Uniform Declaratory Judgments Act have frequently been involved in determining questions arising from the construction and operation of insurance policies, whether such insurance policies delineate accident, fire, health, life, liability, or indemnity insurance.[30] The courts have also utilized the acts to determine whether an insurance policy should be cancelled, reformed, or surrendered.[31] Courts have accepted jurisdiction under both acts to determine questions of insurance coverage[32] and also to determine the existence of an insurer's duty to defend.[33] A few courts have taken the position that it is not an abuse of judicial discretion to postpone a ruling in the declaratory judgment action until the resolution of the underlying controversy, assuming that the former action is independent of the latter action.[34] In *Alliance Mutual Casualty Co. v. Bailey* the Kansas court ruled that the declaratory judgment action brought by the insurer for a declaration that the policy had expired prior to the insured's loss was inappropriate, since there was total disagreement between the insurer and the insured as to the respective issues, the insured having counterclaimed for fraud, mistake, and reformation of the insurance contract.[35] In *Smith v. North River Insurance Co.*[36] the Alabama court found no difficulty in adjudicating a declaratory judgment involving coverage under a homeowner's policy with respect to injuries suffered by a bystander when the insured shot another person, even though the bystander had previously filed a personal injury suit against the insured.[37]

Third parties to the controversy over an insurance contract may also be proper parties to the declaratory judgment action. The Federal Declaratory Judgment Act expressly states that the court may declare the rights of any "interested party,"[38] and the Uniform Act provides that "all persons shall be made parties who have or claim an interest which would be affected by the declaration."[39] The absence of a third party may preclude a declaratory judgment suit by an insurer for declaration of its rights and obligations under a fire insurance policy.[40]

It should be noted that the right to jury trial in declaratory judgment actions is generally preserved; under Rule 57 of the Federal Rules of Civil Procedure, the right to trial by jury may be demanded under the circumstances and in the manner provided. Where only equitable issues of law are presented in the declaratory judgment action, there is no right to a jury trial.[41]

Burden of proof in declaratory judgment actions generally falls upon the party bringing the suit; the insurer seeking to prove breach of warranty or representation or that the loss is within an exclusion from coverage would have the burden of proof.[42]

The declaratory judgment has the force and effect of a final judgment between the parties and is therefore res judicata between the parties.[43] It is interesting to note that the state of California gives priority to declaratory judgment actions by setting such actions down for trial at the earliest possible date.[44]

The New York Supreme Court, New York County, on March 21, 1988, held that declaratory judgment was appropriate by plaintiff hospital against its excess insurer after the latter went insolvent. Plaintiff sought return of its premiums and any possible additional charges, despite the insurance carrier's contention that the hospital had not incurred liability necessitating the excess coverage and therefore the claim was a purely speculative claim. But the court pointed out that the hospital had established through actuarial evidence that present claims against it would probably lead to liability within the scope of the excess insurer's policy coverage. The court concluded: "Although a court is not permitted to render advisory opinions on issues that do not present a current justiciable controversy (see CPLR §3001), in an action to determine the rights and responsibilities of an excess insurance carrier towards coverage of potential claims, declaratory judgment may be appropriate where the judgments on the underlying claims are likely to amount to more than the excess floor, or where the potential liability might well reach into the excess coverage. . . . I find that the hospital has presented a justiciable controversy in which the possibility of damage to plaintiff is not so remote as to render the action for declaratory judgment premature."

The federal district court for the Southern District of New York in *Sutton Hill Associates v. Landes* was involved with a declaratory judgment motion by the plaintiff, who sought a declaration that defendants, tenants of two of plaintiff's theaters, have no right to lease the theaters after expiration of the current lease.[45] Defendants asserted counterclaims against the plaintiff and a counterclaim against Royal Insurance Co., claiming that the insurer had refused to pay on the policy after the collapse of the ceiling of the theater. Defendants also alleged that plaintiff had maliciously interfered with the contractual relationship between them and the insurer. The insurer moved for severance and a separate trial of the counterclaims against it. But the court declined to sever or to order a separate trial or to grant plaintiff's summary judgment. The court found the counterclaims against the insurer were intertwined with 6 counterclaims by the defendants against the plaintiff and also with 11 counterclaims by the plaintiff in response to defendants' counterclaims. The court held that "[a]lthough it makes some sense to separate the claims against Royal from the two original claims in the suit, it makes no sense to separate the claims against Royal from all other claims arising out of the ceiling collapse. [Plaintiff] and [defendants] would risk the possibility of inconsistent determinations if one party is found liable in the action between them, and then, in a separate action against the insurance company, the issue of the ceiling collapse is relitigated and a different or inconsistent determination is reached." Hence, there was no summary judgment in this case.

DECLARATORY JUDGMENTS IN CIVIL RIGHTS MATTERS

The civil rights statute, 42 USC 1983, speaks of the availability of equitable relief, but with no apparent exception for declaratory judgment against state criminal proceedings.[46] However, in *Mitchum v. Foster*[47] the U.S. Supreme Court in 1972 removed the obstacle and held that the Anti-Injunction Act[48] did not apply to the civil rights statute. However, in *Younger v. Harris* the highest court one year earlier had raised substantial questions that revealed a preference for an enhanced state court role, particularly in those cases raising the constitutionality of state statutes.[49] The long-standing rule that state remedies must first be exhausted before resort to declaratory judgment has also impeded the increase of declaratory judgment actions in civil rights matters.[50]

In *Carter v. Hand* the Fifth U.S. Court of Appeals held that the plaintiff's action for declaratory judgment was not "ripe" for judicial examination because, even though the judgment had been unsatisfied for five years, no attempt had been made to collect it, no execution was threatened, and furthermore the plaintiff, seeking the declaratory judgment relief, was judgment-proof![51] On the other hand, in *Kroehler v. Scott*, where the surveillance activities of poice in public restrooms had been halted but were still challenged in a declaratory judgment action, the federal district court granted the motion for declaratory judgment because the threat of future surveillance was sufficiently real.[52] To the same effect is the case of *Buise v. Hudkins*, where it was held that a "jail-house lawyer" transfered from a state prison farm to another state prison was entitled to declaratory judgment relief on the ground that his transfer violated the rights of other state farm inmates![53]

NOTES

1. See Chapter 9.
2. See the section "Injunction" in Chapter 6.
3. See Mullane v. Central Hanover Bank & Trust Co., 339 US 306 (1950).
4. Note Zeitlin v. Arnebergh, 31 Cal. Rptr. 800, 383 P2d 152 (1963).
5. See Liberty Warehouse Co. v. Grannis, 273 US 70 (1927).
6. See Selby Realty Co. v. City of Buena Vista, 514 P2d 111 (1973).
7. 234 NYS2d 435 (AD 4th Dept., 1962).
8. The rights of the parties are to be determined as of the time the rights are declared, Poersch v. Eldridge, 319 NYS2d 749 (1971).
9. 273 US 70 (1927), followed by Willing v. Chicago Auditorium Assn., 277 US 289 (1928).
10. 288 US 249 (1933).
11. 28 USC 2201.
12. 300 US 227 (1937).
13. 367 US 497 (1961) at 504.
14. See Euclid v. Ambler Realty Co., 272 US 365 (1926) and Pierce v. Society of Sisters, 268 US 510 (1925).
15. See Ex parte Young, 209 US 123 (1908).
16. 380 US 479 (1965).
17. Note Younger v. Harris, 401 US 37 (1971).
18. See generally 33 Torts & Ins. C. J. 161 (Fall 1987).
19. See Sumrall v. Preferred Risk Mutual Insurance Co., 339 So2d 568 (Miss., 1976).
20. See Section 1 of the Uniform Act.
21. Supra note 8.
22. See Ripples' of Clearview, Inc. v. Le Havre Associates, 443 NYS2d 824 (1981).
23. See Phelan v. City of Buffalo, 388 NYS2d 469 (1976).
24. 42 NY2d 527, 369 NE2d 1155 (1975).

25. 341 NYS2d 21 (1983), aff. 32 NY2d 878, 299 NE2d 898 (1983).

26. See Lutheran Church in America v. City of New York, 278 NYS2d 1 (1971).

27. Unreported (New York County, Dec. 30, 1987).

28. According to the court, "In order to have standing to maintain a declaratory judgment action, plaintiffs must establish that their rights will be directly and specifically affected by a determination regarding the validity of the notes (see Wein v. City of New York, 47 A.D. 2d 367, mod. on other grounds 36 N.Y. 2d 610; 3 Weinstein-Korn-Miller, N.Y. Prac., para. 3001.04). The Nyland note at issue herein was executed by Bernstein, as attorney in fact for the corporation; the Glockhurst note was executed by a representative of that corporation acting in the same capacity. It is concluded, therefore, that since these two corporations, as primary obligors on the notes, will be directly affected by a judgment determining their validity, they have standing to commence an action seeking to have the notes declared null and void and to obtain the injunctive relief necessary to effectuate such a judgment. . . .

In support of their demand for a declaration that the notes are null and void, plaintiffs rely exclusively upon the federal injunction and their contention that enforcement of any judgment of liability that may be entered on the notes would work to the detriment of the Philippine Government. In making this argument, plaintiffs now accept as true those allegations that they vehemently deny in the federal action, i.e., that Nyland and Glockhurst are instrumentalities of the Marcoses responsible for diverting funds belonging to the people of the Philippines and that Chemical was aware that the funds it loaned to Nyland and Glockhurst were to be diverted to Marcos. Plaintiffs then assert that these facts compel the conclusion that the notes are thus void for lack of consideration.

Even if the allegations relied upon by plaintiffs are true, this court will not permit them to rely upon their own wrongful participation in such diversion to obtain affirmative relief. In so holding, this court accepts the reasoning of Judge Knapp as applied in a related federal action in which Citibank ought to foreclose its mortgage on 40 Wall Street (Citibank, N.A. v. Nyland [CF8] Ltd., et. al., United States Dist. Ct., Southern Dist. of New York, 86 Civ. 9181 [WK]).

Furthermore, it is well established that it is within the discretion of the court to exercise its jurisdiction in a declartory judgment action (see, e.g., Morgenthau v. Erlbaum, 59 N.Y. 2d 173, cert. den. 464 U.S. 993). As a general rule, a declaratory judgment action will not be entertained if the same parties are already engaged in litigation and the first action was brought in an adequate forum where all issues sought to be raised can be resolved (3 Weinstein-Korn-Miller, N.Y. Prac., para. 3001.09a).

29. 561 F. Supp. 1077 (SDNY, Aug. 6, 1987), aff'd, 742 F2d 1434 (2d Cir., 1987).

30. See 33 Torts & Ins. C. J. 161 (Fall 1987) at 163 et seq.

31. See St. Paul Fire & Marine Ins. Co. v. Lawson Bros. Iron Works, 428 F2d 929 (10th Cir., 1970), Hartford Acc. & Indem. Co. v. Northwest Nat. Bank of Chicago, 228 F2d 391 (7th Cir., 1955); Penn. Mut. Life Ins. Co. v. Forcier, 103 F2d 166 (8th Cir., 1939); cert. den., 308 US 571 (1939); Aetna Life Ins. Co. v. Haworth, 300 US 227 (1937); Trinity Universal Ins. Co. v. Willrich, 13 Wash. 2d 263, 124 P2d 450 (1955); Empire Fire & Marine Ins. Co. v. Goodman, 147 Mont. 396, 412 P2d 569 (1966).

On the general issues of construction of insurance policies, note American Interinsurance Exch. v. Commercial Union Assur. Co., 605 F2d 731 (4th Cir., 1979), cert. den., 445 US 929 (1980); United States v. Transport Indem. Co., 544 F2d 393 (9th Cir., 1976); Inland Mut. Ins. Co. v. Eastern Motor Lines, 119 F. Supp. 344 (DCSC, 1954);

Aetna Life Ins. Co. v. Williams, 88 F2d 929 (8th Cir., 1937); Aetna Life Ins. Co. v. Haworth, 300 US 227 (1937); Traders & General Ins. Co. v. Rudco Oil & Gas Co., 129 F2d 621 (10th Cir., 1942); New York Life Ins. Co. v. Roe, 102 F2d 28 (8th Cir., 1939); Aetna Cas. & Sur. Co. v. Yeatts, 99 F2d 665 (4th Cir., 1938); Equitable Life Assur. Soc. v. Hemenover, 100 Colo. 231, 67 P2d 80 (1937); Temperance Ins. Exch. v. Carver, 83 Idaho 487, 365 P2d 824, (1961); Farmers Auto. Ins. Ass'n v. Janusick, 30 Ill. App. 2d 352, 174 N.E.2d 705 (1961); World Ins. Co. v. Perry, 210 Md. 449, 124 A.2d 259 (1956); State Farm Mut. Auto. Ins. Co. v. Skluzacek, 208 Minn. 443, 294 N.W. 413 (1940); Carter v. Bergeron, 102 N.H. 464, 160 A2d 348 (1960); Globe Indem. Co. v. Sterling Corp., 283 N.Y. 582, 27 N.E. 2d 441 (1940); Iowa Mut. Ins. Co. v. Fred M. Simmons, 25 N.C. 69, 128 S.E. 2d 19 (1962); Travelers Indem. Co. v. Cochrane, 155 Ohio St. 305, 98 N.E. 2d 840 (1951); Hartford Fire Ins. Co. v. Aetna Ins. Co., 278 Or. 226, 527 P2d 406 (1974); Malley v. American Indem. Corp., 297 Pa. 216, 146 A. 571 (1929); Standard Cas. Co. v. Boyd, 75 S.D. 617, 71 N.W. 2d 450 (1955); Trinity Universal Ins. Co. v. Willrich, 13 Wash. 2d 263, 124 P2d 950 (1942); Poling v. North American Life and Cas., 593 P2d 568 (Wyo., 1979).

32. See Providence Wash. Indem. Co. v. Edes, 109 F. Supp. 813 (D.C. Me., 1953); Maryland Cas. Co. v. Faulkner, 126 F2d 175 (6th Cir., 1942); Perez v. State Auto Ins. Ass'n, 270 So. 2d 377 (Fla., 1972); Southern Trust Ins. Co. v. Eason, 134 Ga. App. 827, 216 S.E. 2d 667 (1975).

33. See Firestone v. Pverman, 388 F. Supp. 948 (D.C. Conn., 1975); Stout v. Grain Dealers Mut. Ins. Co., 307 F2d 521 (4th Cir., 1962); C.Y. Thomason Co. v. Lumbermen's Mut. Cas. Co., 183 F2d 729 (4th Cir., 1950); Elliott v. Metropolitan Cas. Ins. Co., 250 F2d 680 (10th Cir., 1957), cert. den., 356 US 932 (1958); and Temperance Ins. Exch. v. Carver, 83 Idaho 487, 365 P2d 824 (1961).

34. See Hartford Insurance Group v. District Court, 625 P2d 1013 (Colo., 1981).

35. 380 P2d 413 (Kan., 1963).

36. 360 So2d 313 (Ala., 1978).

37. Also note Hollander v. Nationwide Mutual Insurance Co., 401 NYS2d 336 (1978); and generally 33 Torts & Ins. C. J. 161 (Fall 1987) at 165–166.

38. 28 USC 2201.

39. Section 11 thereof.

40. See Vale Chemical Co. v. Hartford Accident & Indemnity Co., 516 A2d 684 (Pa., 1986).

41. See General Insurance Co. v. Icelandic Builders, Inc., 604 P2d 966 (Wash. App., 1979).

42. See Columbian National Life Insurance Co. v. Goldberg, 138 F2d 192 (6th Cir., 1943), cert. den. 321 US 765 (1944).

43. See Rader v. Manufacturers Casualty Insurance Co., 255 F2d 404 (2d Cir., 1958).

44. Section 1062.3(a) of California Code of Civil Procedure; also supra note 30 at 178–180.

45. 1988 U.S. Dist. LEXIS 4746 (SDNY, May 25, 1988).

46. This obstacle is the Anti-Injunction Act, 28 USC 2283, which states that "a Court of the United States may not grant an injunction to stay proceedings in a State court except as expressly authorized by Act of Congress, or where necessary in aid of its jurisdiction, or to protect or effectuate its judgments."

47. 407 US 225 (1972).

48. Supra note 46.

49. 401 US 37 (1971).

50. See City of Columbus v. Leonard, 565 F2d 957 (5th Cir., 1977).

51. 593 F2d 10 (5th Cir., 1979).

52. 391 F. Supp. 1114 (WD Pa., 1975). See also Detco, Inc. v. McCann, 380 F. Supp. 1366 (Wis., 1974).

53. 584 F2d 223 (6th Cir., 1974).

6

Provisional Remedies: An Overview

Provisional remedies are preclusive devices that often bring litigation to a close, although by definition the remedies are only "provisional" or temporary. The most common provisional remedies are attachment, injunction, receivership, and notice of pendency. Article 60 of the New York Civil Practice Law and Rules (CPL & R) delineates these provisional remedies in action, and under Section 6001 thereof states that "on motion for a provisional remedy, the plaintiff shall state whether any other provisional remedy has been secured or sought in the same action against the same defendant," the point being that only one provisional remedy can be attained at a time! Section 6001 also provides that "a cause of action contained in a counterclaim or cross-claim and a judgment demanded thereon, shall entitle the defendant to the same provisional remedies to which he would be entitled if he were the plaintiff, or the party against whom the judgment is demanded were the defendant and the cause of action were contained in a complaint."

Provisional remedies can be defined as temporary remedies to protect the plaintiff's asserted rights during the pendency of litigation. A provisional remedy is a judicial order obtained at the initial stage of litigation, designed to stabilize the situation pending the final outcome of the case or to provide security to plaintiff so that, if plaintiff succeeds in obtaining judgment, he or she will be able to realize its enforcement. It is interesting to observe that neither the common law nor equity had devices for securing recovery for the plaintiff in advance of final judgment. The thrust of the old common law and equity courts was to coerce the defendant to appear for trial because, at least until the 18th century, a judgment could not be entered in default of an appearance by the defendant.[1] The so-called provisional remedy at that early time was "distraint" at common law and "sequestration" in equity.

ATTACHMENT

Attachment, or seizure of defendant's property, at common law was, as indicated above, designed to compel the defendant's appearance at trial, not for the purpose of securing plaintiff's claim.[2] However, the use of attachment of property to secure the claim of the plaintiff was a local custom in many English towns and villages, and state courts built upon that usage in legislating attachment as a provisional remedy.[3] In some states attachment developed as ''foreign attachment''; that is, it became a means of satisfying a claim against a debtor who was absent from the jurisdiction or who could not be found within the jurisdiction but who had property in the jurisdiction.[4] Today state laws regulating attachment (and garnishment) vary greatly, with some states permitting recourse to this provisional remedy in all situations and other states restricting the use of the provisional remedy only in special circumstances. Pursuant to Rule 64 of the Federal Rules of Civil Procedure, the federal courts, in granting provisional remedies, generally follow the law of the state in which the federal court is sitting.

In the state of New York the grounds for attachment are expressly set forth in Section 6201 of the CPL & R.[5] Attachment in New York is a drastic remedy that is available only upon a showing of specific damages and clear evidence supporting the moving party's cause of action.[6] There is no constitutional infirmity to this provisional remedy, even though it permits a New York resident in an out-of-state automobile accident, for example, to obtain quasi in rem jurisdiction over a nonresident defendant by attachment of the defendant's automobile insurance policy issued by a New York insurance company.[7] In *Cohen v. Carl M. Loeb, Rhoades & Co.* the defendant who asserted a cross-claim in litigation involving the indebtedness of a third-party defendant to the plaintiff was entitled to an attachment against the third-party defendant, even though the defendant's third-party claim was contingent on plaintiff's action.[8] In *Leslee Travel Inc. v. American Coupon Exchange, Inc.* the New York court granted the plaintiff an ex parte order of attachment against the defendant foreign corporation even though the foreign corporation was not authorized to do business in the state of New York.[9] However, the foreign corporation had received such authorization to do business in New York between the time the plaintiff made the application for an attachment and the time the court issued the ex parte order of attachment. The foreign corporation here sought damages[10] against the plaintiff for such mistake of fact and law in seeking attachment knowing that the defendant was not doing business in the state at that time, but the court ruled that the plaintiff was not liable since it would not have been reasonable to require the plaintiff to check daily whether the defendant's status had changed. In *Fair Sky, Inc. v. International Cable Ride Corp.*, where attachment already granted plaintiff was the more appropriate provisional remedy to prevent removal or disposition of property by defendant, the plaintiff was not entitled additionally to invoke the remedy of injunction for the same purpose.[11] A foreign plaintiff or foreign defendant may not bring an action in New York to take advantage of New York's prejudgment attachment statute where the contract between the parties was made, performed, and broken outside the state of New York.[12]

Section 6202 of New York CPL & R provides that "any debt or property against which a money judgment may be enforced . . . is subject to Attachment." A court may order a sheriff to open a safe-deposit box in aid of an attachment against the renter of the safe-deposit box.[13] Levy can be made on debts represented by negotiable instruments by levying on the holder of the negotiable instrument or seizing the instrument itself.[14] But future rents may not be attached or garnisheed since they are so speculative as not to qualify as "debts certain to be due" or even debts at all.[15] Section 6203 deals with attaching creditor's rights in personal property[16] Section 6204 with discharge of garnishee's obligation;[17] Section 6210 with order of attachment on notice;[18] and Section 6211 describes the order of attachment without notice.[19] It is clear that the purpose of these statutes, particularly Section 6204, is to protect a garnishee who pays a debt or delivers property pursuant to an execution or court order against a subsequent claim by the judgment debtor for the same debt or property.[20] In *Cooper v. Ateliers de la Motobecane, S.A.* an ex parte order of attachment of a debt, owed by a New York corporation to defendant French corporation and obtained by the plaintiff when he commenced an action against the defendant for a money judgment, was vacated under Section 6211.[21] The underlying dispute between the parties involved their obligations under a contract which provided that disputes were to be resolved by arbitration in Switzerland and by prearbitral judicial action in cases restricted to determining whether arbitration may be compelled. The court ruled that plaintiff's action for a money judgment was merely an attempt to avoid a prior court ruling denying a stay of arbitration of the same dispute.

Section 6212 details the motion papers, the undertaking, the filing, the demand, and the damages;[22] before an order of attachment can be confirmed, the moving party must demonstrate the probability of success on the merits of the underlying action.[23] Section 6213 delineates the service of the summons and states that "an order of attachment granted before an action is commenced is valid only if within 60 days after the order is granted, a summons is served upon the defendant or first publication of the summons against defendant is made. . . . " The levy upon personal property by service of the attachment order is a complicated process, detailed in Sections 6214,[24] 6215, 6216, and 6217.[25] The annulment of an attachment is described in Section 6224,[26] and other statutory provisions deal with return of property and disposition of attached property after execution is issued.[27]

Thus, the provisional remedy of attachment moves the litigation forward and in many instances actually serves as a preclusive device that brings the parties to the close of litigation. The 1905 U.S. Supreme Court case *Harris v. Balk* is an example thereof; here Harris of North Carolina owed Balk of North Carolina the sum of $180, and Epstein of Maryland claimed that Balk also owed him $300; while Harris was visiting in Maryland, Epstein garnisheed Harris's debt to Balk by serving Harris with process; Harris did not contest the attachment, and the Maryland court found that Balk owed Epstein the money and ordered Harris to pay Epstein the $180 that Harris owed to Balk; Balk then sued Harris in North Carolina for the original $180 debt and Harris claimed as a defense the payment of $180 to Epstein in the Maryland action.[28] The U.S. Supreme Court ruled that Harris's defense was valid and that the Maryland court had properly exercised in rem jurisdiction: "The obligation of the debtor to pay his debt clings to and accompanies him wherever he goes. . . . If there be a law of the State providing for the attachment of the debt, then if the garnishee be found in that State, and process be personally served upon him therein, we think the court thereby acquires jurisdiction over him, and can garnish the debt due from him to the debtor. . . ."[29]

But the U.S. Supreme Court has been critical over the years of the use of attachment, either for purposes of obtaining jurisdiction over a nonresident, or as a provisional remedy against locally situated persons, as evidenced in *Fuentes v. Shevin*, in which case the highest court examined the attachment laws of Florida and Pennsylvania:

> Both states provide for issuance of writs ordering state agents to seize a person's possessions, simply upon the *ex parte* application of any other person who claims a right to them and posts a security bond. Neither statute provides for notice to be given to the possessor of the property, and neither statute gives the possessor an opportunity to challenge the seizure at any kind of prior hearing. The question is whether these statutory procedures violate the Fourteenth Amendment's guarantee that no State shall deprive any person of property without due process of law.[30]

The Court pointed out that

> under the Florida statute challenged here "any person whose goods or chattels are wrongfully detained by any other person. . . . may have a writ of replevin to recover them. . . ." Fla. Stats. § 78.01. There is no requirement that the applicant make a convincing showing before the seizure that the goods are, in fact, "wrongfully detained." Rather, Florida law automatically relies on the bare assertion of the party seeking the writ that he is entitled to one and allows a court clerk to issue the writ summarily. It requires only that the applicant file a complaint, initiating a court action for repossession and reciting in conclusory fashion that he is "lawfully entitled to the possession" of the property, and that he file a security bond "in at least double the value of the property to be replevied conditioned that plaintiff will prosecute his action to effect and without delay and that if defendant recovers judgment against him in the action, he will return the property, if return thereof is adjudged, and will pay defendant all sums of money recovered against plaintiff by defendant in the action." Fla. Stats. § 78.07. On the sole basis of the complaint and bond, a writ is issued "command[ing] the officer to whom it may be directed to replevy the goods and chattels in the posses-

sion of the defendant . . . and to summon the defendant to answer the complaint." Fla. Stats. § 78.08. If the goods are "in any dwelling house or building or enclosure," the officer is required to demand their delivery; but, if they are not delivered, "he shall cause such house, building or enclosure to be broken open and shall make replevin according to the writ. . . . " Fla. Stats. § 78.10.

Thus, at the same moment that the defendant receives the complaint seeking repossession of property through court action, the property is seized from him. He is provided no prior notice and allowed no opportunity whatever to challenge the issuance of the writ. *After* the property has been seized, he will eventually have an opportunity for a hearing, as the defendant in the trial of the court action for repossession, which the plaintiff is required to pursue. And he is also not wholly without recourse in the meantime. For under the Florida statute, the officer who seizes the property must keep it for three days, and during that period the defendant may reclaim possession of the property by posting his own security bond in double its value. But if he does not post such a bond, the property is transferred to the party who sought the writ, pending a final judgment in the underlying action for repossession. Fla. Stats. § 78.13.

The Pennsylvania law differs, though not in its essential nature, from that of Florida. As in Florida, a private party may obtain a prejudgment writ of replevin through a summary process of *ex parte* application, although a prothonotary rather than a court clerk issues the writ. As in Florida, the party seeking the writ may simply post with his application a bond in double the value of the property to be seized. Pa. Rule Civ. Proc. 1073(a). There is no opportunity for a prior hearing and no prior notice to the other party. On this basis, a sheriff is required to execute the writ by seizing the specified property. Unlike the Florida statute, however, the Pennsylvania law does not require that there *ever* be opportunity for a hearing on the merits of the conflicting claims to possession of the replevied property. The party seeking the writ is not obliged to initiate a court action for repossession. Indeed, he need not even formally allege that he is lawfully entitled to the property. The most that is required is that he file an "affidavit of the value of the property to be replevied." Pa. Rule Civ. Proc. 1073(a). If the party who loses property through replevin seizure is to get even a post-seizure hearing, he must initiate a lawsuit himself. He may also, as under Florida law, post his own counterbond within three days after the seizure to regain possession. Pa. Rule Civ. Proc. 1076.[31]

The highest court then asserted that:

[T]he constitutional right to be heard is a basic aspect of the duty of government to follow a fair process of decisionmaking when it acts to deprive a person of his possessions. The purpose of this requirement is not only to ensure abstract fair play to the individual. Its purpose, more particularly, is to protect his use and possession of property from arbitrary encroachment—to minimize substantively unfair or mistaken deprivations of property, a danger that is especially great when the State seizes goods simply upon the application of and for the benefit of a private party. So viewed, the prohibition against the deprivation of property without due process of law reflects the high value, embedded in our constitutional and political history, that we place on a person's right to enjoy what is his, free of governmental interference. . . .

The requirement of notice and an opportunity to be heard raises no impenetrable barrier to the taking of a person's possessions. But the fair process of decisionmaking that it guarantees works, by itself, to protect against arbitrary deprivation of property. For when a person has an opportunity to speak up in his own defense, and when the State must listen to what he has to say, substantively unfair and simply mistaken deprivations of property interests can be prevented. It has long been recognized that "fairness can rarely be obtained by secret, one-sided determination of facts decisive of rights. . . . [And n]o better instrument has been devised for arriving at truth than to give a person in jeopardy of serious loss notice of the case against him and opportunity to meet it." Joint Anti-Fascist Refugee Committee v. McGrath, 341 U.S. 123, 170-172 (Frankfurter, J., concurring).

If the right to notice and a hearing is to serve its full purpose, then, it is clear that it must be granted at a time when the deprivation can still be prevented. At a later hearing, as individual's possessions can be returned to him if it was unfairly or mistakenly taken in the first place. Damages may even be awarded to him for the wrongful deprivation. But no later hearing and no damage award can undo the fact that the arbitrary taking that was subject to the right of procedural due process has already occurred. "This Court has not . . . embraced the general proposition that a wrong may be done if it can be undone." Stanley v. Illinois, 400 U.S. 1020.

This is no new principle of constitutional law. The right to a prior hearing has long been recognized by this Court under the Fourteenth and Fifth Amendments.

The Florida and Pennsylvania prejudgment replevin statutes fly in the face of this principle. To be sure, the requirements that a party seeking a writ must first post a bond, allege conclusorily that he is entitled to specific goods, and open himself to possible liability in damages if he is wrong, serve to deter wholly unfounded applications for a writ. But those requirements are hardly a substitute for a prior hearing, for they test no more than the strength of the applicant's own belief in his rights. Since his private gain is a stake, the danger is all too great that his confidence in his cause will be misplaced. Lawyers and judges are familiar with the phenomenon of a party mistakenly but firmly convinced that his view of the facts and law will prevail, and therefore quite willing to risk the costs of litigation. Because of the understandable self-interested fallibility of litigants, a court does not decide a dispute until it has had an opportunity to hear both sides—and does not generally take even tentative action until it has itself examined the support for the plaintiff's position. The Florida and Pennsylvania statutes do not even require the official issuing a writ of replevin to do that much.

The minimal deterrent effect of a bond requirement is, in a practical sense, no substitute for an informed evaluation by a neutral official. More specifically, as a matter of constitutional principle, it is no replacement for the right to a prior hearing that is the only truly effective safeguard against arbitrary deprivation of property. While the existence of these other, less effective, safeguards may be among the considerations that affect the form of hearing demanded by due process, they are far from enough by themselves to obviate the right to a prior hearing of some kind.

The right to a prior hearing, of course, attaches only to the deprivation of an interest encompassed within the Fourteenth Amendment's protection. In the present cases, the Florida and Pennsylvania statutes were applied to replevy chattels in the appellant's possession. The replevin was not cast as a final judgment; most, if not all of the appellants lacked full title to the chattels; and their claim even to continued possession was a matter in dispute. Moreover, the chattels at stake were nothing more than an assortment of household goods. Nonetheless, it is clear that the appellants were deprived of possessory interests in those chattels that were within the protection of the Fourteenth Amendment. . . .

A deprivation of a person's possessions under a prejudgment writ of replevin, at least in theory, may be only temporary. The Florida and Pennsylvania statutes do not require a person to wait until a post-seizure hearing and final judgment to recover what has been replevied. Within three days after the seizure, the statutes allow him to recover the goods if he, in return, surrenders other property—a payment necessary to secure a bond in double value of the goods seized from him. But it is now well settled that a temporary, nonfinal deprivation of property is nonetheless a "deprivation" in the terms of the Fourteenth Amendment. Sniadach v. Family Finance Corp., supra; Bell v. Burson, supra. Both *Sniadach* and *Bell* involved takings of property pending a final judgment in an underlying dispute. In both cases, the challenged statutes included recovery provisions, allowing the defendants to post security to quickly regain the property taken from them. Yet the Court firmly held that these were deprivations of property that must be preceded by a fair hearing.

The present cases are no different. . . .

The Court concluded:

We hold that the Florida and Pennsylvania prejudgment replevin provisions work a deprivation of property without due process of law insofar as they deny the right to a prior opportunity to be heard before chattels are taken from their possessor. Our holding, however, is a narrow one. We do not question the power of a State to seize goods before a final judgment in order to protect the security interests of creditors so long as those creditors have tested their claim to the goods through the process of a fair prior hearing. The nature and form of such prior hearings, moreover, are legitimately open to many potential variations and are a subject, at this point, for legislation—not adjudication. Since the essential reason for the requirement of a prior hearing is to prevent unfair and mistaken deprivations of property, however, it is axiomatic that the hearing must provide a real test. "[D]ue process is afforded only by the kinds of 'notice' and 'hearing' which are aimed at establishing the validity, or at least the probable validity, of the underlying claim against the alleged debtor *before* he can be deprived of his property. . . . For the foregoing reasons, the judgments of the district courts are vacated and these cases are remanded for further proceedings consistent with this opinion."[32]

Three years later in 1975, in *North Georgia Finishing, Inc. v. Di-Chem, Inc.*, the dissent of Mr. Justice White had apparently become the majority opinion, as he wrote the court's opinion, noting the deficiencies of the Georgia attachment statute, in that it failed to provide for (a) a factual showing based on the affiant's own knowledge; (b) a consideration of that showing by a judge instead of a clerk; and (c) opportunity for early hearing on the questions whether the plaintiff's claim was apparently valid and whether there was risk of dissipation of the property.[33] But it is also apparent that there are situations in which some of these requisites can be dispensed with.[34]

In 1969 the highest court had apparently established an exception for garnishment of an individual's wages in *Sniadach v. Family Finance Corp.*,[35] although due process would still require notice and a hearing prior to application of the garnishment remedy. The case is limited to wages, "a specialized type of property presenting distinct problems in our economic system."[36] Mr. Justice Douglas, who wrote the majority opinion, had concluded:

The result is that a prejudgment garnishment of the Wisconsin type may as a practical matter drive a wage-earning family to the wall. Where the taking of one's property is so obvious, it needs no extended argument to conclude that absent notice and a prior hearing (cf. Coe v. Armour Fertilizer Works, 237 U.S. 413, 423) this prejudgment garnishment procedure violates the fundamental principles of due process.

. . . "For a poor man—and whoever heard of the wage of the affluent being attached?—to lose part of his salary often means his family will go without the essentials. No man sits by while his family goes hungry or without heat. He either files for consumer bankruptcy, and tries to begin again, or just quits his job and goes on relief. Where is the equity, the common sense in such a process?" Congressman Gonzales, 114 Cong. Rec., p. H 690 (1968). For the impact of garnishment on personal bankruptcies see H.R. Rep. No. 1040, 90th Cong., 1st Sess., pp. 20–21.[37]

Attachment in aid of arbitration under New York CPL & R Section 7502(c) was delineated in *Drexel Burnham Lambert Incorporated v. Ruebsamen*, where petitioner, a securites broker and dealer, sought an attachment.[38] Here the petitioner claims that it intends to arbitrate with its former customers, residents of West Germany, pursuant to an account aggreement. Defendants allegedly had failed to comply with a $300,000 margin call. But the New York Supreme Court, New York County, denied the petition upon findinig that the nondomiciliary status of the defendants makes attachment in aid of arbitration impossible, as the court explained:

CPLR 7502[c] in pertinent part provides: "The supreme court . . . may entertain an application for an order of attachment or for a preliminary injunction in connection with an arbitrable controversy, but only upon the ground that the award to which the applicant may be entitled may be rendered ineffectual without such provisional relief."

Thus, the ground available for attachments in aid of arbitration has been limited to the situation described in CPLR 6201(3): "the defendant with intent to defend his creditors or frustrate the enforcment of a judgment that might be rendered in plaintiff's favor, has assigned, disposed of, encumbered or secreted property, or removed it from the state or is about to do any of these acts." Essentially, this confines the attachment to aid of arbitration to a security function whereas in a plenary action the grounds for attachment are broader and can serve a jurisdictional function, as well (CPLR 6201[1] and [2]; Matter of Saferstein v. Wendy, —Misc. 2d—, slip op. p. 5 fn2 [1987]). As in the related provisional remedy of injunction in an arbitration, the reason why the prospective award may become ineffectual must be related to some act that the respondent threatens or performs (cf. CPLR 6301; Matter of Saferstein v. Wendy, supra, slip op. p. 4; 7B McKinney's Consol. Laws of New York CPLR 7502, McLoughlin, 1985 Supplementary Practice Commentaries, C7502; 4 1988 Pocket Part, p. 58; New York State

Bar Association Committee on Civil Practice Law and Rules, Legislation Report No. 57, March 18, 1985).

In the case at bar, neither the ground advanced in the petition nor the possible impact of German law amounts to action that respondents are taking to render the arbitration award ineffectual. Petitioner concedes as much by emphasizing the non-domiciliary status of respondents. But, this status simply brings petitioner within the first ground for an attachment in an action (CPLR 6201[1]); this ground is unavailable for an attachment in aid of arbitration (CPLR 7502[c]).

For an additional reason, petitioner is not entitled to the discretionary remedy of attachment. The doctrine of unclean hands should be as much relevant to the provisional remedy of attachment as it is to the preliminary injunction—Compare 7A Weinstein-Korn-Miller, N.Y. Civil Practice ¶ 6201.03 (''Discretionary character of attachment'') with id. at ¶ 6301.22 (''Elements of discretion—clean hands'').

If the German law is in fact what petitioner claims it to be, barring West German non-merchants from trading in options and futures, the application for this attachment, in effect, is an effort to circumvent that law. Indeed, the petitioner who in its Brussels office accepted this account from respondents, knowing they were West German nationals and residents of Nuremberg, is deemed to have known of the West German legal prohibition. Therefore, petitioner took a risk, after years of profitable transactions, that a time would come that it could not collect a debit balance against respondents in the courts of their own country.

The issue, then, is whether it is equitable to relieve petitioner of the consequence of this risk. The question answers itself. An applicant for such relief, accusing its adversaries of hiding behind the German law, who seeks the assistance of the court to circumvent that law, comes to court with unclean hands.

Another form of attachment is the ''prejudgment attachment''[39] utilized by lenders in order to secure payment of principal and interest. Prejudgment attachments are designed to be instruments of a surprise attack launched against a borrower, and therefore most loan agreements do not expressly mention the prejudgment attachment. In England the courts grant injunctive relief, as shown in the famous *Mareva* case, which was the same relief as a prejudgment attachment.[40] Indeed, the statutory basis upon which the *Mareva* injunction is grounded today is Sectiton 37(3) of England's Supreme Court Act, 1981, which reads: ''The power of the High Court under subsection (1) to grant an interlocutory injunction restraining a party to any proceedings from removing from the jurisdiction of the High Court, or otherwise dealing with, assets located within that jurisdiction shall be exercisable in cases where that party is, as well as in cases where he is not, domiciled, resident or present within that jurisdiction.''[41]

INJUNCTION

The injunction, or restraining order, is another provisional remedy that, in effect, directs the defendant to do an act or refrain from doing an act, with the consequence that the plaintiff's position is made better or its worsening is averted. The injunction, whether temporary or permanent, derives from courts of equity, which exercised their discretion to grant or deny the injunctive remedy. (Generally, the determination of fact issues going to the remedy is for the judge and not for the jury.) The common law historically awarded only the remedy of damages, but the courts of equity granted specific relief in certain situations. The inadequacy of the damages remedy was apparent especially since a judgment for damages did not of itself obligate the defendant to be prompt in paying it; plaintiff had to indulge in discovery to locate defendant's assets through perhaps supplementary proceedings.

In public law litigation it might be pointed out that the provisional remedy of injunction is the normal mode of relief.[42] It is inappropriate to award damages relief in most public law situations—like school desegregation, or civil rights violations, or ecological harms—since the idea of putting a monetary value on such torts or contract violations or constitutional violations is not accepted publicly by many courts.[43] While the damages remedy may have some utility in these public law situations, it is more prudent to direct compliance with the law through an injunction.

There are many caveats about injunctive relief, such as the authority that an injunction should not issue when the threat of harm has terminated.[44] Injunctions can enjoin continuing nuisances,[45] for example, much more effectively than the damage remedies. In *Street v. Vitti* the federal district court granted a preliminary injuntion enjoining the defendant president, the majority stockholder in a closed corporation, from discharging plaintiff minority stockholders from the board of directors and from issuing stock; irreparable harm was said to exist because if defendant discharged plaintiffs the minority stockholders would lose their rights to inspect corporate books.[46] Also, firing plaintiffs would invoke provisions of the shareholders' agreement requiring discharged officers to sell their stock. Indeed, the court found that the sale of the stock would permit defendant to dilute plaintiffs' shareholdings and nullify their statutory rights, all to the irreparable harm of the plaintiffs.

The temporary restraining order may be the first step of relief pendente lite in a suit for an injunction; it may be issued immediately and ex parte upon application of a plaintiff if the plaintiff makes an adequate showing of the apparent necessity for immediate relief, as perhaps illustrated in *Hamilton Watch Co. v. Benrus Watch Co.*,[47] where the Second U.S. Court of Appeals opined that

> interference at any early stage, if possible, seems the paramount aim. . . . The judge's legal conclusions, like his fact-findings, are subject to change after a full hearing and the opportunity for more mature deliberation. For a preliminary injunction—as indicated by the numerous more or less synonomous adjectives used to label it—is, by its very nature, interlocutory, tenative, provisional, ad interim, impermanent, mutable, not fixed or final or conclusive, characterized by its for-the-time-beingness. It serves as an equitable policing measure to prevent the parties from harming one another during the litigation; to keep the parties, while the suit goes on, as far as possible in the respective positions they occupied when the suit began.

For the foregoing reasons, we cannot hold that the judge should have dismissed the complaint on the merits.

. . . There remains the question whether the judge—assuming, as he did, for the time being, that the complaint was not without merit—went outside the bounds of his discretion in ordering a preliminary injunction. We read Section 16 of the Clayton Act, 15 U.S.C.A. § 26, as declaratory of the usual rule relative to the exercise of such discretion: The judge must consider whether irreparable harm is likely to result to plaintiff if *pendente lite* (i.e., "immediately") the injunction is denied, and against this harm he must balance the harm to defendant likely to result if the relief is granted. The "hardship plaintiff will suffer . . . may make interlocutory relief imperative where the same showing at a final hearing would not outweigh the hardship the defendant would suffer from a permanent injunction. Thus in view of the character and extent of the emergency presented, of the provisional and temporary character of the relief sought, of the probable period of its duration, and of the court's tentative opinion on the substantive issues involved, the factor of relative hardship is measured, on an application for interlocutory injunction, with a different yardstick from that used at final hearing." Here no substantial harm from the injunction to defendant is perceptible; but the hardship to plaintiff, were there no injunction, would be very considerable. We agree with the trial judge that the private harm to plaintiff required as a condition of granting injunctive relief under Section 16 need not be at all the same as the public harm condemned by Section 7. In the light of the evidence before the judge and his findings not unreasonably derived therefrom, we hold that he surely did not "abuse" his discretion.[48]

The injunction also makes possible an early determination of the litigation. For example, in New York under Section 6301 of the CPL & R, the grounds for preliminary injunction and temporary restraining order are delineated.[49] The preliminary injunction or restraining order cannot be issued in the absence of a pending action, however.[50] Grounds for denying injunctive relief are numerous and perhaps are best illustrated by the doctrine of "unclean hands," as seen in *C.C.S. Communication Control, Inc. v. Sklar*[51] and in *Samjens Partners v. Burlington Industries, Inc.*[52] In the first case the court denied a preliminary injunction to enforce a covenant not to compete, finding that perjury by plaintiff's chairman during the preliminary injunction hearing was sufficient basis in and of itself to warrant the denial of such provisional relief. In the second case the court relied expressly upon the "unclean hands" delineation of the plaintiff to deny the injunction; plaintiff, a 13% owner of defendant's stock, sought a preliminary injunction against defendant's self-tender offer and against implementation of a merger agreement; but plaintiff had previously been enjoined by a North Carolina court from pursuing its tender offer because of a substantial likelihood that the tender offer had been launched on the basis of inside information.

An injunction does not punish; its only legitimate end is protection for the future.[53] The court in the exercise of its discretion must weigh the relative hardships that may be imposed upon the parties by the issuance or denial of injunctive relief.[54]

The preliminary injunction in New York "may be granted only upon notice to the defendant,''[55] and this statutory language emphasizes the requisite of notice to the adverse party or parties, or the preliminary injunction will be vacated.[56] However, the usual requirements for a preliminary injunction do not apply where the application is to preserve the status quo and the court has jurisdiction, for example, in a tenancy dispute, unless the claim for injunctive relief is totally lacking in merit.[57] Motion papers are described in Section 6312 of the New York CPL & R.[58]

The temporary restraining order is generally issued ex parte, as set forth in Section 6313,[59] and the vacating or modifying rules for both the preliminary injunction and the temporary restraining order are found in Section 6314.[60] In *Komyathy v. Board of Education* the New York court recognized its inherent power to issue ex parte a restraining order pending a determination of the plaintiff–board member's motion for preliminary injunction where the moving papers established prima facie that the defendant school board of education might have been acting illegally if it conducted a hearing on the charges against the plaintiff.[61]

In the field of civil rights, particularly 42 USC 1983, the injunctive relief offered under Rule 65 of the Federal Rules of Civil Procedure has been a popular provisional remedy. In *Allee v. Medrano* the U.S. Supreme Court authorized injunctive relief where workers seeking to organize a lawful union were intimidated by state officials, in that the workers were placed in fear of exercising their First Amendment rights, and where the remedy at law was clearly shown to be inadequate.[62] Injunctive relief requires some evidence that without that provisional remedy the party will suffer irreparable harm.[63] The injunction must be drawn with sufficient specificity to remedy the irreparable harm shown.[64] In *Black Jack Distributors, Inc. v. Beame* the corporate proprietors of ''adult'' bookstores brought suit under 42 USC 1983 alleging that the defendant police officials were engaged in ''bad faith'' enforcement of obscenity laws solely to harass plaintiffs and drive them out of business.[65] The federal district court for the Southern District of New York ruled that plaintiffs were entitled to preliminary injunctive relief from the continued harassment since defendants' own statements and the uncontradicted evidence as to the pattern and timing of arrest raised sufficiently serious questions regarding the bona fide activities of the defendants and also confirmed the likelihood of irreparable damage to plaintiffs as well as the probability of violations of the First Amendment rights of the plaintiffs. A preliminary injunction is a matter of the trial court's discretionary authority, and a grant or denial of a preliminary injunction will only be disturbed on appeal when the court's findings are clearly erroneous.[66] In *City of Los Angeles v. Lyons* a preliminary injunction barring the police from using life-threatening strangleholds on persons stopped in routine police work was upheld by the U.S. Supreme Court.[67] The highest court 13 years earlier in *Adickes v. S. H. Kress & Co.* had set forth two significant grounds for injunctive relief in such civil rights matters, to wit: plaintiff proved that the defendant had denied plaintiff of a right secured by the U.S. Constitution and laws of the United States, and defendant had deprived plaintiff of his constitutional right "under color of any statute, ordinance, regulation, custom or usage, of any State."[68] To be entitled to injunctive relief it is not necessary that a deprivation of civil rights has occurred, for an anticipated violation of civil rights may also be enjoined.[69]

Several 1988 federal district court decisions in the Southern District of New York point up the diversity of views on the injunctive, provisional remedy. In *Republic of Panama v. Republic National Bank of New York*, the political controversy was between General Noriega and President Delvalle of Panama (removed from office by General Noriega) as to who had the right to control funds deposited with U.S. banks by the Republic of Panama.[70] Finding irreparable harm, even though money damages were clearly available, the court acted by concluding that whichever faction gains control of the disputed funds would have a decisive advantage over the other faction for effective control of the government. The injunction was warranted because prospective uncertain money damages could not adequately compensate for the immediate and irreparable loss evident here; there was a real threat that the funds would be dissipated and irretrievably lost if disbursed to persons other than the "lawful representative" of the Republic of Panama. An injunction was granted in *City of New York v. Citisource, Inc.* because the defendant, allegedly with intent to defraud its creditors or to frustrate the enforcment of a judgment that might be rendered in plaintiff's favor, had assigned, disposed of, encumbered, or secreted property, or was about to do any of such acts.[71] In *Bruce v. Martin* the court enjoined the promoters of horse-breeding limited partnerships from filing state court actions to collect on investor notes and from taking any other action to prosecute collection, other than as counterclaims to plaintiff's securities frauds and RICO action pending in the federal district court.[72] But the court rejected plaintiff's argument that they would suffer irreparable harm if they were subject to vexatious litigation in multiple forums, noting that "mere litigation expense, even substantial and unrecoupable cost, does not constitute irreparable injury." However, the potential harm to the court's jurisdiction could arise from multiple actions in different states, and therefore a court "may grant an injunction to avoid multiple actions at law if the actions involve the same issues of law and fact so that decisions in one action will be determinative of all."

RECEIVERSHIP

The appointment of and powers of receivers are described in Article 64 of the New York CPL & R.[73] The avowed purpose of receivership is the conservation and preservation of the property or assets, but the appointment of a receiver may also determine the result of the litigation, although in most instances the mere appointment of a receiver does not constitute adjudication on the merits.[74] Even the duties of a temporary receiver are detailed in the New York statute.[75]

In *Sachs v. Killeen* the California court examined the duties and responsibilities of the receiver:

The appointment of a receiver pendente lite is a matter for the sound discretion of the trial court. (42 Cal.Jur.2d 341). Where there is evidence that the plaintiff has at least a probable right or interest in the property sought to be placed in receivership and that the property is in danger of destruction, removal or misappropriation, the appointment of a receiver will not be disturbed on appeal. . . .

Appellants contend that there was no evidence that plaintiff had an interest in the property placed under receivership. The argument is without merit. The verified complaint and the affidavits submitted by plaintiff furnished ample evidentiary support for a conclusion that Sachs had at least a probable interest in the described property. Appellants urge that the written agreement created neither a partnership nor a joint venture, hence Sachs is in the position of an unsecured creditor suing at law to recover a debt. The action is not one of law, but is essentially an equitable action to obtain an accounting and establish a constructive trust. Furthermore, it is immaterial whether the 1951 agreement created either a partnership or a joint venture. Under the agreement Sachs was to receive 50 per cent of the net profits from the sale of the speed control device. It cannot be doubted that he had an interest in the net profits. The court could properly infer from the facts alleged in the affidavits of Sachs and Alford that the Killeens were systematically falsifying their quarterly statements and diverting to their own use the net profits which belonged to Sachs. It was likewise a reasonable inference, if not a necessary one, from the showing made by plaintiff, that the property of the Killeens was acquired in large part with the funds withheld from plaintiff. Appellants admitted having assets worth $147,000; there was evidence that they had assets valued at only $5,000 in 1951. The court could also consider the accountant's computations that the profits withheld from Sachs were approximately $129,000. In view of the statement in Killeen's affidavit that only 11 per cent of the company's business derived from sources other than the speed control device, the court could well disbelieve his assertions that appellants' property was acquired otherwise than from the profits of the venture. Killeen's denials created merely a conflict in the evidence, which was resolved against appellants by the court. . . .

Another contention of appellants is that the plenary receivership imposed upon them violated due process of law because it deprived them of the means of defending the action. If, however, as we have held, the trial court was warranted in making the order confirming the appointment of the receiver it is of no consequence that its effect may have been to deprive the appellants of the right to use funds, to which it appeared probable that plaintiff was entitled, for the purpose of defending the action. Incidentally it may be noted that pursuant to a stipulation of the parties, the court subsequently made an order directing the receiver to release $10,000 to appellants for the purpose of defending the action.

A final contention of appellants is that the ex parte order exceeded the jurisdiction of the court in that it contained a preliminary injunction without providing that Sachs file a written undertaking, as required by section 529 of the Code of Civil Procedure. We are not persuaded by the argument. The ex parte order provided, inter alia, that "all persons at interest or with interest in the . . . [Killeens] . . . or their business or property . . . are enjoined from "interfering with, transferring, selling or disposing" of any property or income of the Killeens, individually and as copartners, and "from taking possession, or of levying upon or attempting to'' sell or dispose of such property. The property had been ordered into the possession of the receiver. So far as appellants are concerned the so-called injunction was no more than a rerstraint of appellants from defeating the receiver's possession and this would have been implied from other provisions of the order. The order of confirmation reads as follows: ''The ex parte appointment of receiver is confirmed''; it did not purport to confirm the provision we have just quoted. Furthermore, even if that provision were void, its invalidity would not render invalid the appointment of a receiver.

The ex parte order appointing a receiver is not appealable and the purported appeal therefrom is dismissed. The order confirming the appointment of a receiver is affirmed.[76]

NOTICE OF PENDENCY

The notice of pendency is also a provisional remedy in that the filing of same is to protect some right, title, or interest claimed.[77] In New York, Sections 6501, 6511, 6512, and 6513 of the CPL & R delineate in great detail this simple provisional remedy.[78] The lis pendens is constructive notice to any transferee of property involved in litigation,[79] and the mere filing of notice of pendency is equivalent to an ''order'' required in case of other provisional remedies.[80] Section 6514 describes the motion for cancellation of the notice of pendency, and is explicitly to be followed.[81]

It should be noted that at common law a purchaser of property (which was the subject of litigation) was charged with knowledge of the litigation. Today this common law doctrine has largely been replaced with statutory provisions, as described above in New York. However, there is sometimes a question as to whether the common law doctrine or the statutory provisions pertain to personal property.

NOTES

1. See the section ''Default Judgment'' in Chapter 4.

2. Note Millar, Civil Procedure of the Trial Court in Historical Perspective (1952) at chapter 26.

3. See Comment, 38 Yale L J 376 (1929).

4. Note New York Laws 1849, c. 438, section 227, for example.

5. *§6201. Grounds for attachment.*

An order of attachment may be granted in any action, except a matrimonial action, where the plaintiff has demanded and would be entitled, in whole or in part, or in the alternative, to a money judgment againist one or more defendants, when:

1. the defendant is a nondomiciliary residing without the state, or is a foreign corporation not qualified to do business in the state; or

2. the defendant resides or is domiciled in the state and cannot be personally served despite diligent efforts to do so; or

3. the defendant, with intent to defraud his creditors or frustrate the enforcement of a judgment that might be rendered in plaintiff's favor, has assigned, disposed of, en-

cumbered or secreted property, or removed it from the state or is about to do any of these acts; or

4. the cause of action is based on a judgment, decree or order of a court of the United States or of any other court which is entitled to full faith and credit in this state, or on a judgment which qualifies for recognition under the provisions of article 53.

6. See Werner v. Werner, 423 NYS2d 780 (1979).

7. See Rodriguez v. Wolfe, 401 NYSd 442 (1978), citing the U.S. Supreme Court holding in Shaffer v. Heitner, 433 US 186 (1980) to the effect that ''all assertions of State court jurisdiction . . . be evaluated according ''to Minimum contacts standards of due process of law.''

8. 264 NYS2d 463 (1970).

9. Unreported (New York County, March 8, 1988).

10. CPLR 6212(e) provides that plaintiff shall be liable for all costs and damages ''if the defendant recovers judgment or if it is finally decided that the plaintiff was not entitled to an attachment of the defendant's property.

Here attachment was clearly warranted when the ex parte order was applied for. When ACE obtained authorization to do business, that ground fell.

The issue is whether Leslee is liable under CPLR 6212(e) when ACE's certificate to do business was obtained in the 19 day interval between the submission of the ex parte order and its approval by the Court. To sustain such a holding, Leslee's attorney would be obligated to check with the Secretary of State each day to discover if there were a change in ACE's status which would undermine the basis for the attachment. Such a burden is patently unreasonable. Quite apart, if the Court had signed the ex parte order between December 4 and December 14th—a 10 day period—this issue would not even arise. CPLR 6212(e) is not meant to cover the situation where the ex parte application is proper and its signing is not within Leslee's control. Vacature of attachment for a 'technical reason,' other than that plaintiff was not entitled to attachment, does not give rise to liability for damages under the statute (McKinney's Practice Commentaries, Paragraph C6212:3).''

11. 257 NYS2d 351 (1970).

12. See Wachsman v. Craftool Co., 353 NYS2d 78 (1974).

13. See Carples v. Cumberland Coal & Iron Co., 148 NE 185 (N.Y., 1962).

14. See Underwriters Bank, Inc. v. First Chicago International Banking Corp., 262 NYS2d 828 (1971).

15. See Glassman v. Hyder, 23 NY 2d 354, 244 NE2d 259 (1983).

16. *§ 6203. Attaching creditor's rights in personal property.*

Where a plaintiff has delivered an order of attachment to a sheriff, the plaintiff's rights in a debt owed to the defendant or in an interest of the defendant in personal property against which debt or property a judgment may be enforced, are superior to the extent of the amount of the attachment to the rights of any transferee of the debt or property, except:

1. a transferee who acquired the debt or property before it was levied upon for fair consideration or without knowledge of the order of attachment; or

2. a transferee who acquired the debt or property for fair consideration after it was levied upon without knowledge of the levy while it was not in the possession of the sheriff.

17. *§ 6204. Discharge of garnishee's obligation.*

A person who, pursuant to an order of attachment, pays or delivers to the sheriff money or other personal property in which a defendant has or will have an interest, or so pays a debt he owes the defendant, is discharged from his obligation to the defendant to the extent of the payment or delivery.

18. *§6210. Order of attachment on notice; temporary restraining order; contents.*

Upon a motion on notice for an order of attachment, the court may, without notice to the defendant, grant a temporary restraining order prohibiting the transfer of assets by a garnishee as provided in subdivision (b) of section 6214. The contents of the order of attachment granted pursuant to this section shall be as provided in subdivision (a) of section 6211.

19. *§ 6211. Order of attachment without notice.*

(a) *When granted; contents.* An order of attachment may be granted without notice, before or after service of summons and at any time prior to judgment. It shall specify the amount to be secured by the order of attachment including any interest, costs and sheriff's fees and expenses, be indorsed with the name and address of the plaintiff's attorney and shall be directed to the sheriff of any county or of the city of New York where any property in which the defendant has an interest is located or where a garnishee may be served. The order shall direct the sheriff to levy within his jurisdiction, at any time before final judgment, upon such property in which the defendant has an interest and upon such debts owing to the defendant as will satisfy the amount specified in the order of attachment.

(b) *Confirmation of order.* An order of attachment granted without notice shall provide that within a period not to exceed five days after levy, the plaintiff shall move, on such notice as the court shall direct to the defendant, the garnishee, if any, and the sheriff, for an order confirming the order of attachment. If the plaintiff fails to make such motion within the required period, the order of attachment and any levy thereunder shall have no further effect and shall be vacated upon motion. Upon the motion to confirm, the provisions of subdivision (b) of section 6223 shall apply. An order of attachment granted without notice may provide that the sheriff refrain from taking any property levied upon into his actual custody, pending further order of the court.

20. See Oppenheimer v. Dresden Bank A.G., 377 NYS2d 625 (1975).

21. 57 NY2d 408, 442 NE2d 1239 (1982).

22. *Rule 6212. Motion papers; undertaking; filing; demand; damages.*

(a) *Affidavit; other papers.* On a motion for an order of attachment, or for an order to confirm an order of attachment, the plaintiff shall show, by affidavit and such other written evidence as may be submitted, that there is a cause of action, that it is probable that the plaintiff will succeed on the merits, that one or more grounds for attachment provided in section 6201 exist, and that the amount demanded from the defendant exceeds all counterclaims known to the plaintiff.

(b) *Undertaking.* On a motion for an order of attachment, the plaintiff shall give an undertaking, in a total amount fixed by the court, but not less than five hundred dollars, a specified part thereof conditioned that the plaintiff shall pay to the defendant all costs and damages, including reasonable attorney's fees, which may be sustained by reason of the attachment if the defendant recovers judgment or if it is finally decided that the plaintiff was not entitled to an attachment of the defendant's property, and the balance conditioned that the plaintiff shall pay to the sheriff all of his allowable fees. The attorney for the plaintiff shall not be liable to the sheriff for such fees. The surety on the undertaking shall not be discharged except upon notice to the sheriff. . . .

(d) *Demand for papers.* At any time after property has been levied upon, the defendant may serve upon the plaintiff a written demand that the papers upon which the order of attachment was granted and the levy made be served upon him. Not more than one day after service of the demand, the plaintiff shall cause the papers demanded to be served at the address specified in the demand. A demand under this subdivision shall not of itself constitute an appearance in the action.

(e) *Damages.* The plaintiff shall be liable to the defendant for all costs and damages, including reasonable attorney's fees, which may be sustained by reason of the attachment if the defendant recovers judgment, or if it is finally decided that the plaintiff was not entitled to an attachment of the defendant's property. Plaintiff's liability shall not be limited by the amount of the undertaking.

23. See Shearson Hayden Stone, Inc. v. Scrivener, 480 F. Supp. 256 (SDNY, 1979).

24. *§ 6214. Levy upon personal property by service of order.*

(a) *Method of levy.* The sheriff shall levy upon any interest of the defendant in personal property, or upon any debt owed to the defendant, by serving a copy of the order of attachment upon the garnishee, or upon the defendant if property to be levied upon is in the defendant's possession or custody, in the same manner as a summons except that such service shall not be made by delivery of a copy to a person authorized to receive service of summons solely by a designation filed pursuant to a provision of law other than rule 318.

(b) *Effect of levy; prohibition of transfer.* A levy by service of an order of attachment upon a person other than the defendant is effective only if, at the time of service, such person owes a debt to the defendant or such person is in the possession or custody of property in which such person knows or has reason to believe the defendant has an interest, or if the plaintiff has stated in a notice which shall be served with the order that a specified debt is owed by the person served to the defendant or that the defendant has an interest in specified property in the possession or custody of the person served. All property in which the defendant is known or believed to have an interest then in and thereafter coming into the possession or custody of such a person, including any specified in the notice, and all debts of such a person, including any specified in the notice, then due and thereafter coming due to the defendant, shall be subject to the levy. Unless the court orders otherwise, the person served with the order shall forthwith transfer or deliver all such property, and pay all such debts upon maturity, up to the amount specified in the order of attachment, to the sheriff and execute any document necessary to effect the payment, transfer or delivery. After such payment, transfer or delivery, property coming into the possession or custody of the garnishee, or debt incurred by him, shall not be subject to the levy. Until such payment, transfer or delivery is made, or until the expiration of ninety days after the service of the order of attachment upon him, or of such further time as is provided by any subsequent order of the court served upon him, whichever event first occurs, the garnishee is forbidden to make or suffer any sale, assignment or transfer of, or any interference with any such property, or pay over or otherwise dispose of any such debt, to any person other than the sheriff, except upon direction of the sheriff or pursuant to any order of the court. A garnishee, however, may collect or redeem an instrument received by him for such purpose and he may sell or transfer in good faith property held as collateral or otherwise pursuant to pledge thereof or at the direction of any person other than the defendant authorized to direct sale or transfer, provided that the proceeds in which the defendant has an interest be retained subject to the levy. A plaintiff who has specified personal property or debt to be levied upon in a notice served with an order of attachment shall be liable to the owner of the property or the person to whom the debt is owed, if other than the defendant, for any damages sustained by reason of the levy.

(c) *Seizure by sheriff; notice of satisfaction.* Where property or debts have been levied upon by service of an order of attachment, the sheriff shall take into his actual custody all such property capable of delivery and shall collect and receive all such debts. When the sheriff has taken into his actual custody property or debts having value sufficient to satisfy the amount specified in the order of attachment, the sheriff shall notify the defendant and each person upon whom the order of attachment was served that the order of attachment has been fully executed.

(d) *Proceeding to compel payment or delivery.* Where property or debts have been levied upon by service of an order of attachment, the plaintiff may commence a special proceeding against the garnishee served with the order to compel the payment, delivery or transfer to the sheriff of such property or debts, or to secure a judgment against the garnishee. Notice of petition shall also be served upon the parties to the action and the sheriff. A garnishee may interpose any defense or counterclaim which he might have interposed against the defendant if sued by him. The court may permit any adverse claimant to intervene in the proceeding and may determine his rights in accordance with section 6221.

(e) *Failure to proceed.* At the expiration of ninety days after a levy is made by service of the order of attachment, or of such further time as the court, upon motion of the plaintiff on notice to the parties to the action, has provided, the levy shall be void except as to property or debts which the sheriff has taken into his actual custody, collected or received or as to which a proceeding under subdivision (d) has been commenced.

25. *§ 6215. Levy upon personal property by seizure.*

If the plaintiff shall so direct and shall furnish the sheriff indemnity satisfactory to him or fixed by the court, the sheriff, as an alternative to the method prescribed by section 6214, shall levy upon property capable of delivery by taking the property into his actual custody. The sheriff shall forthwith serve a copy of the order of attachment in the manner prescribed by subdivision (a) of section 6214 upon the person from whose possession or custody the property was taken.

§ 6216. Levy upon real property.

The sheriff shall levy upon any interest of the defendant in real property by filing with the clerk of the county in which the property is located a notice of attachment indorsed with the name and address of the plaintiff's attorney and stating the names of the parties to the action, the amount specified in the order of attachment and a description of the property levied upon. The clerk shall record and index the notice in the same books, in the same manner and with the same effect, as a notice of the pendency of an action.

§ 6217. Additional undertaking to carrier garnishee.

A garnishee who is a common carrier may transport or deliver property actually loaded on a conveyance, notwithstanding the service upon him of an order of attachment, if it was loaded without reason to believe that an order of attachment affecting the property had been granted, unless the plaintiff gives an undertaking in an amount fixed by the court, that the plaintiff shall pay any such carrier all expenses and damages which may be incurred for unloading the property and for detention of the conveyance necessary for that purpose.

26. *§ 6224. Annulment of attachment.*

An order of attachment is annulled when the action in which it was granted abates or is discontinued, or a judgment entered therein in favor of the plaintiff is fully satisfied, or a judgment is entered therein in favor of the defendant. In the last specified case a stay of proceedings suspends the effect of the annulment, and a reversal or vacating of the judgment revives the order of attachment.

27. See Sections 6225 and 6226 of New York Civil Practice Law and Rules (CPL & R).

28. 198 US 215 (1905).

29. See 1 Emanuel's Encyclopedia of American Law (1987) at 43–44.

30. 407 US 67 (1972).

31. The court continued:

''Although these prejudgment replevin statutes are descended from the common law replevin action of six centuries ago, they bear very little resemblance to it. Replevin at common law was an action for the return of specific goods wrongfully taken or 'distrained.' Typically it was used after a landlord (the 'distrainor') had seized possessions from a tenant (the 'distrainee') to satisfy a debt allegedly owed. If the tenant then instituted a replevin action and posted security, the landlord could be ordered to return the property at once, pending a final judgment in the underlying action. However, this prejudgment replevin of goods at common law did *not* follow from an entirely *ex parte* process of pleading by the distrainee. For '[t]he distrainor could always stop the action of replevin by claiming to be the owner of the goods; and as this claim was often made merely to delay the proceedings, the writ *de proprietate probanda* was devised early in the fourteenth century which enabled the sheriff to determine summarily the question of ownership. If the question of ownership was determined against the distrainor the goods were delivered back to the distrainee [pending final judgment].' 3 Holdsworth, History of English Law 284 (1927).

Prejudgment replevin statutes like those of Florida and Pennsylvania are derived from this ancient possessory action in that they authorize the seizure of property before a final judgment. But the similarity ends there. As in the present cases, such statutes are most commonly used by creditors to seize goods allegedly wrongfully detained—not wrongfully taken—by debtors. At common law, if a creditor wished to invoke state power to recover goods wrongfully detained, he had to proceed through the action of debt or detinue. These actions, however, did not provide for a return of property before final judgment. And, more importantly, on the occasions when the common law did allow prejudgment seizure of state power, it provided some kind of notice and opportunity to be heard to the party then in possession of the property, and a state official made at least a summary determination of the relative rights of the disputing parties before stepping into the dispute and taking goods from one of them.

For more than a century the central meaning of procedural due process has been clear: 'Parties whose rights are to be affected are entitled to be heard; and in order that they may enjoy that right they must be notified.' Baldwin v. Hale, 68 U.S. 223. See Windsor v. McVeigh, 93 U.S. 274; Hovey v. Elliott, 167 U.S. 409; Grannis v. Ordean, 234 U.S. 385. It is equally fundamental that the right to notice and an opportunity to be heard 'must be granted at a meaningful time and in a meaningful manner.' Armstrong v. Manzo, 380 U.S. 545, 552.

The primary question in the present cases is whether these state statutes are constitutionally defective in failing to provide for hearings 'at a meaningful time.' The Florida replevin process guarantees an opportunity for a hearing after the seizure of goods, and the Pennsylvania process allows a post-seizure hearing if the aggrieved party shoulders the burden of initiating one. But neither the Florida nor Pennsylvania statute provides for notice or an opportunity to be heard *before* the seizure. The issue is whether procedural due process in the context of these cases requires an opportunity for a hearing *before* the State authorizes its agents to seize property in the possession of a person upon the application of another.''

32. The dissent of Mr. Justice White (joined with The Chief Justice and Mr. Justice Blackmun) opined that ''the procedure which the Court strikes down is not some barbaric hangover from bygone days. The respective rights of the parties in secured transactions have undergone the most intensive analysis in recent years. The Uniform Commercial Code, which now so pervasively governs the subject matter with which it deals, provides in Art. 9, § 9–503, that: 'Unless otherwise agreed a secured party has on default the right to take possession of the collateral. In taking possession a secured party may proceed without judicial process if this can be done without breach of peace or may proceed by action. . . . '' Recent studies have suggested no changes in Art. 9 in this respect. See Permanent Editorial Board for the Uniform Commercial Code, Review Committee for Article 9 of the Uniform Commercial Code, Final Report, § 9–503 (April 25, 1971). I am content to rest on the judgment of those who have wrestled with these problems so long and often and upon the judgment of the legislatures that have considered and so recently adopted provisions that contemplate precisely what had happened in these cases.''

33. 419 US 601 (1975).

34. See Calero-Toledo v. Pearson Yacht Leasing Co., 416 US 663 (1974) and Flagg Bros., Inc. v. Brooks, 436 US 149 (1978), for example.

35. 395 US 337 (1969).

36. Note Randone v. Appellate Department, 488 P2d 13 (1973) at 22: ''*Sniadach* does not mark a radical departure in constitutional adjudication. It is not a rivulet of wage garnishment but, part of the mainstream of past procedural due process decisions of the United States Supreme Court.''

37. Note the dissent of Mr. Justice Black: ''The Court here holds unconstitutional a Wisconsin statute permitting garnishment before a judgment has been obtained against the principal debtor. The law, however, requires that notice be given to the principal debtor and authorizes him to present all of his legal defenses at the regular hearing and trial of the case. The Wisconsin law is said to violate the 'fundamental principles of due process.' Of course the Due Process Clause of the Fourteenth Amendment contains no words that indicate that this Court has power to play so fast and loose with state laws. The arguments the Court makes to reach what I consider to be its unconstitutional conclusion, however, shows why it strikes down this state law. It is because it considers a garnishment law of this kind to be bad state policy, a judgment I think the state legislature, not this Court, has power to make. . . . ''

38. Unreported (1987).

39. See generally 21 Int'l Law. (Winter 1987) at 1 et seq.

40. Mareva Compania Naviera, S.A. v. International Bulk Carriers, S.A., (1975) 2 Lloyd's Rep. 509 (C.A.).

41. Ch. 54; supra note 39 at 11.

42. See generally Fiss, The Civil Rights Injunction (1978) and also Note, 91 Harv. L. Rev. 428 (1977).

43. See Vasquez v. Superior Court, 484 P2d 964 (1971).

44. See Rondeau v. Mosiness Paper Corp., 422 US 49 (1975).

45. See Christopher v. Jones, 41 Cal. Rptr. 828 (1964).

46. 1988 U.S. Dist. LEXIS 3630 (SDNY, May 2, 1988).

47. 206 F2d 738 (2d Cir., 1957).

48. The preliminary injunction also protects the defendant against untoward harm while the proceedings go forward. Note the sample Order to Show Cause preceding the issuance of the preliminary injunction:

At a Special Term, Part II of the Supreme Court of the State of New York, held in and for the County of New York at 60 Centre Street, New York, New York, on the 17th day of April 1969.

PRESENT:

HONORABLE JAWN A. SANDIFER

Justice

THE TRUSTEES OF COLUMBIA UNIVERSITY IN THE CITY OF NEW YORK

Plaintiffs

ORDER TO SHOW CAUSE

— against —

STUDENTS FOR A DEMOCRATIC SOCIETY, Columbia University Chapter, et alii and "JOHN DOE" NUMBERS 1 to 100, the latter being unknown persons present in or adjacent to Philosophy Hall, Columbia University, in connection with the unlawful occupation of that building,

Defendants

Upon the annexed summons, verified complaint, and the affidavit of Ralph S. Halford, sworn to on April 17, 1969, and sufficient reason appearing therefor, it is

ORDERED that the defendants show cause before this Court at Special Term, Part I, New York County Court House, 60 Centre Street, New York, New York, on 29th April 1969 at 10:00 a.m. why an order should not be entered herein pending the hearing and determination of the issues in this action:

1. Restraining and enjoining each and all of the defendants and all other persons receiving notice of this injunction from congregating or assembling within or adjacent to any of plaintiff's academic or administrative buildings, dormitories, recreation rooms or athletic facilities or in any corridors, stairways, doorways and entrances thereto, in such manner as to disrupt or interfere with normal functions conducted by plaintiff in such place or to block, hinder, impede or interfere with ingress to or egress from any of such properties by plaintiff's faculty, administrators, students, employees or guests;

2. Restraining and enjoining each and all of the defendants and all other persons receiving notice of this injunction from creating or broadcasting on plaintiff's Morningside Heights campus or in the streets adjacent thereto, any loud or excessive noise that hinders, impedes, prevents or interferes with the conduct of normal activities by members of the University community;

3. Restraining and enjoining each and all of the defendants and all other persons receiving notice

of this injunction from employing force or violence, or the threat of force or violence, against persons or property on plaintiff's campus;

4. Restraining and enjoining each and all of the defendants and all other persons receiving notice of this injunction from threatening to do or inciting or counselling others to do any of the abovementioned acts; and

5. Granting plaintiff such other relief as may be proper; and it is further

ORDERED that pending the hearing and determination of this motion, the defendants and all other persons receiving notice of this injunction be and they hereby are restrained and enjoined:

1. From congregating or assembling within or adjacent to any of plaintiff's academic or administrative buildings, dormitories, recreation rooms or athletic facilities or in any corridors, stairways, doorways and entrances thereto, in such manner as to disrupt or interfere with normal functions conducted by plaintiff in such place or to block, hinder, impede or interfere with ingress to or egress from any of such properties by plaintiff's faculty, administrators, students, employees or guests;

2. From creating or broadcasting on plaintiff's Morningside Heights campus or in the streets adjacent thereto, any loud or excessive noise that hinders, impedes, prevents or interferes with the conduct of normal activities by members of the University community;

3. From employing force or violence, or the threat of force or violence, against persons or property on plaintiff's campus;

4. From threatening to do or inciting or counselling others to do any of the abovementioned acts; and it is further

ORDERED that service of this order and the papers upon which it is made be accomplished by serving the defendants personally, and by serving the parents of those defendants who have not yet attained the age of twenty-one years by registered mail, on or before April 19th, 1969 at 4 P.M.

ENTER
(S) *Jawn A. Sandifer*

In the federal courts the form and scope of injunctions is set forth in Rule 65(d) of Federal Rules of Civil Procedure (FRCP): "*Form and Scope of Injunction or Restraining Order*. Every order granting an injunction and every restraining order shall set forth the reasons for its issuance; shall be specific in terms; shall describe in reasonable detail, and not by reference to the complaint or other document, the act or acts sought to be restrained; and is binding only upon the parties to the action, their officers, agents, servants, employees, and attorneys, and upon those persons in active concert or participation with them who receive actual notice of the order by personal service or otherwise."

49. *§ 6301. Grounds for preliminary injunction and temporary restraining order.*

A preliminary injunction may be granted in any action where it appears that the defendant threatens or is about to do, or is doing or procuring or suffering to be done, an act in violation of the plaintiff's rights respecting the subject of the action, and tending to render the judgment ineffectual, or in any action where the plaintiff has demanded and would be entitled to a judgment restraining the defendant from the commission or continuance of an act, which, if committed or continued during the pendency of the action, would produce injury to the plaintiff. A temporary restraining order may be granted pending a hearing for a preliminary injunction where it appears that immediate and irreparable injury, loss or damage will result unless the defendant is restrained before the hearing can be had.

50. See McCampbell v. Di Nuzzo, 270 NYS2d 685 (1968).

51. 628 F. Supp. 1457 (SDNY, June 1, 1987).

52. 663 F. Supp. 614 (SDNY, June 22, 1987).

53. See Sanfield v. Goldstein, 308 NYS2d (1969), aff'd 28 NY2d 794, 270 NE2d 723 (1969). Injunctive relief is available in actions involving real property, although traditionally injunctive relief as an extraordinary remedy would be granted only when another form of relief was unavailable. Today it does not require such a pleading, as illustrated in Republic Aviation Corp. v. Republic Lodge, 169 NYS2d 651 (1957). Even where the plaintiff can be compensated by monetary damages, the difficulty and complexity of calculating those damages may warrant the injunctive relief, according to Gulf & Western Corp. v. Craftique Productions, Inc., 523 F. Supp. 603 (SDNY, 1981). See generally Block and Mellon, "Availability of Injunctive Relief in Actions Involving Real Property," NYLJ (March 16, 1988) at 31 et seq. In South Ferry Building v. J. Henry Schroder Bank, 458 NYS2d 584 (1st Dept., 1983) a preliminary injunction was granted which precluded the tenant from making any alteration to the building's electrical distribution system. In City of New York v. Narod Realty Corp., 471 NYS2d 757 (1983) the New York court issued an injunction enjoining the use of a portion of the premises as a "bodega."

54. See Western New York Motor Lines, Inc. v. Rochester-Genesee Regional Transportation Authority, 340 NYS2d 252 (1974).

55. *§ 6311. Preliminary Injunction.*

1. A preliminary injunction may be granted only upon notice to the defendant. Notice of the motion may be served with the summons or at any time thereafter and prior to judgment. A preliminary injunction to restrain a public officer, board or municipal corporation of the state from performing a statutory duty may be granted only by the supreme court at a term in the department in which the officer or board is located or in which the duty is required to be performed.

2. Notice of motion for a preliminary injunction to restrain state officers or boards of state officers under the provisions of this section must be upon notice served upon the defendant or respondent, state officers or board of state officers and must be served upon the attorney general in the county in which venue of the action is designated or if there is no office of the attorney general in such county, at the office of the attorney general nearest such county.

56. See Re Utica Teachers Assn., 325 NYS2d 587 (1974).

57. See First National Stores v. Yellowstone Shopping Center, 21 NY2d 630 (1940).

58. *Rule 6312. Motion papers; undertaking.*

(a) *Affidavit; other papers.* On a motion for a preliminary injunction the plaintiff shall show, by affidavit and such other evidence as may be submitted, that there is no cause of action, and either that the defendant threatens or is about to do, or is doing or procuring or suffering to be done, an act in violation of the plaintiff's rights respecting the subject of the action and tending to render the judgment ineffectual; or that the plaintiff has demanded and would be entitled to a judgment restraining the defendant from the commission or continuance of an act, which, if committed or continued during the pendency of the action, would produce injury to the plaintiff.

(b) *Undertaking.* Except as provided in section 2512, prior to the granting of a preliminary injunction, the plaintiff shall give an undertaking in an amount to be fixed by the court, that the plaintiff, if it is finally determined that he was not entitled to an injunction, will pay to the defendant all damages and costs which may be sustained by reason of the injunction, including,

1. if the injunction is to stay proceedings in another action, on any ground other than that a report, verdict or decision was obtained by actual fraud, all damages and costs

which may be, or which have been, awarded in the other action to the defendant as well as all damages and costs which may be awarded him in the action in which the injunction was granted; or

2. if the injunction is to stay proceedings in an action to recover real property, or for dower, on any ground other than that a verdict, report or decision was obtained by actual fraud, all damages and costs which may be, or which have been, awarded to the defendant in the action in which the injunction was granted, including the reasonable rents and profits of, and any wastes committed upon, the real property which is sought to be recovered or which is the subject of the action for dower, after the granting of the injunction; or

3. if the injunction is to stay proceedings upon a judgment for a sum of money on any ground other than that the judgment was obtained by actual fraud, the full amount of the judgment as well as all damages and costs which may be awarded to the defendant in the action in which the injunction was granted.

The New York Supreme Court, New York County, in *Liz Claiborne, Inc. v. Avon Products, Inc.*, on March 24, 1988, had occasion to discuss the New York view on "injunctive relief":

"Plaintiffs claim that irreparable harm will befall plaintiffs if the preliminary injunction requested by plaintiffs is not granted. On the other hand, defendants contend that any harm that may befall plaintiffs can be adequately compensated by money damages. Each of the agreements expressly recites that the parties acknowledge 'that the other may suffer great and irreparable harm as the result of the breach . . . of any covenant or agreement to be performed or observed by it,' and each acknowledges that 'the other shall be entitled to apply for and, if granted, receive from any court of competent jurisdiction a temporary restraining order, preliminary injunction, [or] permanent injunction without any necessity of proving damages or any requirement for the posting of a bond or other security, enjoining the other from further breach of this Agreement.' While injunctive relief under this clause is not assured, for it is still up to the court to decide if to grant it, clearly the parties contemplated that injunctive relief could be called for to keep the contract going, even though they, as joint venturers and partners, might be in fundamental disagreement.

Defendants' claim that money damages are adequate in the event of a breach overlooks such intangible considerations as how the possible destruction of the Liz Claiborne cosmetics line may effect the other businesses carried on under the Liz Claiborne name. The closing of a much publicized venture by Liz Claiborne and its failure to supply stores would do nothing to enhance its reputation with suppliers, distributors, retailers and customers. Money damages would be inadequate to compensate for such damage as Liz Claiborne's reputation may suffer.

The argument advanced by defendants that plaintiffs' application for injunctive relief is premature is equally without merit. If plaintiffs were to await the very last moment for its application to the court, it might indeed be too late to enable plaintiffs to plan their 1988 Fall/Christmas distribution and sales. This court is not convinced, moreover, that such application is premature when one considers the lead time necessary in ordering seasonal merchandise or merchandise to be sold during a particular season.

U.C.C. Sec 2–716 provides that " . . . [s]pecific performance may be decreed where the goods are unique or in other proper circumstances." See Dexter Bishop C. v. B.

Redmond & Don, Inc. 58 A.D.2d 755. The uniqueness of the plaintiffs' cosmetics line including its distinctive packaging, is obvious.

Avon grudgingly concedes that while it may be obligated to honor orders placed prior to what it claims were acts of dissolution so that there can be an orderly liquidation, it argues that the orders here involved go far beyond Cosmetics' requirements for a reasonable liquidation period, and are in fact an attempt to stockpile merchandise for sales well into 1989. It insists that the Cosmetics Board of Directors, divided equally between Claiborne and Avon designees, had not approved any annual plan for 1988, so the orders were unauthorized.

Claiborne replies that with respect to the 1988 plan, the only disagreement on the Board was concerning budget and promotional expenses, and that it was agreed the venture would continue functioning in accordance with existing procedures, and with no dispute as to sales projections. Avon's internal schedule called for all purchase orders from Cosmetics for the Fall/Christmas 1988 season to be placed not later than March 21, 1988, so that procurement of materials and manufacturing could proceed with delivery to Cosmetics by August, preparatory to retail distribution. Claiborne contends there was inventory on hand in 1987, which makes its orders for 1988 noncomparable, and that in light of favorable actual sales experience, an 18% sales experience, an 18% sales increase over 1987 is realistic. They concede orders placed will give them inventory to cover the first three months of 1989, since they claim no business can permit its inventory to go down to zero.

Under the circumstances, there appears to be no pressing necessity for Avon to be compelled to fill orders calling for November and December deliveries on this temporary injunction application. Twenty weeks lead time appears to be ample, pending resolution of the entire case. Should the filling of further orders become necessary, further application can be made to this court.

Injunctive relief, as required by plaintiffs, is a form of specific performance and this court grants plaintiffs the relief requested to the extent of requiring defendants and those under their control to fulfill and otherwise service, fill and deliver in timely and diligent fashion all purchase orders previously placed by plaintiff Cosmetics with defendants in accordance with the terms of such orders which call for delivery up to and including the end of August, 1988. Division of Triple T Service Inc. v. Mobil Oil Corp., 60 Misc. 2d 720, affd. 34 A.D. 2d 618.

The fact that Avon may have breached its covenant does not mean that Claiborne Cosmetics must drop its venture in cosmetics so auspiciously begun. It has not, as claimed, 'abandoned' the venture. It is entitled to claim a breach and still get its requirements to remain an ongoing factor in the market. Declaration of a default does not terminate the contract, it creates an option to do so. Until, and under the contract even after that is done, the right to be supplied continues. It follows that plaintiffs' motion, to the extent indicated, must be granted."

59. *§ 6313. Temporary restraining order.*

(a) *Generally.* If, on a motion for a preliminary injunction, the plaintiff shall show that immediate and irreparable injury, loss or damages will result unless the defendant is restrained before a hearing can be had, a temporary restraining order may be granted without notice. Upon granting a temporary restraining order, the court shall set the hearing for the preliminary injunction at the earliest possible time. No temporary restraining order may be granted in an action arising out of a labor dispute as defined in section eight hundred seven of the labor law, nor against a public officer, board or municipal corporation of the state to restrain the performance of statutory duties.

(b) *Service.* Unless the court orders otherwise, a temporary restraining order together with the papers upon which it was based, and a notice of hearing for the preliminary injunction, shall be personally served in the same manner as a summons.

(c) *Undertaking.* Prior to the granting of a temporary restraining order the court may, in its discretion, require the plaintiff to give an undertaking in an amount to be fixed by the court, containing terms similar to those set forth in subdivision (b) of rule 6312, and subject to the exception set forth therein.

60. *§ 6314. Vacating or modifying preliminary injunction or temporary restraining order.*

A defendant enjoined by a preliminary injunction may move at any time, on notice to the plaintiff, to vacate or modify it. On motion, without notice, made by a defendant enjoined by a temporary restraining order, the judge who granted it, or in his absence or disability, another judge, may vacate or modify the order. An order granted without notice and vacating or modifying a temporary restraining order shall be effective when, together with the papers upon which it is based, it is filed with the clerk and served upon the plaintiff. As a condition to granting an order vacating or modifying a preliminary injunction or a temporary restraining order, a court may require the defendant, except where the defendant is a public body or officer, to give an undertaking, in an amount to be fixed by the court, that the defendant shall pay to the plaintiff any loss sustained by reason of the vacating or modifying order.

61. 348 NYS2d 28 (1974).

62. 416 US 802 (1974).

63. See Bonner v. Circuit Court, 526 F2d 1331 (6th Cir., 1975), cert. den. 424 US 946, and reh'g den. 425 US 926 (1976).

64. See Winpisinger v. Watson, 628 F2d 133 (4th Cir., 1980).

65. 433 F. Supp. 1297 (SDNY, 1977).

66. See Supreme Court of Virginia v. Consumers Union of the United States, 446 US 719 (1980).

67. 103 S. Ct. 1660 (1983). It is interesting to observe that "ineffectuality" is a prime reason for a court to issue or even refuse to issue an injunction as a provisional remedy. See Cooper v. Ateliers de la Motobecane, 57 NY2d 408, 456 NYS2d 728 (1982). In Matter of Denihan, 119 AD2d 144, 506 NYS2d 39, the New York Appellate Division, First Dept., the injunction was applied to a situation where any award would be ineffectual without it. And in Matter of Saferstein v. Wendy, 523 NYS2d 725 (1987) the New York Supreme Court, New York County, faced a situation where the petitioner had developed a plastic comb with an adjustable metal comb; the money was put up by respondent, and the parties entered into a licensing agreement that provided for payment of royalties to the respondent, the licensor, on sales made by petitioner, the licensee. The agreement was terminable by the licensee on 6 months' notice and by the licensor on 30 days' notice. The agreement was in effect for a number of years until respondent, dissatisfied with the royalty payments, gave notification of intention to terminate the agreement, and at the same time sought an accounting. The licensee made a demand for arbitration under the broad arbitration clause in the agreement. But the licensor obtained a temporary restraining order pending the court's decision on petitioner's application for a temporary injunction preventing respondent from terminating the agree-

ment. The argument that without an injunction the arbitration would be ineffectual was based on the fact that without it respondent could simply declare the agreement at an end and license someone else to market the combs, which apparently were used to delouse! The New York court issued the preliminary injunction on the ground that "the award to which the applicant may be entitled may be rendered ineffectual without such provisional relief."

68. 398 US 144 (1970).

69. See Hosey v. Club Van Cortlandt, 299 F. Supp. 501 (SDNY, 1969).

70. 682 F. Supp. 1544 (SDNY, 1988); also 681 F. Supp. 1066 (SDNY, 1988).

71. 676 F. Supp. 546 (SDNY, 1988); also 679 F. Supp. 393 (SDNY, 1988).

72. Unreported (SDNY, 1988).

73. *§ 6401. Appointment and powers of temporary receiver.*

(a) *Appointment of temporary receiver; joinder of moving party.* Upon motion of a person having an apparent interest in property which is the subject of an action in the supreme or a county court, a temporary receiver of the property may be appointed, before or after service of summons and at any time prior to judgment, or during the pendency of an appeal, where there is danger that the property will be removed from the state, or lost, materially injured or destroyed. A motion made by a person not already a party to the action constitutes an appearance in the action and the person shall be joined as a party.

(b) *Powers of temporary receiver.* The court appointing a receiver may authorize him to take and hold real and personal property, and sue for, collect and sell debts or claims, upon such conditions and for such purposes as the court shall direct. A receiver shall have no power to employ counsel unless expressly so authorized by order of the court. Upon motion of the receiver or a party, powers granted to a temporary receiver may be extended or limited or the receivership may be extended to another action involving the property.

(c) *Duration of temporary receivership.* A temporary receivership shall not continue after final judgment unless otherwise directed by the court.

74. See Hahn v. Wylie, 387 NYS2d 255 (1975).

75. *§ 6404. Accounts.*

A temporary receiver shall keep written accounts itemizing receipts and expenditures, and describing the property and naming the depository of receivership funds, which shall be open to inspection by any person having an apparent interest in the property, the court may require the keeping of particular records or direct or limit inspection or require presentation of a temporary receiver's accounts. Notice of a motion for the presentation of a temporary receiver's accounts shall be served upon the sureties on his undertaking as well as upon each party.

§ 6405. Removal.

Upon motion of any party or upon its own initiative, the court which appointed a receiver may remove him at any time.

76. 331 P2d 735 (Cal. App., 1958).

77. See Mageloff v. Sarkin, 276 NYS2d 708 (1971).

78. *§ 6501. Notice of pendency; constructive notice.*

A notice of pendency may be filed in any action in a court of the state or of the United States in which the judgment demanded would affect the title to, or the possession, use or enjoyment of, real property. The pendency of such an action is constructive notice, from the time of filing of the notice only, to a purchaser from, or incumbrancer against, any defendant named in a notice of pendency indexed in a block index against a block in which property affected is situated or any defendant against whose name a notice of pendency is indexed. A person whose conveyance or incumbrance is recorded after the filing of the notice is bound by all proceedings taken in the action after such filing to the same extent as if he were a party.

Rule 6511. Filing, content and indexing of notice of pendency.

(a) *Filing.* In a case specified in section 6501, the notice of pendency shall be filed in the office of the clerk of any county where property affected is situated before or after service of summons and at any time prior to judgment. Unless it has already been filed in that county, the complaint shall be filed with the notice of pendency.

(b) *Content; designation of index.* A notice of pendency shall state the names of the parties to the action, the object of the action and a description of the property affected. A notice of pendency filed with a clerk who maintains a block index shall contain a designation of the number of each block on the land map of the county which is affected by the notice. Except in an action for partition a notice of pendency filed with a clerk who does not maintain a block index shall contain a designation of the names of each defendant against whom the notice is directed to be indexed.

(c) *Indexing.* Each county clerk with whom a pendency is filed shall immediately record it and index it against blocks or names designated. A county clerk who does not maintain a block index shall index a notice of pendency of an action for position against the names of each plaintiff and each defendant not designated as wholly fictitious.

§ 6512. Service of summons.

A notice of pendency filed before an action is commenced is effective only if, within thirty days after filing, a summons is served upon the defendant or first publication of the summons against the defendant is made pursuant to an order and publication is subsequently completed. If the defendant dies within thirty days after filing and before the summons is served upon him or publication is completed, the notice is effective only if the summons is served upon his executor or administrator within sixty days after letters are issued.

§ 6513. Duration of notice of pendency.

A notice of pendency shall be effective for a period of three years from the date of filing. Before expiration of a period or extended period, the court upon motion of the plaintiff and upon such notice as it may require, for good cause shown, may grant an extension for a like additional period. An extension order shall be filed, recorded and indexed before expiration of the prior period.

79. See Tubbs v. Hendrickson, 390 NYS2d 791 (1976).

80. See King v. Quinn, 256 NYS2d 823 (1970).

81. *§ 6514. Motion for cancellation of notice of pendency.*

(a) *Mandatory cancellation.* The court, upon motion of any person aggrieved and upon such notice as it may require, shall direct any county clerk to cancel a notice of pendency, if service of a summons has not been completed within the time limited by section 6512; or if the action has been settled, discontinued or abated; or if the time to appeal from a final judgment against the plaintiff has expired; or if enforcement of a final judgment against the plaintiff has not been stayed pursuant to section 5519.

(b) *Discretionary cancellation.* The court upon motion of any person aggrieved and upon such notice as it may require, may direct any county clerk to cancel a notice of pendency, if the plaintiff has not commenced or prosecuted the action in good faith.

(c) *Costs and expenses.* The court, in an order cancelling a notice of pendency under this section, may direct the plaintiff to pay any costs and expenses occasioned by the filing and cancellation, in addition to any costs of the action.

(d) *Cancellation by stipulation.* At any time prior to entry of judgment, a notice of pendency shall be cancelled by the county clerk without an order, on the filing with him of

1. an affidavit by the attorney for the plaintiff showing which defendants have been served with process, which defendants are in default in appearing or answering, and which defendants have appeared or answered and by whom, and

2. a stipulation consenting to the cancellation, signed by the attorney for the plaintiff and by the attorneys for all the defendants who have appeared or answered including those who have waived all notices, and executed and acknowledged, in the form required to entitle a deed to be recorded, by the defendants who have been served with process and have not appeared but whose time to do so has not expired, and by any defendants who have appeared in person.

(e) *Cancellation by plaintiff.* At any time prior to the entry of judgment a notice of pendency of action shall be cancelled by the county clerk without an order, on the filing with him of an affidavit by the attorney for the plaintiff showing that there have been no appearances and that the time to appear has expired for all parties.

7

Requests for Admission and Other Time-Saving Devices

THE CONCEPT OF ADMISSIONS

The core of the concept of requests for admission, which aid in resolving issues and save time, is Rule 36 of the Federal Rules of Civil Procedure.[1] This federal rule finds its counterpart in state statutes like Section 3123 of New York Civil Practice Law & Rules.[2] Both plaintiffs and defendants can and do utilize these statutes and rules to gain a decided advantage in a dispute. There are also other time-saving devices, like the request to produce documents[3] and the demand for a physical and mental examination of the adversary party.[4]

Historically, the right to seek admissions probably originated in England with the Hilary Rules of 1834 on the genuineness of documents. Within 15 years the state of New York adopted the concept, and after many other states followed suit, the federal Equity Rules of 1912 were put into effect. The latter opened the door to provisions in the Federal Rules of Civil Procedure, which were enacted in 1938. But admissions as to evidentiary facts probably did not originate in English legislation until 1883. They were later adopted here in the statutes of the several states and then in the Federal Rules of Civil Procedure.

RULE 36 OF THE FEDERAL RULES OF CIVIL PROCEDURE

Rule 36 of the Federal Rules of Civil Procedure can be shown in action in *Lumpkin v. Meskill*, where the federal district court in Connecticut was deeply involved in a school desegregation dispute.[5] The court expressed the problem as follows:

> Germane to the issues in this case is the racial balance of the Hartford school system from approximately 1950 to the present. Before 1964 the school system did not maintain

statistics regarding the racial composition of either individual schools or the system as a whole. Thus, for the 1950–1964 period plaintiffs have been forced to compile these statistics on their own. Apparently the school system maintained individual records on all students throughout the period which indicated the child's race and such other data (pertinent for the purpose of determining whether a child was a Latino) as the child's place of birth and the language spoken in his home.

In compiling their statistics, plaintiffs were faced with the choice of either reading through the files of 321,000 students who attended Hartford elementary schools during the period in question or else employing a random sampling technique to arrive at an accurate approximation of the racial composition of the schools. Not unreasonably, they chose the latter alternative which, according to their statistical expert, Dr. Paul Hadden of the University of Connecticut, required the examination of only 11,000 files to reach an accuracy level of 5 percent with a confidence level of 95 percent. It is clear that an actual reading of all 321,000 files would have involved incalculable time and expense.

Having completed their statistical survey, the plaintiffs then submitted the results in tabular form to the defendant school board and the state defendant on March 4, 1974, with a request to admit their accuracy pursuant to F.R. Civ. P. 36(a).

The defendant school admitted the accuracy of the results but the state of Connecticut refused to admit or deny the accuracy of the result:

Within the 30 days required by the rule, the defendant did submit a response in which it stated that it could not "truthfully admit or deny the accuracy of the contents of the table because it is based on a statistical formulation employing random sampling to obtain estimates of the racial composition of the schools so that the conclusions reached are not verifiable facts."

Upon receipt of this response, plaintiffs conferred with the defendant and agreed to break down their request for admission into three parts. As so drafted, they now read:

1. Where the Hartford Board of Education maintains that actual figures for the racial composition of the Hartford Public Schools were not kept, a formulation based on statistically valid random sampling techniques is a reliable means of approximating the racial composition of those individual schools.

2. The methodology employed by Dr. Kenneth Paul Hadden as set out in the "Affidavit of Kenneth Paul Hadden in Support of the Attached Document 'Racial Composition of Hartford Public Schools, Determined by Sample Count of Student Population' " is a statistically valid random sampling technique.

3. The results of the methodology referred to in item #2 above and depicted in the table entitled, "Racial Composition of Hartford Public Schools, Determined by Sample Count of Student Population" are accurate as a reliable means of approximating the racial composition of the schools listed in that table.

The defendant responded to these revised requests by admitting that the table of results was "obtained in accordance with the methodology described in the affidavit of Kenneth Paul Hadden. . . . " However, again it stated that it could not "truthfully admit or deny the accuracy of the contents of the table." Presumably, its difficulty was still chiefly based upon the notion that Rule 36(a) only requires a response to a request to admit "verifiable facts." This assumption is borne out by the argument of defendant's counsel in his brief and in the hearing held before this Court on this matter.

The court thereupon delineated the scope of Rule 36(a), pointing out the following:

The defendant refuses to answer on the grounds that the rule only requires it to admit or deny "verifiable facts." It argues that the plaintiffs are asking it to express an opinion as to the validity of sampling techniques in general, the validity of the particular technique used in this case and the accuracy of the results obtained. It firmly maintains that Rule 36(a) does not contemplate that kind of request.

In light of the recent amendment to Rule 36(a), this Court is somewhat perplexed by the defendant's argument. Prior to 1970, the rule read, in relevant part: "After commencement of an action a party may serve upon any other party a written request for the admission by the latter of the genuineness of any relevant documents described in and exhibited with the request or of the truth of any *relevant matters of fact* set forth in the request. . . . " (Emphasis added.)

It is true that under this language there was some confusion and division among the courts as to the type of material which could be the subject matter of an admission. Some courts, viewing the scope of the rule broadly, held that requests in the shadowy area between fact and opinion were proper. Photon, Inc. v. Harris Intertype, 28 F.R.D. 327 (D. Mass. 1961), aff'd on other grounds 349 F.2d 856 (1st Cir. 1965), cert. denied sub nom. Tansel v. Photon, Inc., 382 U.S. 1011 (1966); Jones v. Boyd Truck Lines, Inc., 11 F.R.D. 67 (W.D. Mo. 1951). Others, narrowly restricting the rule, held that requests for admission of matters of opinion or conclusion were not proper. Trabon Engineering Corp. v. Eaton Mfs. Co., 37 F.R.D. 51 (N.D. Ohio 1964); Kasar v. Miller Printing Machinery Co., 36 F.R.D. 200 (W.D. Pa. 1964).

In revising Rule 36(a), the Advisory Committee on Rules was well aware of this problem area. As revised, the rule now reads in pertinent part: "A party may serve upon any other party a written request for the admission, for purposes of the pending action only, *of the truth of any matters within the scope of Rule 26(b) set forth in the request that relate to statements or opinions of fact or of the application of law to fact*, including the genuineness of any document described in the request. . . . " (Emphasis added.)

Thus, the revised rule on its face embraces requests for admissions of opinions of fact. As the parties admit, there is virutually no case law on the impact of the revision upon practice under Rule 36(a). However, the Advisory Committee on Rules itself discussed the intent of the change as follows:

> Subdivision (a). As revised, the subdivision provides that a request may be made to admit any matters within the scope of Rule 26(b) that relate to statements or opinions of fact or of the application of law to fact. It thereby eliminates the requirement that the matters be "of fact." This change resolves conflicts in the court decisions as to whether a request to admit matters of "opinion" and matters involving "mixed law and fact" is proper under the rule. . . .
>
> Not only is it difficult as a practical matter to separate "fact" from "opinion," see 4 Moore's Federal Practice 36.04 (2d ed. 1966); cf. 2A Barron & Holtzoff, Federal Practice and Procedure 317 (Wright ed. 1961), but an admission on a matter of opinion may facilitate proof or narrow the issues or both. An admission of a matter involving the application of law to fact may, in a given case, even more clearly narrow the issues. 48 F.R.D. 487, 532 (1970).

In view of this clear language, it becomes rather apparent why virtually no other court has been forced to resolve the chimerical problem presented here.

The court ruled that for purposes of this litigation, "the first two requests [for admissions are] admitted." And the court concluded:

> At the hearing, however, the defendant was not willing to admit the accuracy of the statistics, even assuming its construction of Rule 36 to be wrong. It cited a number of valid concerns with the way in which the research may have been conducted. For example, it did not understand why Dr. Hadden had sampled only 17 of the 30 schools in Hartford or know the degree of Dr. Hadden's supervision over the students who actually did the field research. Valid as these concerns are, there seems to be no apparent reason why through "reasonable inquiry" the defendant would not be able to obtain those facts which it contends are necessary to put it in a position to make a judgment as to the accuracy of plaintiffs' statistics. Plaintiffs point out that they have offered to make Dr. Hadden available to the defendant for the purpose of a deposition. In addition, the defendant could inspect the field notes and working papers of Dr. Hadden. In this way, it could obtain information regarding the way in which the study was conducted. Its expert(s) could then advise whether plaintiffs' statistics are reliable within the range indicated Dr. Hadden's affidavit.
>
> The burden which this places upon the State of Connecticut is not unduly heavy. The defendant argues that the "reasonable inquiry" requirement of Rule 36 does not contemplate the kind of inquiry which would be required of it in this case. Again, this objection is answered by the Report of the Advisory Committee on Rules in reference to this requirement in the amended Rule 36. . . .
>
> In the instant case, the defendant is only being asked to "secure such knowledge and information as are readily obtainable by [it]." In addition, it is clear that if the defendant finds that it cannot admit the accuracy of the statistics, the research required of it here will not have been wasted. It will be "necessary either to [its] own case or to preparation for rebuttal." Indeed, it does not even seem unreasonable to require the defendant to conduct independent research if necessary to verify the accuracy of the raw data obtained by Dr. Hadden's field workers.

The expansiveness of Rule 36 of the Federal Rules of Civil Procedure is the result of many amendments, the most recent being effective August 1, 1987.[6] The request for admission is not really a discovery device since the requesting party generally has the information beforehand; but the request for admission potentially can simplify the proof and narrow the issues before trial. A party may serve upon any other party (but not upon nonparties) a written request for admission, for the purpose of the pending action only, of the truth of any matters within the scope of Rule 26(b) of the Federal Rules of Civil Procedure. The statements include statements or opinions of fact, or of the application of law to fact. (An admission of the genuineness of such statements may be requested.)[7] In *Yates v. Dow Chemical Co.* defendant Chrysler cross-claimed against Dow, whereupon Dow requested that Chrysler admit, inter alia, that Chrysler "has no document which indicates" that Dow used faulty materials, that Chrysler has "no document which supports its cross-claim," and that Chrysler is "aware of no fact which supports its cross-claim."[8] The New York court held that these requests to admit were improper, for the purpose of a request to admit is "not to obtain information in lieu of other disclosure devices, but to eliminate from the issues matters which will not really be in dispute at the trial." An admission of the genuineness of any documents described in the request may also be sought.

The party served with the request for admissions is obligated to make a reasonable inquiry before responding; failure to answer constitutes an admission, but the answerer may admit, deny, or state that he or she lacks knowledge or information sufficient to permit an admission or denial, or simply object to the request for admission. The admission is solely for the purpose of the pending action, but it is conclusive, not merely evidentiary, unless the court grants the answerer leave to withdraw the admission or to amend the admission. Requests for admission can "distill the significant concepts and facts from an otherwise meandering deposition, economizing proofs and emphasizing important issues."[9] The fact that a particular request to admit concerns an issue in dispute is not per se grounds for objection under Rule 36. A clear, unambiguous, and unequivocal answer is desired.[10] A denial that does not constitute a denial of the essential truth of a request to admit, but that disputes its accuracy or is evasive, may be deemed an admission.[11] Argumentative answers injecting theories of the defense into matters where there is no genuine or good faith dispute are "defective" answers, and hence are admissions.[12] The federal district court in *Chess Music, Inc. v. Bowman* summed it up: "It is well settled that a failure to respond to requests for admission is deemed to be an admission of the matters set forth."[13]

The time to serve or answer requests for admission was delineated in *Steadham v. United States Leasing Corp.*, where the Alabama appellate court affirmed a summary judgment for the plaintiff based upon defendant's failure to answer the request to admit.[14] After defendant had failed to answer, the trial court gave defendant 10 days to answer; approximately 40 days later defendant responded, and this late response was held not to detract from the admissions, especially since defendant did not seek to withdraw or amend the admissions. In sum, the defendant had ignored a valid request for admissions and also refused to obey an order of the court directing him to answer that request for admissions. The trial court did not abuse its discretion here,[15] nor in *Wagner v. Carex Investigation and Security, Inc.*, where the Nevada court ruled that "oversight" was not sufficient reason for excusing the plaintiffs from not responding to requests for admission in this action for false arrest.[16] In *Brown v. Arlen Management Corp.* the Fifth U.S. Court of Appeals affirmed the admission of certain elements of negligence in a personal injury action against the defendant whose inquiry to obtain information in order to respond to plaintiff's request to admit had not been reasonable; the defendant had located certain former employees from whom defendant could have formulated reasonable admissions or denials or at least demonstrated to the court what knowledge the former employees possessed.[17] Late answers under particular circumstances have been excused, as illustrated in *Gutting v. Falstaff Brewing Corp.*, where defendant failed to show that it would be prejudiced in maintaining its defense by plaintiff's late answers to the requests for admission.[18]

Under Rule 36 a party must answer requests to admit within 30 days after service, except that a defendant has at least 45 days after service of the complaint in which to answer. If a party fails to admit the truth of any matter requested for admission, and if the party making the request proves the truth of the matter at trial, the court, upon proper motion, may require the party who had refused to admit the matter to pay reasonable expenses sustained by the moving party in proving the truth of the matter.[19] On the other hand, abusively burdensome requests to admit may be readily set aside by the court or even trigger sanctions against the wrongdoer.[20] Rule 36 requires that the answer to a request to admit be signed manually by the party or by the party's attorney; however, in view of Rule 11 against frivolous complaints and frivolous answers,[21] the attorney for the party may well be the proper person to sign the papers giving an office address and office telephone number for the mandatory certification of the complaint or answer.[22] Note that even objections to requests to admit must be in writing and signed by the answering party and/or his or her attorney; objections based upon privileged communications must be clearly set forth.[23] In *LeBlanc v. Spector*[24] the Fifth Amendment privilege against self-incrimination was invoked in an objection to a request for admission, since the admission could have led to evidence that might have been used against the answering party in a subsequent criminal action.[25]

The granting of a motion for summary judgment can be based on admissions obtained under Rule 36, as illustrated in *First National Bank of Clinton v. Insurance Company of North America*.[26] Although requests to admit will be deemed admitted in the absence of a formal reply, and although summary judgment can be entered on the basis of an unanswered request to admit, courts may, in fairness, take into consideration the nonanswering party's affidavit in ruling on the motion for summary judgment, and the requests to admit may be taken as admitted only insofar as the facts so admitted are uncontroverted by the affidavit.[27] Note that an admission may be withdrawn or amended with the permission of the court,[28] and that the denial of that motion to withdraw or amend the request for admissions may be reviewed for an abuse of judicial discretion.[29] In *Gardner v. Southern Railway Systems* the Seventh U.S. Court found that the trial court's granting of defendant's motion to amend its answer to deny that the deceased stopped the vehicle prior to crossing the railroad tracks was held to be tantamount to permission to withdraw its admission regarding the deceased's stopping, which was contained in its own request for admissions.[30] The court reasoned that the purpose of Rule 36 is to permit the person obtaining the admission to rely thereon in preparation for trial, and that there is no way in which the plaintiff could have relied on the admission contained in defendant's original answer and request for admissions to her prejudice in view of the amendment to the defendant's answer as permitted by the court. In short, the admission need not be specifically withdrawn or amended in order to be negated.

Rule 36 places no limitation on the number and the detail of requests to admit; in *Photon, Inc. v. Harris Intertype Inc.* the plaintiff in a patent case was served with requests to admit covering 114 legal-size papers calling for 704 separate answers.[31] In *Moscowitz v. Baird*[32] the federal district court for the Southern District of New York denied a motion to strike as "prolix" a set of requests to admit containing 267 items: the number was "large, to be sure, but not unreasonably so in the circumstances of the case."[33] But in *Misco, Inc. v. United States Steel Corp.*, a federal antitrust and breach of contract action, the Sixth U.S. Court of Appeals ruled that the 2,000 requests for admission (comprising 225 pages) submitted by the plaintiff were in reality interrogatories as defined in Rule 33 of the Federal Rules of Civil Procedure, and therefore that the trial court had properly excluded all but 30 of the "requests for admission."[34]

Sanctions delineated under Rule 37(c) are designed to insure the successful operation of Rule 36.[35] Note that violation of a court order compelling answers to a request for admissions is not a prerequisite to imposition of sanctions. In *Gutting v. Falstaff Brewing Corp.* counsel failed to respond to requests for admission; it seems that, while preparing for depositions, he discovered a conflict of interest, and quietly withdrew as counsel.[36] The new attorney sought permission to respond late to the requests for admission, but the court denied the motion. The Eighth U.S. Court of Appeals reversed, pointing out that the discovery of the conflict of interest was a factor that should have been taken into consideration by the trial court before imposing sanctions. Rule 37(c) is the exclusive sanction for failure to comply with Rule 36 requests for admissions.[37] In *Bradshaw v. Thompson*[38] the federal appellate court imposed a substantial monetary penalty "for the amount claimed . . . as reasonable expenses incurred in making proof of this fact denied upon the request for admissions."[39]

REQUESTS TO ADMIT UNDER STATE STATUTE

Section 3123 of the New York Civil Practice Law & Rules is but one example of comparable legislation at the state level dealing with requests for admission.[40] Its intent decidedly is to narrow the issues and save the time of the court and the litigants.[41] But the request for admission is limited in scope and intendment and is not to be used in lieu of other disclosure devices; an alleged failure to respond to requests for admission under Section 3123 cannot be resolved by the court summarily.[42] The comparable "discovery" statute in New York is Section 3124 dealing with failure to disclose, motion to compel disclosure, and penalty for unreasonable demands or refusals.[43]

In *Lumpkin v. Meskill*, Federal District Court Judge Blumenfeld discussed requests for admission in terms of state considerations under the Federal Rules of Civil Procedure, though without describing the Connecticut statute on such requests.[44] He pointed out that the issue had a "substantial bearing on the speed with which this prolonged litigation can finally reach the state of adjudication and the length of the trial which must ultimately be conducted." He ordered the defendant to "make reasonable inquiry . . . to acquire the facts necessary to admit or deny the request submitted by the plaintiffs. It is directed to respond within 30 days of the date of this order to plaintiff's request for admission unless good cause be shown why time to respond should be enlarged. If no response is made within that time period, the matter shall be deemed admitted."

PHYSICAL AND MENTAL EXAMINATIONS

Related to the requests for admission under Rule 36 are the physical and mental examinations authorized under Rule 35 of the Federal Rules of Civil Procedure, which provides that, when the physical or mental condition of a party or a nonparty over whom a party has custody or legal control is in controversy, the court may on motion of the party order a physical or mental examination. A showing of good faith is a prerequisite, and the party against whom the order is made is entitled on request to a copy of the examining physician's report. In return, the party receiving the report must make available to the moving party his or her own reports of physical or mental examination. Rule 35, however, raised questions as to constitutionality in that the court order invaded privacy, but that issue was resolved by pronouncements of the U.S. Supreme Court in *Sibbach v. Wilson & Co.*[45] and *Schlagenhauf v. Holder.*[46] Note that Rule 35 does not exclusively govern the exchange of medical reports, for a request for production of the medical report can also be made under Rule 34.[47] The court can order a mental examination subject to protective restrictions, and can even restrict disclosure of the report.[48] Rule 35 is obviously not limited to personal injury actions,[49] and a party does not place mental conditions "in controversy" for purposes of Rule 35(a) by asserting a claim for damages for emotional distress.[50] A court may deny the party's own physician access to the psychiatric examination where warranted;[51] nor does a party have a right to the presence of an attorney during the physical examination by a doctor for an adverse party.[52]

NOTES

1. *Rule 36. Requests for Admission.*

(a) *Request for Admission.* A party may serve upon any other party a written request for the admission, for purposes of the pending action only, of the truth of any matters within the scope of Rule 26(b) set forth in the request that relate to statements or opinions of fact or of the application of law to fact, including the genuineness of any documents described in the request. Copies of documents shall be served with the request unless they have been or are otherwise furnished or made available for inspection and copying. The request may, without leave of court, be served upon the plaintiff after commencement of the action and upon any other party with or after service of the summons and complaint upon that party.

Each matter of which an admission is requested shall be separately set forth. The matter is admitted unless, within 30 days after service of the request, or within such shorter or longer time as the court may allow, the party to whom the request is directed serves upon the party requesting the admission a written answer or objection addressed to the matter, signed by the party or by the party's attorney, but, unless the court shortens the time, a defendant shall not be required to serve answers or objections before the expiration of 45 days after service of the summons and complaint upon the defendant. If objection is made, the reasons therefor shall be stated. The answer shall specifically deny the matter or set forth in detail the reasons why the answering party cannot truthfully admit or deny the matter. A denial shall fairly meet the substance of the requested admission, and when good faith requires that a party qualify an answer or deny only a part of the matter of which an admission is requested, the party shall specify so much of it as is true and qualify or deny the remainder. An answering party may not give lack of information or knowledge as a reason for failure to admit or deny unless the party states that the party has made reasonable inquiry and that the information known or readily obtainable by the party is insufficient to enable the party to admit or deny. A party who considers that a matter of which an admission has been requested presents a genuine issue for trial may not, on that ground alone, object to the request; the party may, subject to the provisions of Rule 37(c), deny the matter or set forth reasons why the party cannot admit or deny it.

The party who has requested the admissions may move to determine the sufficiency of the answers or objections. Unless the court determines that an objection is justified, it shall order that an answer be served. If the court determines that an answer does not comply with the requirements of this rule, it may order either that the matter is admitted or that an amended answer be served. The court may, in lieu of these orders, determine that final disposition of the request be made at a pre-trial conference or at a designated time prior to trial. The provisions of Rule 37(a)(4) apply to the award of expenses incurred in relation to the motion.

(b) *Effect of Admission.* Any matter admitted under this rule is conclusively established unless the court on motion permits withdrawal or amendment of the admission. Subject to the provisions of Rule 16 governing amendment of a pre-trial order, the court may permit withdrawal or amendment when the presentation of the merits of the action will be subserved thereby and the party who obtained the admission fails to satisfy the court that withdrawal or amendment will prejudice that party in maintaining the action or defense on the merits. Any admission made by a party under this rule is for the purpose of the pending action only and is not an admission for any other purpose nor may it be used against the party in any other proceeding.

2. *§ 3123. Admissions as to matters of fact, papers, documents and photographs.*

(a) *Notice to admit; admission unless denied or denial excused.* At any time after service of the answer or after the expiration of twenty days from service of the summons, whichever is sooner, and not later than twenty days before the trial, a party may serve upon any other party a written request for admission by the latter of the genuineness of any papers or documents, or the correctness or fairness of representation of any photographs, described in and served with the request, or of the truth of any matters of fact set forth in the request, as to which the party requesting the admission reasonably believes there can be no substantial dispute at the trial and which are within the knowledge of such other party or can be ascertained by him upon reasonable inquiry. Copies of the papers, documents or photographs shall be served with the request unless copies have already been furnished. Each of the matters of which an admission is requested shall be deemed admitted unless within twenty days after service thereof or within such further time as the court may allow, the party to whom the request is directed serves upon the party requesting the admission a sworn statement either denying specifically the matters of which an admission is requested or setting forth in detail the reasons why he cannot truthfully either admit or deny those matters. If the matters of which an admission is requested cannot be fairly admitted without some material qualification or explanation, or if the matters constitute a trade secret or such party would be privileged or disqualified from testifying as a witness concerning them, such party may, in lieu of a denial or statement, serve a sworn statement setting forth in detail his claim and, if the claim is that the matters cannot be fairly admitted without some material qualification or explanation, admitting the matters with such qualification or explanation.

(b) *Effect of admission.* Any admission made, or deemed to be made, by a party pursuant to a request made under this rule is for the purpose of the pending action only and does not constitute an admission by him for any other purpose nor may it be used against him in any other proceeding; and the court, at any time, may allow a party to amend or withdraw any admission on such terms as may be just. Any admission shall be subject to all pertinent objections to admissibility which may be interposed at the trial.

(c) *Penalty for unreasonable denial.* If a party, after being served with a request under subdivision (a) does not admit and if the party requesting the admission thereafter proves the genuineness of any such paper or document, or the correctness or fairness of representation of any such photograph, or the truth of any such matter of fact, he may move at or immediately following the trial for an order requiring the other party to pay him the reasonable expenses incurred in making such proof, including reasonable attorney's fees. Unless the court finds that there were good reasons for the denial or the refusal otherwise to admit or that the admissions sought were of no substantial importance, the order shall be made irrespective of the result of the action. Upon a trial by jury, the motion for such an order shall be determined by the court outside the presence of the jury.

3. See Rule 34 of Federal Rules of Criminal Procedure (FRCP).

4. See Rule 35 of FRCP.

5. 64 FRD 673 (Conn., 1974).

6. The 1987 amendments were purely technical, no substantive change was intended: (matter stricken out is in brackets and new matter is in italics)

(a) . . . Each matter of which an admission is requested shall be separately set forth. The matter is admitted unless, within 30 days after service of the request, or within such shorter or longer time as the court may allow, the party to whom the request is directed serves upon the party requesting the admission a written answer or objection addressed to the matter, signed by the party or by [his] *the party's* attorney, but, unless the court shortens the time, a defendant shall not be required to serve answers or objections before the expiration of 45 days after service of the summons and complaint upon [him] *that defendant.* If objection is made, the reasons therefore shall be stated. The answer shall specifically deny the matter or set forth in detail the reasons why the answering party cannot truthfully admit or deny the matter. A denial shall fairly meet the substance of the requested admission, and when good faith requires that a party qualify [his] *an* answer or deny only a part of the matter of which an admission is requested, [he] *the party* shall specify so much of it as is true and qualify or deny the remainder. An answering party may not give lack of information or knowledge as a reason for failure to admit or deny unless [he] *the party* states that [he] *the party* has made reasonable inquiry and that the information known or readily obtainable by [him] *the party* is insufficient to enable [him] *the party* to admit or deny. A party who considers that a matter of which an admission has been requested presents a genuine issue for trial may not, on that ground alone, object to the request; [he] *the party* may, subject to the provisions of Rule 37(c), deny the matter or set forth reasons why [he] *the party* cannot admit or deny it.

(b) *Effect of Admission*. Any matter admitted under this rule is conclusively established unless the court on motion permits withdrawal or amendment of the admission. Subject to the provision of Rule 16 governing amendment of a pretrial order, the court may permit withdrawal or amendment when the presentation of the merits of the action will be subserved thereby and the party who obtained the admission fails to satisfy the court that withdrawal or amendment will prejudice [him] *that party* in maintaining [his] *the* action or defense on the merits. Any admission made by a party under this rule is for the purpose of the pending action only and is not an admission [by him] for any other purpose nor may it be used against [him] *the party* in any other proceeding.

7. See 1 Emanuel's Encyclopedia of American Law (1987) at 145 et seq.

8. 414 NYS2d 34 (1979).

9. See Atkinson and White, "Requests to Admit," Trial Mag. (April 1987) at 45.

10. See United States v. Kenealy, 646 F2d 699 (1st Cir., 1981), cert. den. 102 S. Ct. 478 (1981).

11. See Adley Express Co. v. Highway Truck Drivers, 349 F. Supp. 436 (ED Pa., 1972).

12. Note United States Plywood Corp. v. Hudson Lumber Co., 127 F. Supp. 489 (SDNY, 1954).

13. 474 F. Supp. 184 (Neb., 1979) at 185.

14. 382 So2d 563 (Ala. App., 1980).

15. Note Boyter v. MCR Construction Co., 673 SW2d 938 (Tex Civ. App., 1984).

16. 572 P2d 921 (Nev., 1977).

17. 663 F2d 575 (5th Cir., 1981).

18. 710 F2d 1309 (8th Cir., 1983).

19. See Rule 37(c) of FRCP; also supra note 7 at 146.

20. See Rules 26(b)(1) and 26(g); also see Misco, Inc. v. United States Steel Corp., 784 F2d 198 (6th Cir., 1986).

21. See Warren Freedman, Frivolous Law Suits and Frivolous Defenses (1987).

22. Rules 11 and 26(g) of FRCP.

23. See Kenyatta v. Kelly, 375 F. Supp. 1175 (D Pa., 1974).

24. 378 F. Supp. 310 (Conn., 1974).

25. See McSparran v. Hannigan, 225 F. Supp. 628 (ED Pa., 1963) where court had occasion to make these comments:

"An answer to a request under Rule 36 is unlike a statement of fact by a witness made in the course of oral evidence at a trial, or in oral pre-trial depositions, or even in written answers to interrogatories. It is on the contrary a studied response, made under sanctions against easy denials, to a request to assert the truth or falsity of a relevant fact pointed out by the request for admission. The purpose of the Rule is not the discovery of information but the elimination at trial of the need to prove factual matters which the adversary cannot fairly contest. This is analogous to the older style pleading in which so-called ultimate facts were alleged under oath by the plaintiff and were conclusively taken to be true unless specifically denied by defendant. Having adopted a simpler form of pleading the Federal Rules preserved in the request for admission the means for obtaining a conclusive admission of any relevant fact and did not limit the remedy to so-called 'ultimate' facts. Were this otherwise then the much vaunted improved Federal Rules would be without a well-known and usefull mode of limiting factual disputes, and this under a system which has reduced the significance of pleadings as the means of limiting issues of fact.

Language in textbooks and decisions declaring that admissions under Rule 36 have the effect of 'sworn testimony' serve to confuse the problem. In every case such language either was dictum or the problem of the binding effect of answers to requests for admission was not presented, or there were present peculiar circumstances not here involved. One case which is cited in all the subsequent decisions starts with the assumption that answers to requests for admission 'stand in the same relation to the case that sworn evidence bears,' emphasizing that such answers must be sworn to and signed by the litigant himself. But the presence of the party's oath in both instances, with its sanction of the penalty for perjury, does not make an admission of a request the same in all respects as sworn testimony. For requests for admission, although answered under the oath of a party, are normally made under the direction and supervision of counsel, who has full professional realization of their significance. Therefore, their similarity to sworn testimony in one respect should not reduce their effect from conclusive admissions to merely evidential ones."

26. 606 F2d 760 (7th Cir., 1979).

27. See De Leon v. Ramirez, 465 F. Supp. 698 (SDNY, 1979).

28. See Rule 36(b) of FRCP.

29. Once the trial has begun, a more restrictive standard is to be applied in permitting a party to withdraw or amend the request for admission.

30. 675 F2d 949 (7th Cir., 1982).

31. 28 FRD 327 (Mass., 1961).

32. 10 FRD 233 (SDNY, 1959).

33. See United States v. Schine Chain Theatres, Inc., 4 FRD 109 (WDNY, 1944): "From the pleadings and from the interrogatories heretofore answered, it is apparent that there must be many matters, transactions and acts which are not and will not be in dispute. The theatres in question were or are in six states. Unless Rule 36 were invoked, it is reasonably certain that the government would be required to bring numerous witnesses from these several states and many documents would be required to be proved and large expense would necessarily be incurred, but the expense incident to the prolongation of the trial would be most considerable."

34. 784 F2d 198 (6th Cir., 1986).

35. "If a party fails to admit the genuineness of any document or the truth of any matter as requested under Rule 36, and if the party requesting the admissions thereafter proves the genuineness of the document or the truth of the matter, the requesting party may apply to the court for an order requiring the other party to pay the reasonable

expenses incurred in making that proof, including reasonable attorney's fees. The court shall make the order unless it finds that (1) the request was held objectionable pursuant to Rule 36(a), or (2) the admission sought was of no substantial importance, or (3) the party failing to admit had reasonable ground to believe that the party might prevail on the matter, or (4) there was other good reason for the failure to admit.''

36. Supra note 18.

37. See J. F. Edwards Construction Co. v. Anderson Safeway Guard Rail Corp., 542 F2d 1318 (7th Cir., 1976).

38. 454 F2d 76 (6th Cir., 1972).

39. The court concluded: ''This rule requires the Court to award expenses including reasonable attorney's fees to a party whose request for the admission of the truth of any matter under Rule 36 is denied and who thereafter proves the truth of the matter, unless any one of four conditions is found to exist. The District Court found that none of the four enumerated conditions was present in this case, and we will not disturb that finding, and we do not find any abuse of discretion in the amount of the award. The determinative fact upon which Beech's liability would depend was whether he had received a no sale instruction from the appellant *before* the horse had been taken from the ring, and the entirety of Beech's defense was directed toward establishing this one fact.''

40. Supra note 2.

41. See Barnes v. Shul Private Car Service, Inc., 301 NYS2d 907 (1974).

42. See Spawton v. James E. Strates Shows, Inc., 349 NYS2d 295 (1974).

43. *Rule 3124. Failure to disclose; motion to compel disclosure; penalty for unreasonable demands or refusals.*

If a person, without having made timely objection, fails to appear at an examination for questioning or fails to answer any question propounded upon oral or written depositions or interrogatories or fails to respond to a demand for addresses under rule 3118 or fails to produce a thing as provided by rule 3111 or fails to permit examination or inspection of property or things as provided by rule 3120 or fails to submit to or produce a person for an examination as provided by section 3121, or fails to exchange reports as provided in subdivision (b) of section 3121, the discovery, inspection or examination shall be completed on other matters or adjourned, as the proponent of the discovery, inspection, question or examination may elect. Thereafter, in addition to any remedies available to him according to laws of the place where the examination is held, he may, on reasonable notice to all persons affected, apply to the court to compel disclosure.

44. Supra note 5.

45. 312 US 1 (1942).

46. 379 US 104 (1964).

47. See Buffington v. Wood, 351 F2d 292 (3d Cir., 1965).

48. See Bodnar v. Bodnar, 441 F2d 1103 (5th Cir., 1971), cert. den. 404 US 913 (1972); note Swift v. Swift, 64 FRD 440 (EDNY, 1974).

49. See Winters v. Travia, 495 F2d 839 (2d Cir., 1974).

50. See Cody v. Marriott Corp., 103 FRD 421 (Mass., 1984).

51. See Brandenberg v. El Al Israel Airlines, 79 FRD 543 (SDNY, 1978).

52. See Warrick v. Brode, 46 FRD 427 (Del., 1969).

8

The Art of Intervention

According to the New York Judicial Council's *Recommendations Relating to the Extension of the Remedy of Intervention* (1946), intervention may be defined as

> the procedural device whereby a stranger can present a claim or defense in a pending action or in a proceeding incidental thereto, and become a party for the purpose of the claim or defense presented. . . . The chief utility of intervention lies in affording to the vast and undefined group of non-parties the means of protecting their interests which may be affected by a particular law suit. . . . The practice of allowing a stranger to intervene was first developed in the civil, the ecclesiastical, and the admiralty courts. Apparently, intervention practice in Roman law was rather extensive, although intervention seems to have taken place only at the appeal stage and then on the theory that the losing party might refuse to appeal or might not be vigilant in prosecuting the appeal and the petitioner's interest thus be inadequately protected. . . . Indigenous to the old common law and tending to restrict the extension of rights of intervention, was an unusual concern that the plaintiff be enabled by the courts to control his action; the modern common law theories of joinder and intervention of parties, however, brings us toward a raprochement with the theories of the civil law. . . . The practice of intervention developed slowly in the English and American law, but by the middle of the nineteenth century was permitted in equity by a device known as an examination *pro interesse suo* and at law by an analagous but more limited practice.[1]

Third parties were frequently allowed at common law to enter a pending lawsuit, but actions in equity greatly limited intervention, so that it was not until the 19th century that intervention came to be a useful tool in bringing the lawsuit to an adjudication.[2] In the development of the doctrine of intervention a distinction was immediately drawn between intervention as of right, i.e., where the absentee would be prejudiced by the exclusion, and permissive intervention, i.e., where the advantages and disadvantages would be weighed by the court. In England the distinction is between the absolute right to intervene and the discretionary right to intervene.[3] Rule 24 of the Federal Rules of Civil Procedure sets forth both forms of the art of intervention in the federal courts.[4] As the Second U.S. Court of Appeals in *United States v. Board of Education* expressed it, "the purpose of intervention, whether of right or permissive, is to enable those satisfying the requirements of Rule 24 to assert their interests in all pending aspects of the lawsuit, within the limitations of purpose imposed at the time of intervention."[5] Rule 24 was designed to "foster economy of judicial administration and to protect non-parties from having their interests adversely affected by litigation conducted without their participation."[6] Intervention involves the statutory intervention of right, the nonstatutory intervention of right, the statutory permissive intervention, and the nonstatutory permissive intervention.[7]

Intervention as of right is dependent upon showing sufficiently that the intervenor (a) has an interest in the transaction, (b) which the intervenor may be impeded in protecting because of the pending action, and (c) which interest is not adequately protected by others.[8] The intervention as of right is done without leave of the court. Permissive intervention, as set forth in Rule 24(b), means that anyone may be permitted to intervene if his or her claim and the main action have a common question of law or fact. Permissive intervention may be denied, however, in order to avoid the likelihood of undue delay.[9] Rule 24(b) permits, upon timely application, a governmental officer or agency to intervene "when a party to an action relies for ground of claim or defense upon any statute or executive order administered by a federal or state governmental officer or agency or upon any regulation, order, requirement, or agreement issued or made pursuant to the statute or executive order."[10] Of the federal statutes giving certain outsiders the right to intervene, the most common are those that allow the U.S. government to intervene.[11]

Intervention as of right was delineated in *Atlantis Development Corp. v. United States*, where the defendant, a general contractor, began work on certain uninhabited coral reefs without the permission of the federal government, and the federal government brought suit contending that the coral reefs were federal properties.[12] The plaintiff, claiming that it bought the reefs from their discoverer, sought to intervene as of right. The Fifth U.S. Court of Appeals agreed that the plaintiff did indeed have that kind of interest which as a practical matter would be impaired by the adjudication of the lawsuit in the absence of the plaintiff. The Fifth U.S. Court of Appeals began its opinion with this dramatic opening:

> This case involves a little bit of nearly everything—a little bit of oceanography, a little bit of marine biology, a little bit of the tidelands oil controversy, a little bit of international law, a little bit of latter day Marco Polo exploration. But these do not command

our resolution since the little bits are here controlled by the less exciting bigger, if not big, problem of intervention. The District Court declined to permit mandatory intervention as a matter of right or to allow intervention as permissive. As is so often true, a ruling made to avoid delay, complications, or expense turns out to have generated more of its own. With the main case being stayed by District Court pending this appeal, it is pretty safe to assume that the case would long have been decided on its merits (or lack of them) had intervention of either kind been allowed. And this seems especially unfortunate since it is difficult to believe that the presence of the attempted intervenor would have added much to the litigation. All of this becomes the more ironic, if not unfortunate, since the intervenor and the Government, sparring over why intervention ought or ought not to have been allowed, each try to persuade us the one was bound to win, the other lose on the merits which each proceeds to argue as though the parties were before or in the court. Adding to the problem, or perhaps more accurately, aiding in the solution of it, are the mid-1966 amendments to the Federal Rules of Procedure including specifically those relating to intervention. We reverse.

The federal appellate court, in holding in favor of intervention as of right, pointed out that

F.R.Civ.P.24(a)(2) requires both the existence of an interest which may be impaired as a practical matter and an absence of adequate representation of the intervenor's interest by existing parties. There can be no difficulty here about the lack of representation. On the basis of the pleadings, Atlantis is without a friend in this litigation. The Government turns on the defendants and takes the same view both administratively and in its brief here toward Atlantis. The defendants, on the other, are claiming ownership in and the right to develop the very islands claimed by Atlantis.

Nor can there be any doubt that Atlantis "claims an interest relating to the property or transaction which is the subject of the action." The object of the suit is to assert the sovereign's exclusive dominion and control over two out of a group of islands publicly claimed by Atlantis. This identity with the very property at stake in the main case and with the particular transaction therein involved (the right to build structures with or without permission of the Corps of Engineers) is of exceptional importance. For 24(a)(2) is in the conjunctive requiring both an interest relating to the property or transaction and the practical harm if the party is absent. This sharply reduces the area in which stare decisis may, as we later discuss, supply the element of practical harm.

This brings us then to the question whether these papers reflect that in the absence of Atlantis, a disposition of the main suit may as a practical matter impair or impede its ability to protect that interest—its claim to ownership and the right to control, use and develop without hindrance from the Government, the Department of Defense, or other agencies. Certain things are clear. Foremost, of course, is the plain proposition that the judgment itself as between Government and defendants cannot have any direct, immediate effect upon the rights of Atlantis, not a party to it.

But in a very real and practical sense is not the trial of this lawsuit the trial of Atlantis' suit as well?

It has been said that the prototypical intervention case during the early development of intervention was *Freeman v. Howe*.[13] Here a creditor of the railroad attached certain railroad cars, and the highest court ruled that other creditors, holding liens against the railroad cars, could have properly intervened in the attachment proceeding based upon a claimed interest in the property involved in the pending action. The recent amendments to Rule 24 of the Federal Rules of Civil Procedure add "interest relating to the property or transaction" and thus extend the reach of possible intervention. In *Cascade Natural Gas Corp. v. El Paso Natural Gas Co.*, the U.S. Supreme Court acknowledged the right of a natural gas company to intervene as of right because that company's interest was not adequately represented by the existing parties, because all the parties wanted settlement, and settlement of the pending lawsuit would have cut off this company's supply of natural gas.[14] Incidentally, it has generally been held that no independent-subject matter jurisdictional grounds are required for an intervention as of right, for such intervention readily falls within the court's ancillary jurisdiction.[15] Of course, an indispensable party may intervene as of right without the court's ancillary jurisdiction.[16] But in *Vietnamese Fishermen's Association v. Knights of the Ku Klux Klan*[17] the court opined: "There is no question here that the intervenor's claim . . . arises out of the same 'common nucleus of operative fact' as the plaintiffs' claims . . . [and] it is clear that there is no independent jurisdictional base for intervenor's action against defendants. . . . [R]elevant case law makes clear, however, that under proper circumstances, permissive intervention is allowed, in the absence of an independent federal jurisdictional base where 'pendant party' jurisdiction exists."[18] In the intervention as of right the interest is typically a property interest,[19] but other interests have sufficed.[20]

Permissive intervention requires the permission of the court for the intervenor who has a "claim or defense" involving a "question of law or fact in common" with the pending lawsuit. It is a matter of the court's discretion, and permissive intervention may be denied if the claim does not, for example, meet the relevant amount-in-controversy requirement or satisfy the diversity requisites.[21] Again, the primary factor in the exercise of the court's discretion is "whether the intervention will unduly delay or prejudice the adjudication of the rights of the original parties."[22]

On the state level, it should be noted that some states like New York have a "narrow" type of intervention statute,[23] and other states like California have "broad" types that permit intervention by "any person, who has an interest in the matter in litigation, or in the success of either of the parties, or an interest against both."[24] Texas permits anyone to intervene in a pending action, subject to being stricken out by the court.[25] However, in Illinois a public interest group that sought to intervene as defendants was required by the Seventh U.S. Court of Appeals in *Charles v. Daley* to pay plaintiffs more than $206,000 in attorney fees.[26] The intervenors had sided with state officials in defending the Illinois Abortion Control Act, taking the case to the U.S. Supreme Court when the governmental defendants declined to do so.[27]

INTERVENTION IN ACTION

The Iowa Supreme Court in *Wharff v. Wharff* was called upon to allow children to intervene in a divorce action brought by the husband against their mother with respect to certain real estate held under a tenancy in common by the parties.[28] Defendant wife contended that the real estate had been purchased with money that she held in trust for her children by a previous marriage. The court opined:

> It is true that persons not parties to the litigation would not be bound by its result and might bring a separate action. But we think the rule that a multiplicity of suits will be avoided wherever possible has a direct application. It might also happen that if the plaintiff and defendant here should try out their action first, and intervenors be relegated to a separate suit, different and contradictory results would be reached. A division of the property of the original parties without the benefit of such evidence as the intervenors might produce could very well be inequitable, resulting, at the best, in an action to modify the divorce decree by the litigant whose rights were adversely affected by a later trial of the separate action to enforce a trust. . . . There seems every reason in policy why, if there are third parties claiming an interest in either the real or personal property, the entire matter should be decided at once. Such a course will do away with a multiplicity of suits and will enable the court to make orders concerning property of the litigants. In the case at bar, if the court is not to be permitted to know the real interest of the plaintiff and defendant in the realty and personalty now owned by them, if this must be left to determination in a future and separate suit brought by the proposed intervenors, it will be greatly hampered in making a fair order. . . .

And in *Brune v. McDonald* the Oregon Supreme Court summarized the issue of intervention, noting that intervention is largely statutory in nature and that it undercuts the traditional notion that a plaintiff is allowed to control his or her own suit:

> The question here is whether said complaint in intervention states facts sufficient to warrant the court in granting the relief sought by the intervener, which is an injunction restraining the prosecution of plaintiff's cause of action until it can be determined whether defendant has breached the terms and conditions of said policy of insurance, as alleged by intervener.
>
> The view usually expressed by the courts is that originally, in jurisdictions in which the common law prevailed, intervention was unknown except that it was in use to some extent in the ecclesiastical courts, and that apparently it is derived from the civil law. Therefore, in common-law jurisdictions intervention is usually regarded as of purely statutory origin. . . .
>
> The generally accepted rule is that the right or interest which will authorize a third person to intervene must be of such a direct and immediate character that the intervener will either gain or lose by the direct legal operation of the judgment. . . .

It is obvious that the direct legal operation of the judgment in the case at bar would not cause intervener either to gain or lose anything.

It is equally apparent that the complaint in intervention herein tenders an entirely new and different issue from those of the complaint. . . .

It will be noted that the intervener does not seek to interpose an answer to the complaint of plaintiff upon the merits of her alleged claim at law. Tested by a demurrer, the clause, "thereby presenting an appearance of liability on the part of the defendant to plaintiff where none in truth and fact existed," does not constitute a statement of any defense to plaintiff's legal demand against defendant.

The relief sought by intervener is equitable. Intervener prays for an injunction restraining the further prosecution of plaintiff's action against defendant, until it can be determined whether the intervener would be liable to defendant upon its policy of insurance in case plaintiff should secure a judgment against defendant herein.

The reason assigned for seeking this relief is that by the time the judgment, if any, is procured by plaintiff against defendant, and proceedings are instituted to recover on intervener's policy, the intervener's witnesses to the alleged conspiracy will have become scattered and difficult, if not impossible, to procure, and that intervener will be confronted by a woman claimant whose feminity will render it much harder for intervener than if the same issue should be tried before plaintiff's claim against defendant has been adjudicated.[29]

INTERVENTION AND CIVIL RIGHTS

As stated in Rule 24(b)(1) of the Federal Rules of Civil Procedure, intervention, upon timely application, may be permitted when a federal law grants a conditional right to intervene.[30] Statutory permissive intervention pursuant to the Civil Rights Act of 1964 is also existent.[31] But in *Lumbermen's Mutual Casualty Co. v. Rhodes*, the bonding company insuring the prison guard who allegedly deprived the plaintiff prisoner of his civil rights was not permitted to intervene because the bonding company had delayed four months before attempting to intervene in the suit.[32] Similarly, the wholesale distributor of nudist magazines in *Dale Book Co. v. Leary* was denied the right to intervene in a wholesale distributor's action against city and county officials for an injunction; the fact that the attempted intervenor suffered financial loss because of the criminal prosecution of magazine dealers was insufficient reason for permissive intervention.[33] In *Eley v. Morris* the motion by two former Georgia employees to intervene in an action challenging the regulatory scheme governing termination of classified Georgia state employees was allowed because the defendants failed to oppose substantially the intervention; furthermore, the intervenors raised similar questions of law and fact, and there was no indication that intervention would cause undue delay or prejudice to the rights of the defendants.[34] On the other hand, in *Louis v. Pennsylvania Industrial Development Authority*, the mere allegation that plaintiff intervenors were either fired or not hired because they were black was insufficient to establish that the parties were intervenors who were victims of racial discrimination by the employer, who had applied for aid under the state economic development program.[35]

THE INSURER'S TOOL OF INTERVENTION

Intervention is a useful tool for insurance companies, especially with regard to the control and disposition of insurance claims involving questions of contract coverage.[36] Avoidance of liability of noncovered claims is an important consideration for the insurance carrier, and courts have premised successful interventions not only upon Rule 24 of the Federal Rules of Civil Procedure and state statutes like Section 387 of the California Code of Civil Procedure,[37] but also upon such other factors as avoiding relitigation of issues and multiplicity of actions,[38] and prevention of fraud or collusion or other criminal wrong.[39] Without the insurer's intervention there is always the possibility of inconsistent results if two actions are tried separately.[40] Ideally, all the "players," that is, the injured party or parties, the insurance carriers, the insured party or parties, and all other potential defendants, would participate in the one proceeding where every issue could be fully resolved.[41] But in *Home Insurance Co. v. Lorelei Restaurant Co.* the Illinois appellate court denied intervention to the insurer; here the defendant restaurant lessee allegedly committed arson, and the insurance carrier sought to have a determination that there was no coverage under its policy because of a justifiable fear that the insured owner of the restaurant might not raise the issue of arson.[42] In denying the insurer's intervention as of right, the court held that the conflict of interest between the insured and its insurer was too serious to permit the insurer to participate in the insured's defense, much less to allow the insurer to intervene. Intervention was also inappropriate because the insurer would not be bound by any order or judgment in the pending action. The court similarly denied permissive intervention on the ground that whether certain activity on the part of the insured is or is not covered by the insurance policy or contract is a "new" issue, the introduction of which in the pendinig lawsuit "would complicate and delay trial of the issues."[43] But in *Plough, Inc. v. International Flavors & Fragrances, Inc.*, the federal district court in Tennessee permitted the insurer to intervene for the limited purpose of submitting written questions for the jury in order to determine the coverage question and answer the insurer's obligation to indemnify.[44] Courts have sanctioned intervention where insurance carriers have sought to enforce their lien interests arising from the payment of workers' compensation benefits.[45] Intervention was permitted in *Johnson v. Cape Industries, Ltd.*, where no appearance had been entered on behalf of an insured defendant in an action concerning the sale and use of asbestos; after the default judgment was entered against the insured, the insurer's intervention was approved since the representation in the underlying action was clearly inadequate![46] In *Guaranty National Insurance Co. v. Pittman*,[47] the Mississippi Supreme Court in 1987 approved the insurer's intervention as of right, since it was timely, the insurer's interest in the suit was not contingent, the insurer could have been sued directly by the plaintiff originally, and the insurer's interest was not adequately represented.[48] Intervention was allowed by the insurance carrier in *McGough v. Insurance*

Company of North America because the intervenor "claim[ed] an interest relating to the property or transaction."[49]

Generally, insurance carriers have pursued their right to intervention as of right, but they have been more successful by pursuing permissive intervention.[50] In *State of Missouri v. McKelvey* the insurer sought to intervene on behalf of its insured who allegedly defaulted by not answering the complaint; the Missouri court denied the intervention, but suggested that the insurer could on its own behalf file an application for a stay of proceedings![51] And in *Knapp v. Hankins* the federal district court in Illinois respected the wishes of the parties that intervention by the insurer "will introduce new issues in the controversy between plaintiffs and defendant, and that the plaintiffs are not interested in the controversy between the Company and the defendant. . . . The allowance of intervention in the suit will not change the issues between the plaintiffs and the defendant one iota, but before these issues are tried the Company and the defendant will be permitted to determine the validity of the policy. A separate trial will no doubt be had on the issues raised by the intervening petition."[52]

The 1986 New York decision of *Kaczmarek v. Shoffstall* denied the insurer's motion to intervene as a matter of right and by permission.[53] The original action arose after the defendant had allegedly poured boiling water on the plaintiff's back, and the defendant's insurer disclaimed coverage due to the intentional tort, though the insurer provided defendant with counsel. The gravamen of the insurer's request to intervene was that the counsel has an obligation to protect the defendant insured's interest first. The appellate court held that the issue of whether the insurer could intervene as of right would be determined by the potential res judicata effect upon the insurer as proposed intervenor. The court ruled that the underlying trial would not be res judicata, and therefore intervention as of right was denied. The court also opined that the trial court had not abused its discretion in denying the insurer intervention by permission.[54]

NOTES

1. At 218–225.

2. See generally Millar, Civil Procedure of the Trial Court in Historical Perspective (1952) at 143–152.

3. For the "absolute right," see In re Metropolitan Amalgamated Estates, Ltd., (1912) 2 Ch. 497, and Wilson v. Church, 9 Ch. D 552 (1878). For the "discretionary right," see Vavasseur v. Krupp, 9 Ch. D 351 (1878).

4. "(a) *Intervention of Right.* Upon timely application anyone shall be permitted to intervene in an action: (1) when a statute of the United States confers an unconditional right to intervene; or (2) when the applicant claims an interest relating to the property or transaction which is the subject of the action and the applicant is so situated that the disposition of the action may as a practical matter impair or impede the applicant's

ability to protect that interest, unless that applicant's interest is adequately represented by existing parties.

(b) *Permissive Intervention.* Upon timely application anyone may be permitted to intervene in an action: (1) when a statute of the United States confers a conditional right to intervene; or (2) when an applicant's claim or defense and the main action have a question of law or fact in common. When a party to an action relies for ground of claim or defense upon any statute or executive order administered by a federal or state governmental officer or agency or upon any regulation, order, requirement or agreement issued or made pursuant to the statute or executive order, the officer or agency upon timely application may be permitted to intervene in the action. In exercising its discretion the court shall consider whether the intervention will unduly delay or prejudice the adjudication of rights of the original parties.

(c) *Procedure.* A person desiring to intervene shall serve a motion to intervene upon the parties as provided in Rule 5. The motion shall state the grounds therefor and shall be accompanied by a pleading setting forth the claim or defense for which intervention is sought. The same procedure shall be followed when a statute of the United States gives a right to intervene. When the constitutionality of an act of Congress affecting the public interest is drawn in question in any action to which the United States or an officer, agency, or employee thereof is not a party, the court shall notify the Attorney General of the United States as provided in Title 28, U.S.C. §2403."

5. 605 F2d 573 (2d Cir., 1979) at 576.

6. See Stallworth v. Monsanto Co., 558 F2d 257 (5th Cir., 1977) at 265.

7. See Brown v. Board of Education 84 FRD 383 (Kan., 1979) at 396.

8. See Nuesse v. Camp, 385 F2d 694 (DC Cir., 1967):

"An applicant for intervention must have an 'interest' in the 'transaction' which is the subject of the action. Contending that the Commissioner has no such interest as the Rule requires, the defendants rely on cases rejecting attempts by states and municipalities to intervene in lawsuits by virtue of their status as *parens patriae* in order to promote the general welfare of some of their citizens. Federal courts have frequently held that this type of concern does not rise to the stature of a definable legal right that constitutes a litigable 'interest' in another's lawsuit, although the cases are by no means uniform. We need not wade into the general *parens patriae* fray, however, for we conclude that in this action the Commissioner has distinct legal rights of his own in his official station, rights more precise and definable than merely derivative interests arising because of his office as superintendent of the state's banking industry.

First we declare that a state banking commissioner does have sufficient standing to bring an action to enjoin the Comptroller from unlawfully authorizing a national bank to open a branch where state law would not permit branching by state banks.

We hold that there is a serious possibility that the Commissioner's interest may not be adequately represented by any existing party, and that he is entitled to participate as a party and not merely as a friend of court."

9. Id.

10. See Halderman v. Pennhurst State School & Hospital, 612 F2d 84 (3d Cir., 1979). In Nuesse v. Camp, supra note 8, the court commented:

"It is a significant fact that the applicant for permissive intervention is a government official. Rule 24(b) was expressly amended in 1946 so as to permit intervention by a state or federal governmental official charged with administering a state statute or regulation on which any party relies for his claim or defense. The amendment was added to avoid 'exclusionary constructions' where public officials seek permission to intervene, and 'the amendment in effect expands the concept of "claim or defense" insofar as intervention by a governmental officer or agency is concerned.' It is perhaps more accurate to say that it considers the governmental application with a fresh and more hospitable approach.

. . . [W]e are of the view that Rule 24 is part of an evolving jurisprudence. Even prior to the 1946 amendment, SEC v. United States Realty & Improvement Corp., 310 U.S. 434, 60 S. Ct. 1044, 84 L.Ed. 1293 (1940), stressed that intervention to promote a relevant public interest is permissible when the public official charged with primary responsibility for vindicating that interest seeks to defend it. There the Court approved intervention by the SEC to ensure that a proposed reorganization was carried out under a statute providing for SEC scrutiny. . . .

Underlying this decision is a broad concern that courts should mold their traditional methods in order to advance the 'public interest,' a concern that Justice Stone, teacher and lifetime student of Equity, voiced and implemented in other historic decisions of the Supreme Court. E.g. Virginian Ry. v. System Federation No. 40, 300 U.S. 515, 552, 57 S.Ct. 592, 81 L.Ed. 789 (1937); United States v. Morgan, 307 U.S. 183, 194, 59 S.Ct. 795, 83 L.Ed. 1211 (1939). A kindred concern provided the impetus to the 1946 amendment, and clarified for the stragglers the leading edge of the doctrine of United States Realty. Rules adopted to bring the courts in line with an evolving jurisprudence are not properly read so as to freeze the pattern of decisions and preclude any further evolution. As we noted in connection with another rule, see Smith v. Katzenbach, 122 U.S. App. D.C. 113, 117, 351 F.2d 810, 814 (1965): 'That Rule is a crystallization of a principle of equity jurisdiction. That equity jurisdiction persists as to situations not specifically covered by the Rule. Alternatively the same result can be reached by a broad reading of the Rule.'

It is a living tenet of our society and not mere rhetoric that a public office is a public trust. While a public official may not intrude in a purely private controversy, permissive intervention is available when sought because an aspect of the public interest with which he is officially concerned is involved in the litigation. Notwithstanding this public interest the official may be denied intervention in the exercise of a sound judicial discretion finding that intervention would unduly expand the controversy or otherwise lead to improvident delay or expense. No such exercise of discretion was involved here. Intervention was denied, on the authority of Judge Kent's ruling, solely because of lack of appropriate interest. That was error."

11. See 28 USC 2403, for example.

12. 379 F2d 818 (5th Cir., 1967) See 1 Emanuel's Encyclopedia of American Law (1987) at 252 et seq.

13. 65 US (How.) 450 (1860).

14. 386 US 129 (1967).

15. See Babcock & Wilcox Co. v. Parsons Corp., 430 F2d 531 (8th Cir., 1970).

16. See Rule 19(b) of Federal Rules of Civil Procedure (FRCP).

17. 543 F. Supp. 198 (SD Tex., 1982).

18. See Marmon/Keystone Corp. v. Rowley, 100 FRD 384 (Kan., 1984).

19. See F. W. Woolworth Co. v. Miscellaneous Warehousemen's Local, 629 F2d 1204 (7th Cir., 1980).

20. See Idaho v. Freeman, 625 F2d 886 (9th Cir., 1980). Note the court opinion:

"this is not a situation where specific property rights are being determined in such a way that for all practical purposes the initial judicial decision will foreclose the absent party's claims to an interest in the property. . . . Likewise, the stare decisis problem is greatly lessened where there are parties already in the suit whose position on the issues is the same as the absent party's. . . . Mere inconvenience to the . . . [intervenor applicant] caused by requiring him to litigate separately is not the sort of adverse practical effect contemplated by Rule 24(a)(2)."

21. Supra note 15.

22. See Reeves v. International Tel. & Tel. Corp., 616 F2d 1342 (5th Cir., 1980) at 1349.

23. Note Section 193(4) of CPA: "Where a person not a party to the action has an interest in the subject thereof, or in real property the title to which may in any manner be affected by the judgment, or in real property for injury to which the complaint demands relief, and makes application to the court to be made a party, it must direct him to be brought in by the proper amendment."

24. Note Section 387 of Cal. Code of Civ. Proc.

25. Rule 60 of Texas Rules of Civ. Proc.

26. Unreported (7th Cir., May 5, 1988).

27. See ABAJ (Sept. 1, 1988) at 35.

28. 56 NW2d 1 (Iowa, 1953).

29. 75 P2d 10 (Ore., 1938).

30. See Sisneros v. Corpus Christi Independent District, 560 F2d 190 (5th Cir., 1977), cert. den. 434 US 1075 (1978).

31. Section 706(f)(1), as amended by 42 USC 2000e et seq.

32. 403 F2d 2 (8th Cir., 1968), cert. den. 394 US 965 (1969).

33. 233 F. Supp. 754 (Pa., 1964), aff'd 389 F2d 40 (3d Cir., 1965).

34. 390 F. Supp. 913 (Ga., 1975).

35. 371 F. Supp. 877 (Pa., 1974) aff'd 505 F2d 730 (3d Cir., 1975).

36. See Augustyn, "Intervention: The Insurer's Effective Litigation Tool," For the Defense (March 1988) at 5 et seq.

37. "a. Upon timely application, any person, who has an interest in the matter in litigation, or in the success of either of the parties, or an interest against both, may intervene in the action or proceeding. An intervention takes place when a third person is permitted to become a party to an action or proceeding between other persons, either by joining the plaintiff in claiming what is sought by the complaint, or by uniting with the defendant in resisting the claims of the plaintiff, or by demanding anything adversely to both the plaintiff and the defendant. . . .

b. . . . if the person seeking intervention claims an interest relating to the property or transaction which is the subject of the action and that person is so situated that the disposition of the action may as a practical matter impair or impede that person's interest is adequately represented by existing parties, the court shall, upon timely application, permit that person to intervene."

38. See Fidelity Bankers Life Insurance Co. v. Wedco, Inc., 102 FRD 41 (Nev., 1984).

39. See Eakins v. Burton, 423 SW2d 787 (Mo., 1968).

40. See Su Duk Kim v. H. V. Corp., 668 P2d 1158 (Haw., 1984).

41. See Kohane and Clark, "Intervention—Letting all the Players Play," For the Defense (April 1987) at 20 et seq.

42. 404 NE2d 895 (Ill. App., 1980).

43. To the same effect is Restor-A-Dent Laboratories, Inc. v. Certified Alloy Products, Inc., 725 F2d 871 (2d Cir., 1984).

44. 96 FRD 136 (WD Tenn., 1982).

45. See Miller v. Employers Mutual Liability Insurance Co., 349 So2d 1353 (La. App., 1977), and Schmidt v. Clothier, 338 NW2d 256 (Minn., 1983).

46. 414 NE2d 470 (Ill. App., 1981).

47. 501 So2d 377 (Miss., 1987).

48. The Mississippi Supreme Court concluded:

"In the final analysis we consider our task as arbiters of the practice of intervention of right under Rule 24(a)(2) as 'not to require an elaborate legal minuet in the courts below, but to support the efforts of those courts to insure that litigation moves sensibly and purposefully forward.'

We think there is much to be said for an overall attitude which gives the benefit of the doubt to the one seeking intervention, particularly where intervention of right under Rule 24(a)(2) is claimed. . . . This attitude is expressed in the Comment to Rule 24 which describes the rule as 'represent[ing] a judgment that . . . justice demands that the interest of the absentee [intervenor] should predominate over the interests of the absentee parties and of trial convenience.' "

49. 691 P2d 738 (Ariz., 1984).

50. Rule 24(b) of FRCP.

51. 666 SW2d 457 (Mo. App., 1984).

52. 106 F. Supp. 43 (ED Ill., 1952).

53. 119 AD 2d 1001, 500 NYS 2d 902 (1986).

54. See For the Defense (Dec. 1988) at 28–29.

9

The Act of Interpleader

The act of interpleader describes a technique whereby a party who owes something to one of two or more persons (but does not know to whom the debt or thing is owed) may force those persons to argue out their respective claims among themselves before attempting to recover the debt or thing from the party. As a "stakeholder" the party seeks both to preclude anyone from suing him or her, and to keep from having to pay the same claim twice. Historically, interpleader was a remedy well established under the English system of jurisprudence; interpleader was known at early common law as well as in courts of chancery, and suits for interpleader were acceptable in early American law and practice.[1] The equitable bill of interpleader has traditionally been said to embrace four essential elements: (1) the same thing, debt, or duty had to be claimed by both or all the parties against whom the relief is demanded; (2) all of the adverse title or claims had to be dependent or derived from a common source; (3) the one seeking the relief could neither have nor claim any interest in the subject matter; and (4) he or she could have incurred no independent liability to either of the claimants. If the stakeholder was not disinterested, equity courts permitted him or her to proceed by way of a petition in the nature of a bill of interpleader rather than by a strict bill of interpleader, but only if the stakeholder sought affirmative relief independent of the conflicting claims of the defendants.[2] The U.S. Supreme Court in *Texas v. Florida* explained the difference:

> The peculiarity of the strict bill of interpleader was that the plaintiff asserted no interest in the debt or fund, the amount of which he placed at the disposal of the court and asked that the rival claimants be required to settle in the equity suit the ownership of the claim among themselves. But as the sole ground for equitable relief is the danger of

injury because of the risk of multiple suits when the liability is single . . . and as plaintiffs who are not mere stakeholders may be exposed to that risk, equity extended its jurisdiction to such cases by the bill in the nature of interpleader. The essential of the bill in the nature of interpleader is that it calls upon the court to exercise its jurisdiction to guard against the risks of loss from the prosecution in independent suits of rival claims where the plaintiff himself claims an interest in the property or fund which is subjected to the risk. The object and ground of the jurisdiction are to guard against the consequent depletion of the fund at the expense of the plaintiff's interest in it and to protect him and the other parties to the suit from the jeopardy resulting from the prosecution of numerous demands, to only one of which the fund is subject. While in point of law or fact only one party is entitled to succeed, there is danger that recovery may be allowed in more than one suit. Equity avoids the danger by requiring the rival claimants to litigate before it the decisive issue, and will not withhold its aid where the plaintiff's interest is either not denied or he does not assert any claim adverse to that of the other parties, other than the single claim, determination of which is decisive of the rights of all.(406–407)[3]

The U.S. Congress, at the behest of insurance companies, enacted the first interpleader statute, culminating in the Federal Interpleader Act of 1936:

Title 28, United States Code Annotated

§ 1335. Interpleader

(a) The district courts shall have original jurisdiction of any civil action of interpleader *or in the nature of interpleader* filed by any person, firm, corporation, association, or society having in his or its custody or possession money or property of the value of $500 or more, or having issued a note, bond, certificate, policy of insurance, or other instrument of value or amount of $500 or more, or providing for the delivery or payment or the loan of money or property of such amount or value, or being under any obligation written or unwritten to the amount of $500 or more, if

(1) Two or more adverse claimants, of diverse citizenship as defined in section 1332 of this title, are claiming or may claim to be entitled to such money or property, or to any one or more of the benefits arising by virtue of any note, bond, certificate, policy or other instrument, or arising by virtue of any such obligation; and if (2) the plaintiff has deposited such money or property or has paid the amount of or the loan or other value of such instrument or the amount due under such obligation into the registry of the court, there to abide the judgment of the court, or has given bond payable to the clerk of the court in such amount and with such surety as the court or judge may deem proper, conditioned upon the compliance by the plaintiff with the future order or judgment of the court with respect to the subject matter of the controversy.

(b) Such an action may be entertained although the titles or claims of the conflicting claimants do not have a common origin, or are not identical, but are adverse to and independent of one another.

§ 1397. Interpleader

Any civil action of interpleader or in the nature of interpleader under section 1335 of this title may be brought in the judicial district in which one or more of the claimants reside.

§ 2361. Process and procedure

In any civil action of interpleader or in the nature of interpleader under section 1335 of this title, a district court may issue its process for all claimants and enter its order restraining them from instituting or prosecuting any proceeding in any State or United States court affecting the property, instrument or obligation involved in the interpleader action until further order of the court. Such process and order shall be returnable at such time as the court or judge thereof directs, and shall be addressed to and served by the United States marshals for the respective districts where the claimants reside or may be found.

Such district court shall hear and determine the case, and may discharge the plaintiff from further liability, make the injunction permanent, and make all appropriate orders to enforce its judgment.

FEDERAL INTERPLEADER

As is evident from noting the foregoing federal interpleader statutes, interpleader has readily been recognized in the federal courts.[4] Many years ago the U.S. Supreme Court, in *Liberty Oil Co. v. Condon National Bank*,[5] gave its approval to the act of interpleader.[6] In its 1967 decision in *State Farm Fire & Casualty Co. v. Tashire,*[7] the Court observed that the federal interpleader statute

> cannot be used to solve all vexing problems of multiparty litigation arising out of a mass tort. But interpleader was never intended to perform such a function, to be an all-purpose 'bill of peace.' Had it been so intended, careful provision would necessarily have been made to insure that a party with little or no interest in the outcome of a complex controversy should not strip truly interested parties of substantial rights—such as the right to choose the forum in which to establish their claims, subject to generally applicable rules of jurisdiction, venue, service of process, removal and change of venue. None of the legislative and academic sponsors of a modern federal interpleader device viewed their accomplishment as a 'bill of peace,' capable of sweeping dozens of lawsuits out of the various State and federal courts in which they were brought and into a single interpleader proceeding.[8]

The highest court did not agree that, in the absence of state law or contractual provision for "direct action" suits against the insurance company, the insurance company must wait until persons asserting claims against its insured have reduced those claims to judgment before seeking to invoke the benefits of federal interpleader.[9] The dissent of Mr. Justice William O. Douglas was precisely based upon that point, that the insurance company can have no liability until judgment is obtained against the insured, and therefore federal interpleader was unnecessary.[10]

Other U.S. Supreme Court decisions on federal interpleader include *Griffin v. McCoach*,[11] which held that in a statutory interpleader suit based on diversity jurisdiction, a federal court is bound to apply the conflict-of-laws rules of the state in which the federal court sits.[12] In *Western Union Telegraph Co. v. Pennsylvania,* the Commonwealth of Pennsylvania sought to escheat disbursed monies held by Western Union from money orders bought in Pennsylvania offices of Western Union.[13] In holding that Pennsylvania had no power to escheat the money the court opined:

> our prior opinions have recognized that when a state court's jurisdiction purports to be based, as here, on the presence of property within the State, the holder of such property is deprived of due process of law if he is compelled to relinquish it without assurance that he will not be held liable again in another jurisdiction or in a suit brought by a claimant who is not bound by the first judgment. Anderson National Bank v. Luckett, 321 U.S. 233, 242–243, 64 S.Ct. 599, 604, 88 L.Ed. 692; Security Savings Bank v. California, 263 U.S. 282, 286–290, 44 S.Ct. 108, 110–111, 68 L.Ed. 301. Applying that principle, there can be no doubt that Western Union has been denied due process by the Pennsylvania judgment here unless the Pennsylvania courts had power to protect Western Union from any other claim, including the claim of the State of New York that these obligatitons are property "within" New York and are therefore subject to escheat under its laws. But New York was not a party to this proceeding and could not have been made a party, and, of course, New York's claims could not be cut off where New York was not heard as a party. Moreover, the potential multistate claims to the "property" which is the subject of this escheat make it not unlikely that various States will claim *in rem* jurisdiction over it. Therefore, Western Union was not protected by the Pennsylvania judgment, for a state court judgment need not be given full faith and credit by other States as to parties or property not subject to the jurisdiction of the court that rendered it.

In *National Union Fire Insurance Co. v. Ambassador Group*, the federal district court for the Eastern District of New York faced an interesting dollar issue under the federal interpleader statute.[14] The insurer had insured the officers and directors of Ambassador under an "errors and omissions" policy. By the policy's terms, the insurer's liability was limited to $3 million for "claims made" during each year of the policy's 3-year term. During the first year of the policy, two lawsuits were commenced, and in the second year two more lawsuits against the insured were started. Thereupon, the insurer filed an interpleader action under 28 USC 1335 and deposited a $3 million bond with the court. The insurer then moved for summary judgment, but the defendants pointed out that the $3 million bond was insufficient to invoke the statutory interpleader jurisdiction, which required a $6 million bond. The court agreed with defendants that the intervenor must deposit with the court the highest amount claimed by defendants!

"RULE INTERPLEADER" V. "STATUTORY INTERPLEADER"

The conflict between the "statutory interpleader" pursuant to 28 USC 1335 and the "rule interpleader" under Rule 22 of the Federal Rules of Civil Procedure is apparent in *New York Life Insurance Co. v. Dunlevy*.[15] Here the insured and his daughter the plaintiff were both residents of Pennsylvania, and plaintiff claimed that her father had assigned the life insurance policy to her. Two of her creditors held a valid personal judgment against her, and they sued in Pennsylvania to garnishee the policy. The insured thereupon denied the assignment of the policy to his daughter, who had in the meantime moved to California. The plaintiff insurer brought interpleader to establish which of the three parties had the valid claim on the policy. The Pennsylvania court held that the assignment of the policy was not valid, and therefore the insurer paid the cash surrender value to the insured. Subsequently, the daughter sued the insurer in a California court and the insurer removed the action to the federal court where the insurer claimed that the daughter was estopped by the Pennsylvania interpleader from claiminig that the assignment of the policy was valid. But the federal district court in California under "rule interpleader" held that the Pennsylvania court had no jurisdiction over her in California, and therefore she was not bound by the decision of the Pennsylvania court. The U.S. Supreme Court affirmed, aggreeing that the Pennsylvania court decision had not bound the daughter, and therefore the insurer had to pay twice, both the insured and the assignee of the policy! The highest court ruled that the Pennsylvania interpleader proceeding was not "quasi in rem proceeding" but an "in personam proceeding," and therefore was invalid without personal jurisdiction over the assignee of the policy who was then in California![16]

In short, subject-matter jurisdiction requirements for Rule 22[17] and statutory interpleader under 28 USC 1335 are different. Rule 22 requires the traditional bases for jurisdiction: federal question under 28 USC 1331 or diversity of citizenship under 28 USC 1332. Statutory interpleader merely requires a stake of more than $500 and at least two adverse claimants from different states; complete diversity and citizenship of the stakeholder is irrelevant.[18] Furthermore, under federal interpleader, nationwide service of process is permitted, that is, a court in which the stakeholder has filed an interpleader under 28 USC 1335 may serve its process on any claimant, no matter where in the United States that claimant dwells or is found.[19] Diversity is satisfied for federal court jurisdiction as long as two claimants are citizens of different states.[20] The federal interpleader statute also simplifies the venue requirements since suit is permitted to be brought "in the judicial district in which one or more of the claimants reside," regardless of where the cause of action arose or regardless of the district where all defendants or all plaintiffs reside.[21]

The federal interpleader statutory suit under 28 USC 1335 is commenced by the stakeholder who deposits in the federal district court the amount of the property or thing or money in question, or posts a bond for that amount. Interestingly, the stakeholder is not estopped from claiming subsequently at trial that he or she or it does not owe the money or property or thing to any claimant at all![22] A basic requirement of the statutory interpleader action is that there must be adverse claimants to the particular fund.[23] And in *Hebel v. Ebersole* the court pointed out that "adversity may also exist if the various claims against the stakeholder, while not theoretically mutually exclusive, in the aggregate exceed the limits on the stakeholder's liability. . . . Prospective claims may still satisfy interpleader requirements.[24] Once the federal district court has taken jurisdiction, the court may enjoin or restrain all claimants from starting or continuing in any state or federal court any other action that may affect the property or thing or money deposited in the federal district court by the stakeholder. The stakeholder seeks a discharge of the indebtedness, or a least to be shielded from claimants for "potential double liability. . . . A discharge in interpleader permits the neutral stakeholder having no claim to the subject matter of the action, to retire from the action and requires competing claimants to interplead their claims.[25] Apparently, there is no right to a jury trial in the interpleader action,[26] although in *Pan Am Fire & Casualty Co. v. Revere* the court referred "the questions of liablilty and damages" to the jury: "Each claimant can be given a full opportunity to prove his case before a jury reserving to the court the task of apportioning the fund between those who are successful if the aggregate of the verdicts exceed the amount of the insurance proceeds."[27] Note that a stakeholder may in the discretion of the court recover attorneys' fees and court costs.[28] The court does not have ancillary jurisdiction over cross-claims filed in an insurer's interpleader action seeking to invalidate a purported change of beneficiary forms, power of attorney, or a will executed by the insured prior to his or her death, since the cross-claims do not have any independent basis of federal jurisdiction and are not logically dependent upon the resolution of the interpleader action.[29]

Rule 22 provides that, whenever a person "is or may be exposed to double or multiple liability," he or she may demand interpleader in an actiton as a plaintiff or by counter-claiming or cross-claiming as a defendant in an action already commenced. This "rule interpleader" mandates complete diversity of citizenship,[30] valid service of process within the state where the federal district court is located or pursuant to the state's long-arm statute,[31] and also that the amount in controversy must exceed $10,000.[32] But the stakeholder in the rule interpleader is not required as is the stakeholder in "statutory interpleader," to deposit the property or thing or money into the court.[33]

A federal district court in Maryland in *Builders & Developers Corp. v. Manassas Iron & Steel Co.* was concerned about motions to dismiss a "complaint for interpleader."[34] The court, on its own, determined that "the suit is not brought to, and could not qualify under, the general diversity of citizenship jurisdiction." But on the second question, "whether a plaintiff, having an independent liability to a defendant-claimant can successfully maintain an action in the nature of an interpleader," was answered affirmatively:

> Entirely apart from the special Federal Interpleader Statute the equitable remedy of interpleader has long been a well known ground of equity jurisdiction. "During its

evolution many technical restrictions were placed upon equitable interpleader. (1) The same thing, debt or duty must have been claimed by both or all the parties against whom the relief was demanded. (2) All their adverse titles or claims must have been dependent upon or be derived from a common source. (3) The person seeking relief—the plaintiff—must not have had or claimed any interest in the subject matter. (4) The plaintiff must have incurred no independent liability to either of the claimants, that is, he must have stood perfectly indifferent between them in the position of a mere stakeholder. This was the strict bill of interpleader.'' 2 Barron & Holtzoff, Federal Practice and Procedure § 551, pages 227–228.

A bill in the nature of interpleader was also recognized and differed from strict interpleader in that the plaintiff need not be disinterested in the subject mamtter. Federal interpleader statutes were enacted in 1917, 1925, 1926 and 1936. The latest statute is codified in §§ 1335, 1397, and 2361 of Title 28 U.S.C.A. Each successive statute ''shows very clearly the legislative intent to greatly extend the remedial scope of interpleader in the federal courts to meet situations where the equitable relief is greatly needed because impossible of achievement in the courts of any one State, and the Act should be liberally interpreted as remedial legislation.'' (John Hancock Mutual Life Insurance Company v. Kegan, D.C.D.Md. 1938, 22 F. Supp. 326, 330—an opinion by Judge Chestnut).

The diversity of citizenship issue was raised in *Haynes v. Felder*, an interpleader suit; the Fifth U.S. Court of Appeals, in holding that the trial court properly entertained jurisdiction, took the occasion to expound at length on the issue:

Here, with common citizenship between the bank and Haynes, entirely aside from the mixed citizenship of the Felder group and the original participation of Davis, also a Texan, such diversity as is required under §1332 is lacking. Thus the only basis of federal jurisdiction here which is, or might be, claimed is the Interpleader Act, 28 U.S.C.A. §1335. The pertinent language of this statute is:

(a) The district courts shall have original jurisdiction of any civil action of interpleader or in the nature of interpleader . . . if

(1) Two or more adverse claimants, of diverse citizenshsip as defined in section 1332 of this title, are claiming or may claim to be entitled to such money or property. . . .

This statute does not appear to require any diversity between the plaintiff and the defendant-claimants, and such an interpretation of the similarly conceived 1936 Interpleader Act was held to be both correct and constitutional in Treinies v. Sunshine Mining Co., 308 U.S. 66, 60 S.Ct. 44, 84 L.Ed. 85. However, as the Court there held, the Act is bottomed on the diversity jurisdiction of the United States courts, permitted by Art. III, §2, cl. 1(7) of the Constitution, and thus it was necessary for Congress to specify some alternative form of diversity on which jurisdiction in particular cases could be grounded. This it did in the present Act by requiring ''claimants, of diverse citizenship.''

The question therefore is whether the diversity here existing among the claimants is sufficient to support jurisdiction. . . .

In analyzing the cases and authorities that have dealt with aspects of this question it must be kept in mind that many that appear to be superficially similar or use language broad enough to include the present situation actually involve a distinguishable jurisdictional issue. Interpleader suits may be attempted under Rule 22(1) (normal diversity—§1332) or 22(2) (statutory interpleader—§1335), or both, by plaintiffs (or defendants) who are disinterested (strict interpleader) or interested (bill in the nature of interpleader), and whose citizenship is totally, partially, or not at all diverse from that of all or some of the claimants. . . .

An analysis of the leading appellate cases interpreting the statutory requirement shows that the "complete diversity" test has been rejected under every one of the interpleader acts.[35]

The historical limitations on the use of interpleader were echoed by the California Supreme Court in *Hancock Oil v. Independent Distributing Co*,[36] where the court stated that interpleader would have been denied if the party had asserted an obligation to pay rent that constituted an independent liability that would bar the remedy of interpleader:

The rule concerning independent liability is stated in Corpus Juris as follows: "Interpleader will not lie if the stakeholder has incurred some personal obligation to either of the claimants, independent of the title or the right to possession, because such claimant would in that event have a claim against him which could not be settled in a litigation with the other claimant." 33 C.J. 439. . . . The Supreme Court of Maine put the matter most convincingly when it said: "The mere fact that a contractual relation exists between plaintiff and one of the defendants, under which the fund is required to be paid to such claimant, does not of itself defeat the right of interpleader. . . . If such were the law, it would be difficult to conceive of any set of facts which would enable a bank, a trustee, or other custodian of funds, or even a bailee, to maintain interpleader. The obligation referred to in the rule must be independent of the title or right of possession of the fund or property in question. . . ." First National Bank v. Reynolds, 127 Me. 340, 143 A. 266, 268, 60 A.L.R. 712. . . . Although Professor Pomeroy declares that an independent liability "arises from the very nature of the original relation subsisting between" the landlord and tenant, he states that such a suit is proper whenever there is some privity between the claimant and the lessor, as, for example, when the relation of trustee and *cestui que trust* has been created between them. It seems, therefore, that the reason why the author asserts that the relationship of the landlord and tenant precludes interpleader by the tenant is not that, under the lease, there is an independent liability but because there is no privity between the landlord and the one joined with him as defendant. . . .

From what has been said, then, it is clear that, in the present case, as according to the facts alleged in the complaint, the relations inter se of the respondents and the copartners are such that the decision will determine the liability of the lessees to each of them, there is no independent liability which will bar the remedy of interpleader; accordingly the appellant's complaint is sufficient with respect to those of the four common law requirements for interpleader not abolished or modified by the amendment in 1881 to section 386 of the Code of Civil Procedure.[37]

A passing reference should be made to *impleader* under Rule 14 of the Federal Rules of Civil Procedure. Impleader, or third party practice, allows the defendant to bring in a potentially liable person not joined by the plaintiff. Impleader historically can be traced to the ''voucher to warranty'' of the common law real property actions. Rule 14 provides that a defendant may implead a third party on his or her own behalf against the plaintiff or another defendant. Impleader is ancillary to the main claim for purposes of jurisdiction over subject matter and venue. The impleaded party must be available in the forum, although the court still exercises discretion in allowing or denying impleader. Impleader may give rise to the assertion of other claims, and even the impleader may join other claims under Rule 18 of the Federal Rules of Civil Procedure; the third party defendant may counterclaim against the defendant or defendants in conformity with Rule 13. Rule 14 authorizes claims between plaintiff and the third party defendant arising out of the transaction that is the subject matter of plaintiff's claim against the defendant or defendants.

Impleader is not the only means for avoiding the risk that a secondarily liable party may be caught between inconsistent fact findings. Section 2–607(a)(5) of the Uniform Commercial Code provides: ''Where the buyer is sued for breach of warranty or other obligations for which the seller is answerable over he may give his seller written notice of the litigation. If the notice states that the seller may come in and defend and that if the seller does not do so he will be bound in any action against him by his buyer by any determination of fact common to the two litigations, then unless the seller after reasonable receipt of the notice does come in and defend he is so bound.''

NOTES

1. See generally 48 Harv. L. Rev. 854 (1948); also Rogers, ''Historical Origins of Interpleader,'' 51 Yale L J 924 (1949).
2. Note 4 Pomeroy's Equity Jurisprudence, Sections 1322 and 1481 (1941).
3. 306 US 398 (1939).
4. See U.S. Fidelity & Guaranty Co. v. McGhee, 345 F. Supp. 288 (ND Miss., 1972).
5. 260 US 235 (1918). For example, note 28 USC 1335, delineating the jurisdiction of federal district courts in certain interpleader actions where two or more adverse claimants of diverse citizenship are claiming property of value of $500 or more deposited in court. Also note 38 USC 784(a), relating to interpleader by the Veterans Administration, and 49 USC 97, concerning interpleader by carrier of conflicting claimants.
6. See generally Hazard and Moskowitz, ''An Historical and Critical Analysis of Interpleader,'' 52 Calif. L. Rev. 706 (1964).
7. 386 US 523 (1967).
8. The highest court concluded: ''In light of the evidence that federal interpleader was not intended to serve the function of 'bill of peace' in the contest of multiparty litigation arising out of a mass tort, of the anomalous power which such a construction of the statute would give the stakeholder, and of the thrust of the statute and the purpose it was intended to serve, we hold that the interpleader statute did not authorize the injunction entered in the present case. Upon demand, the injunction is to be modified consistently with this opinion.''

9. Id. "Before considering the issues presented by the petition for certiorari, we find it necessary to dispose of a question neither raised by the parties nor passed upon by the courts below. Since the matter concerns our jurisdiction, we raise it on our own motion. Treinies v. Sunshine Mining Co., 308 U.S. 66, 70, 60 S. Ct. 44, 47, 84 L.Ed. 85 (1939). The interpleader statute, 28 U.S.C. §1335, applies where there are 'Two or more adverse claimants, of diverse citizenship. . . . ' This provision has been uniformly construed to require only 'minimal diversity,' that is, diversity of citizenship between two or more claimants, without regard to the circumstance that other rival claimants may be co-citizens. The language of the statute, the legislative purpose broadly to remedy the problems posed by multiple claimants to a single fund, and the consistent judicial interpretation tacitly accepted by Congress, persuade us that the statute requires no more. There remains, however, the question whether such a statutory construction is consistent with Article III of our Constitution, which extends the federal judicial power to 'Controversies . . . between citizens of different States . . . and between a State, or the Citizens thereof, and foreign States, Citizens or Subjects.' In Strawbridge v. Curtiss, 3 Cranch 267, 2 L.Ed. 435 (1806), this Court held that the diversity of citizenshsip statute required 'complete diversity': where co-citizens appeared on both sides of a dispute, jurisdiction was lost. But Chief Justice Marshall there purported to construe only 'The words of the act of congress,' not the Constitution itself. And in a variety of contexts this Court and the lower courts have concluded that Article III poses no obstacle to the legislative extension of federal jurisdiction, founded on diversity, so long as any two adverse parties are not co-citizens. Accordingly, we conclude that the present case is properly in the federal courts.

10. "I feel that the use which we today allow to be made of the federal interpleader statue, 28 U.S.C. §1335, is, with all deference, unwarranted. How these litigants are 'claimants' to this fund in the statutory sense is indeed a mystery. If they are not 'claimants' of the fund, neither are they in the category of those who 'are claiming' or who 'may claim' to be entitled to it.

This insurance company's policy provides that it will 'pay on behalf of the insured all sums which the insured shall become legally obligated to pay.' To date the insured has not become 'legally obligated' to pay any sum to any litigant. Since nothing is owed under the policy, I fail to see how any litigant can be a 'claimant' as against the insurance company. If that is doubtful the doubt is resolved by two other conditions:

(1) The policy states '[n]o action shall lie against the company . . . until the amount of the insured's obligation to pay shall have been finally determined either by judgment against the insured after actual trial or by written agreement of the insured, the claimant and the company.'

(2) Under California law where the accident happened and under Oregon law where the insurance contract was made, a direct action against the insurer is not allowable until after a litigant receives a final judgment against the insured.

Thus under this insurance policy as enforced in California and in Oregon a 'claimant' against the insured can become a 'claimant' against the insurer only after final judgment against the insured or after a consensual written agreement of the insurer, a litigant, and the insured. Neither of those two events has so far happened.

This construction of the word 'claimant' against the fund is borne out, as the Court of Appeals noted, by Rule 22(1) of the Federal Rules of Civil Procedure. That Rule, also based on diversisty of citizenship, differs only in the district where the suit may be brought and in the reach of service of process, as the Court points out. But it illuminates the nature of federal interpleader for it provides that only '[p]ersons having claims against the plaintiff [insurer] may be joined as defendants and required to interplead.'

Can it be that we have two kinds of interpleader statutes as between which an insurance company can choose: one that permits 'claimants' against the insurer ('persons having claims against the plaintiff') to be joined and the other that permits 'claimants' against the insured to be joined for the benefit of the insurer even though they may never be 'claimants' against the insurer? I cannot believe that Congress launched such an irrational scheme.''

11. 313 US 498 (1941).

12. See 71 Harv. L. Rev. 874 (1958).

13. 368 US 71 (1961).

14. Unreported (EDNY, July 20, 1988).

15. 241 US 518 (1916).

16. See 1 Emanuel's Encyclopedia of American Law (1987) at 256–257.

17. ''(1) Persons having claims against the plaintiff may be joined as defendants and required to interplead when their claims are such that the plaintiff is or may be exposed to double of multiple liability. It is not ground for objection to the joinder that the claims of the several claimants or the titles on which their claims depend do not have a common origin or are not identical but are adverse to and independent of one another, or that plaintiff avers that the plaintiff is not liable in whole or in part to any or all of the claimants. A defendant exposed to similar liability may obtain such interpleader by way of cross-claim or counterclaim. The provisions of this rule supplement and do not in any way limit the joinder of parties permitted in Rule 20.

(2) The remedy herein provided is in addition to and in no way supersedes or limits the remedy provided by Title 28, U.S.C. §§1335, 1397, and 2361. Actions under those provisions shall be conducted in accordance with these rules.''

18. Supra note 4. On the requisite of complete diversity under Rule 22 see Lincoln Income Life Insurance Co. v. Harrison, 71 FRD 27 (WD Okla., 1976): ''Plaintiff stated that the instant interpleader action was being brought pursuant to 28 U.S.C. §1335. It has been determined that as both Defendants are citizens of Oklahoma, the instant action does not lie under said statute. . . . However, the plaintiff is a Kentucky corporation with its principal place of business in Kentucky and jurisdiction of this Court is proper under 28 U.S.C. §1332 wherein diversity . . . exists between Plaintiff and both Defendants and the amount in controversy exceeds $10,000. . . . The interpleader procedure in this . . . case is governed by Rule 22.''

19. 28 USC 2361.

20. See 28 USC 1335(a)(1).

21. Supra note 15 at 258.

22. See Wright, Law of the Federal Courts (4th ed., 1983).

23. See Libby, McNeil & Libby v. City National Bank, 592 F2d 504 (9th Cir., 1979).

24. 543 F2d 14 (7th Cir., 1976).

25. See Aliuga v. Perara Co., 494 F. Supp. 18 (SDNY, 1979) at 20.

26. See Hyde Properties v. McCoy, 507 F2d 301 (6th Cir., 1974).

27. 188 F. Supp. 474 (ED La., 1960).

28. See Skandia American Reinsurance Co. v. Schenck, 441 F. Supp. 715 (SDNY), 1977): ''The federal courts . . . have long exercised the equitable power to permit a party preserving a fund for the benefit of others to recover his costs, including reason-

able attorney's fees, either from the fund itself or directly from the parties enjoying the benefit. . . . [C]osts and counsel fees have been awarded to a stakeholder-plaintiff who commences an interpleader action as a matter of the court's sound discretion . . . . There is some question whether a federal court exercising statutory interpleader jurisdiction must apply the forum state's law as to the recovery of attorney's fees. . . . In this case, however, there is no conflict between the federal rule and the applicable state rule. New York courts, too, . . . have permitted a stakeholder to recover costs and reasonable attorney's fees.'' Cf. Bandura v. Fidelity & Guarantee Life Insurance Co. 443 F. Supp. 829 (WD Pa., 1978) at 833: ''Such awards are within the discretion of the court. . . . However, we do not think it appropriate in this case to do so because the defendant . . . did not initiate this action . . . as an interpleader action in the first instance. Suit was brought against it . . . and . . . it joined a third party defendant and asserted an interpleader cause of action. . . . Its own inattention to the instructions of the insured and its clerical error . . . contrary to the clear instructions of the insured . . . was the cause of this litigation. . . . [W]e will deny the request . . . for costs and attorney's fees.''

29. See Travelers Insurance Co. v. First National Bank of Shreveport, 675 F2d 633 (5th Cir., 1982).

30. Supra note 21 at 497.

31. Id.

32. Id. at 498–499.

33. However, Rule 67 of the Federal Rules of Civil Procedure (FRCP) should be a sufficient basis upon which to receive a deposit incident to Rule 22 of FRCP. See generally General Atomic Co. v. Duke Power Co., 553 F2d 53 (10th Cir., 1977).

34. 208 F. Supp. 485 (Md., 1962).

35. 239 F2d 868 (5th Cir., 1957).

36. 150 P2d 463 (Cal., 1944).

37. The California court set forth the following dissertation on the historical implications: ''The common law bill of interpleader had four essential elements: (1) The same thing, debt, or duty must be claimed by both or all the parties against whom the relief is demanded; (2) all of the adverse titles or claims must be dependent, or be derived from a common source; (3) the one seeking relief must not have nor claim any interest in the subject matter; and (4) he must have incurred no independent liability to either of the claimants. See 4, Pomeroy's Equity Jurisprudence, 5th Ed. 1941, §1322, p. 906.

These requirements have been termed historical limitations upon this otherwise expeditious equitable proceeding . . . and in 1881 section 386 of the Code of Civil Procedure was amended to broaden the remedy. The statute . . . declares . . . : 'And whenever conflicting claims are or may be made upon a person for or relating to personal property, or the performance of an obligation, or any portion thereof, such person may bring an action against the conflicting claimants to compel them to interplead and litigate their several claims among themselves. The order of substitution may be made and the action of interpleader may be maintained, and the applicant or plaintiff be discharged from liability to all or any of the conflicting claimants, although their titles or claims have not a common origin, or are not identical, but are adverse to and independent of one another.' The provision of this enactment, that interpleader lies 'although their titles or claims have not a common origin . . . but are adverse to and independent of one another,' directly abrogates the common law requirement that all the adverse titles or claims must be dependent or be derived from a common source, and it is therefore clear that privity between the conflicting claimants need not be shown to invoke the remedy under the code. . . .

Early in the history of interpleader, it was held that one who sought to maintain such a suit must show outstanding claims, identical in every respect and without the slightest degree of variation, to the same thing, debt or duty. In this case of conflicting claims to specific personal property, this rigid formalism did not seriously interfere with the effectiveness of the proceeding. But where, as is generally the situation modernly, the subject matter of the conflicting claims was an obligation, a debt or a duty, the requirement as to the identity of the defendant's demands very often prevented a stakeholder from using interpleader where he was doubly vexed with respect to one liability. For example, under the narrow rule of the common law, if one person claimed all of the fund held by a bank and another person asserted the right to only a portion of that fund, the bank could not secure a determination of its liability by means of the equitable proceeding. The Legislature has removed this restriction, yet the very rationale of the interpleader compels the conclusion that the amendment does not allow the remedy where each of the claimants asserts the right to a different debt, claim or duty. If the conflicting claims are mutually exclusive, interpleader cannot be maintained, but the fact that an identical right is not asserted by each of the claimants does not preclude the use of the remedy. . . .

In the present case, the plaintiffs have alleged that each of the two groups against whom interpleader is sought claims the right to receive the rents and royalties reserved in the lease. If Independent Distributing Co. and the members of the copartnership should assert that they are entitled to the reasonable value of the use and occupation of the land leased to the plaintiffs, together with the mesne profits or damages for waste, the trial court would be required to deny the plaintiffs the right to interplead those parties with their lessors. Under such circumstances the claims of the parties would not relate to the same obligation. But as the appellants' complaint pleads that there are conflicting claims concerning their obligation to pay the rents and royalties reserved by the lease, the lessors and the thid parties must answer and, if each of them agrees that his claim concerns the right to those rents and royalties, the lessees should be discharged from liability upon payment of their obligations under the lease''.

10

Release-Dismissal and Settlement Agreements

Settlement agreements are obviously preclusive devices because they bring the litigation to a close, but questions may readily be raised with respect to the fairness or equity of the settlement agreement. In *Davis v. American Commercial Lines, Inc.*, the Sixth U.S. Court of Appeals precluded a grant of summary judgment against plaintiffs who were not represented by counsel during settlement negotiations.[1] Furthermore, the federal appellate court noted the genuine issues of material fact regarding the fairness of the settlement agreement and the overreaching and misrepresentation by the defendants. Aggregate settlements, in which one law firm represents a class, also may not be fair,[2] as shown in *Hayes v. Eagle-Picher Industries*, where the 10th U.S. Court of Appeals critized a settlement agreement by 18 plaintiffs and their attorney that a majority vote could govern the acceptance of the settlement, since the settlement agreement was entered into *before* the negotiations leading to settlement.[3] The court cited Rule 5–106A of the Code of Professional Responsibility,[4] which precludes a lawyer from representing "both the clients who favored the settlement and those who opposed it."[5] Note also the restraints upon lawyers under Rule 1.8(a) of Model Rules of Professional Conduct to the effect that "a lawyer who represents two or more clients shall not participate in making an aggregate settlement of the claims of or against the clients . . . unless each client consents after consultation, including disclosure of the existence and nature of all the claims . . . involved and of the participation of each person in the settlement."

In *Smith & Wesson v. Birmingham Fire Insurance Co.*, the New York Appellate Division, First Dept., held that "a settlement agreement between insurer and insured, made without the participation of the injured third party, should not be given the broad effect of barring the third-party judgment creditor's rights. Such agreement might readily be collusively entered into between the insurer and its insured. . . . Consequently, if a settlement is recognized as binding upon the non-participating injured third party, the insurer and the insured would have a strong incentive to settle, merely to limit the amount the injured third party could collect against the insurer. This would defeat the beneficial purpose of Insurance Law.''[6]

Release-dismissal agreements, such as where a criminal defendant releases his or her right to file a civil rights action under 42 USC 1983 in exchange for a prosecutor's dismissal of pending criminal charges, may be enforceable. The U.S. Supreme Court in *Town of Newton v. Rumery* ruled that the release of civil rights claim in exchange for the dismissal of criminal charges was not per se valid.[7] Yet under federal law ''a promise is unenforceable if the interest in its enforcement is outweighed in the circumstances by a public policy harmed by enforcement of the agreement.'' The court opined that release-dismissal agreements are not ''inherently coercive,'' even though such agreements ''may not be the product of an informed decision.'' Conceivably, the prosecutor may improperly give more weight to the private interest in settling the civil rights claim than to the public interest in enforcing the criminal law. And conceivably the release-dismissal agreement may have not been signed by the defendant voluntarily, in which event the court would undoubtedly not enforce the settlement agreement.[8]

Courts are reluctant to disturb settlements unless there was fraud or duress in the making of the settlement contract:

> The focus of attention in cases where the plaintiff attacks a release for mistake or fraud is often in the wrong place. In the fraud cases the only question is: did the defendant or his agent commit any unconscionable act? If so, we need not inquire whether the act amounts to actionable fraud or even the kind that would merit equitable relief. He should not be permitted to minimize the tort liability imposed on him by law by any but the most scrupulous conduct. Concern over ''misrepresentations of law'' or over ''opinion'' is out of place. It is enough if the plaintiff executed the release in reliance on some unfair statement or concealment or because of some unfair conduct. In the mistake cases the focus of attention has sometimes gone even further afield from the real problems. Vision is often concentrated on sterile rules that are not based upon the needs involved, the need for finality and the need to hold the tortfeasor to his tort. Nothing could be less important in answering these problems than the spurious issue whether the plaintiff made a mistake in prognosis or diagnosis, in fact or prediction, or whether he offered to restore the consideration received. Even the fundamental theory of relief, the old contract term, ''mutual mistake,'' is itself out of place, and in fact has little to do with relief granted in release cases. In the end the law can be simplified and improved by eliminating these catch phrases and beginning each case with an inquiry into the policies of finality and fairness. Beyond that, a study of the factors indicated above as applied to the particular case should be of some assistance. The application of sense, experience, and good will may avoid many of the pitfalls. There can be in these cases little certainty or predictability—probably no more than as to what amounts to negli-

gence or contributory negligence. But there can be some rational basis for decision, and that would be progress.[9]

Release-dismissal and settlement agreements are undoubtedly the most popular preclusive documents, and any extended delineation of the myriad factors entering into the agreements would not be fruitful. Indeed, settlements are a broad subject matter that encompass the warp and woof of the law! Every effort to settle or release means an end to litigation in the public interest.

NOTES

1. 823 F2d 1006 (6th Cir., 1987).
2. See Trial Mag. (March 1988) at 13.
3. 513 F2d 892 (10th Cir., 1975).
4. "A lawyer who represents two or more clients shall not make or participate in the making of an aggregate settlement of the claims of or against his clients, unless each client has consented to the settlement after being advised of the existence and nature of all the claims involved in the proposed settlement, of the total amount of the settlement, and of the participation of each person in the settlement."
5. The court concluded: "We hold that the arrangement presented allowing the majority to govern the rights of the minority is violative of the basic tenets of the attorney-client relationship in that it delegates to the attorney powers which allow him to act not only contrary to the wishes of his client, but to act in a manner disloyal to his client and to his client's interests. Because of this, it is essential that the final settlement be subject to the client's ratification particularly in a non-class action case as the present one."
6. 510 NYS2d 603 (App. Div., 1st Dept., 1987).
7. 107 S.Ct. 1187 (1987).
8. See Sexton v. Ryan, 804 F2d 26 (2d Cir., 1986).
9. See Dobbs, "Conclusiveness of Personal Injury Settlement: Basic Problems," 41 N. Car. L. Rev. 665 (1965) at 743–744.

11

The Preclusive Doctrines of Res Judicata and Collateral Estoppel

PRECLUSION: AN OVERVIEW

Res judicata and collateral estoppel offer two of the best means for bringing litigation to a swift and definitive end.[1] Res judicata delineates claim preclusion and collateral estoppel describes issue preclusion, although this distinction may in any given situations be meaningless.[2] In a New York case, *Nellen v. F. J. Wilkes & Co., Inc.*, decided by the New York Supreme Court, New York County, on February 16, 1988, the question was "whether the doctrines of collateral estoppel or res judicata bar this action by reason of a prior administrative determination rendered after a full hearing." Plaintiff was told by an administrative judge of the unemployment insurance administration that she had received "all the payment from her employer to which she was entitled during her (maternity) leave and that she had voluntarily left her job without good cause." In her lawsuit she contended that her employer was guilty of sexual discrimination by refusing to pay plaintiff full salary less disability and by failing to maintain full benefits during her maternity leave. Defendant contended that plaintiff's sexual discrimination claim should have been dismissed under the doctrines of res judicata and collateral estoppel. The court thereupon opined:

> It is beyond dispute that in the proper circumstances, res judicata and collateral estoppel are applicable to give conclusive effect to quasi-judicial determinations of administrative agency's adjudication using procedures similar to those used in a court of law. In order to be given conclusive and binding effect by the court, the determination of the agency must be final. Furthermore, the court must examine whether an identity of issue exists such that the issue raised in the second proceeding is an issue that was necessarily

decided in the prior action or proceeding and whether the party against whom collateral estoppel is asserted had a full and fair opportunity to litigate the issue in the prior proceeding (Ryan v. New York Telephone, 62 NY2d 494).

The court concluded:

Application of the above listed standards leads the court to conclude that collateral estoppel is not applicable here. First, under the Labor Law, if an appeal is taken the final decision maker in the administrative process is the Unemployment Insurance Appeal Board and not the administrative law judge (Labor Law §623; Matter of O'Leary v. Roberts, 93 AD2d 915). Therefore, the decision sought to be given preclusive effect in this case is not the final decision of the agency. In addition, there is not an identity of issues in both proceedings. While determination of plaintiff's entitlement to unemployment benefits and whether defendant is guilty of sexual discrimination or retaliation presumably requires both the administrative agency and the court to address the issue of whether plaintiff voluntarily left her job, the administrative agency is not specifically charged with determining sexual discrimination claims. Moreover, a review of the record of proceedings before the administrative law judge makes it clear that plaintiff's sexual discrimination claims were not raised or actually determined by the administrative law judge. In other words, the issue of whether plaintiff voluntarily left her job under the Labor Law is not identical to the issue of whether she voluntarily left her job under the Human Rights Law. In addition, it is not at all clear that the issues of whether plaintiff received the payments and benefits to which she is entitled during her leave or whether defendant's demands for an examination by a physician of its choice were issues necessarily decided by the administrative law judge or those issues should be decided the same way in the context of a sex discrimination claim under the Human Rights Law. In view of the foregoing, the court finds that the defendant has failed to meet its burden to demonstrate the identicality and decisiveness of the issues and therefore, preclusive effect cannot be given to the determinations of the administrative law judge.

Issue preclusion, and not claim preclusion, was the determination of the New York Court.

The New York decision in *Gilroy v. New York University Medical Center* is illustrative of the issue as to whether an administrative determination should be given preclusive effect to bar counterclaims and affirmative defenses of the defendant university, which was a party too an earlier proceeding.[3] Here plaintiff employee was discharged and an administrative determination disqualified her from receiving unemployment benefits on the ground that she had lost her employment through her misconduct; allegedly, she "did not act in her employer's best interest in that money for which she was responsible was unaccounted for." In the present suit defendant university counterclaims to recover all salary payments made and all employee benefits provided plaintiff for breach of her "lawful obligations as an employee." Plaintiff argues that such counterclaims are barred under the doctrine of collateral estoppel; defendants contend that their failure to contest the unemployment insurance claim should not deprive them of the opportunity to prove in this litigation their assertion that plaintiff did in fact convert defendant's funds. The court opined:

"The doctrine of collateral estoppel precludes a party from relitigating "an issue which has previously been decided against him in a proceeding in which he had fair opportunity to fully litigate the point." . . . It is . . . based upon the general notion that it is not fair to permit a party to relitigate an issue that has already been decided against it. There are now but two requirements which must be satisfied before the doctrine is invoked. First, the identical issue necessarily must have been decided in the prior action and be decisive of the present action, and second, the party to be precluded from relitigating the issue must have had a full and fair opportunity to contest the prior determination. . . . " Kaufman v. Eli Lilly and Company, 65 N.Y. 2d 449, 455 (1985).

With regard to identity of parties, the prior determination will be binding not only on the parties to the first action, but on those in privity with them. "Generally, to establish privity the connection between the parties must be such that the interests of the nonparty can be said to have been represented in the prior proceeding . . . " or "when the party to be precluded can be said to have controlled the conduct of the prior action to further his own interests. . . . " (Green v. Santa Fe Industries Inc., 70 N.Y. 2d 244, 253–254 [1987]).

Here, it is clear that neither Dr. Breinin, his wife, nor Ms. Kahn was a party or in privity with a party to the unemployment benefits administrative proceeding, nor in any way controlled the conduct thereof. Even if Dr. Breinin testified at the hearing, which is unclear in this case, such fact is of no moment (see: Liss v. Trans Auto System, Inc., 68 N.Y. 2d 15, 22 [1986]). Thus, they are not precluded from asserting their counterclaims alleging conversions and theft by plaintiff.

In considering whether the party against whom estoppel is sought to be invoked had a full and fair opportunity to contest the issue in the prior forum, courts "consider the 'realities of the (prior) litigation,' including the context and other circumstances which, although not legal impediments, may have had the practical effect of discouraging or deterring a party from fully litigating the determination which is now asserted against him. . . . "(People v. Plevy, 52 N.Y. 2d 58, 65 [1980]).

After noting that "whether a party has had a full and fair opportunity to contest a prior determination cannot be reduced to formula," the court in Gilberg v. Barbieri (53 N.Y. 2d 285 [1981]), stated (p. 292) that the factors to be considered include "the size of the claim, the forum of the prior litigation, the use of initiative, the extent of the litigation, the competence and experience of counsel, the availability of new evidence, indications of a compromise verdict, differences in the applicable law and foreseeability of future litigatiton." . . . In a medical malpractice action where defendant had interposed the defense of collateral estoppel because he had prevailed on default in an earlier action for professional services rendered to his patient, Justice Gibbons (concurring) opined that New York should follow the majority rule and deny preclusive effect to default (Kossover v. Trattler, 82 A.D. 2d 610, 612 [2d Dept. 1981]).

Then, in Kaufman v. Eli Lilly Co., supra, the Court of Appeals joined with the critics by stating (pp. 456–457) that "if the issue has not been litigated, there is no identity of issues between the present action and the prior determination. An issue is not actually litigated if, for example, there has been a default . . ." [citing Restatement 2d of Judgments §27 comments d, e at 255–257]. (Such comments discuss motives for litigants' defaults, clearly contemplating situations, such as in the case at bar, where the defaults are purposeful.)

Even if the fact that a prior determination had been rendered upon default were one of several factors to be considered, rather than the dispositive one, collateral estoppel would not be applied in this case because the administrative determination herein is sought to be used offensively. . . . The reason for the denial of preclusive effect in both those cases was that both employees had been terminated for breach of their employment contracts which, while constituting discharge "for cause," did not necessarily rise to the level of disqualifying misconduct. Estoppel was therefore denied in both cases because the issue before the court had not been necessary to the administrative determination. . . .

Here, in light of the fact that the issue of whether plaintiff misappropriated funds of defendants was not actually litigated, the defendants' motion to strike the affirmative defenses to the counterclaims of res judicata or collateral estoppel is granted, and plaintiff's cross-motion to dismiss the counterclaims is denied.

RES JUDICATA

In *Brown v. City of New York* the action stemmed from injuries allegedly suffered by the plaintiff when he was assaulted in a building in 1978.[4] Plaintiff believed the building was owned by defendant municipality but the defendant brought a third-party suit against the actual owner of the building, and so the complaint was amended in 1981 to make Covenant a direct defendant. Thereupon, the municipality moved to dismiss the amended complaint, and Covenant filed a pre-answer motion for dismissal on the ground that the suit against Covenant was barred as it was filed more than three years after the assault. The motions were granted in October 1981, with the court observing that "significantly, plaintiff did not oppose" the dismissal motions. In July 1987, after the plaintiff served the amended complaint for a second time, the New York court prohibited the allegedly injured plaintiff from taking what amounted to a "second bite" when the court applied the doctrine of res judicata (on an unusual procedural point) to prohibit relitigating a case that was dismissed almost six years previously. The unusual problem here was that no judgment was ever entered after the parties had been directed to settle an order within three months of the October 1981 dismissal. According to the court, "an order entered on a motion for dismissal is ordinarily entitled to the same res judicata and collateral estoppel treatment that a judgment gets as long as the other requisites of those doctrines, i.e., finality, opportunity to contest, identity of issue and the like, are met."[5] The court concluded: "Having freely elected not to oppose . . . the prior motion to dismiss the plaintiff's complaint, this Court cannot think of any cogent reason why plaintiff should now be able to resurrect the same complaint against the same defendant more than 5 years later, particularly when it is remembered that where, as here, a dismissal is based on the statute of limitations it is considered to be on the merits." But in *Platt v. Jakubowicz*, where the defendants moved for an order dismissing the complaint on the ground that res judicata barred the action, the New York court opined that "it would be grossly inequitable to employ the doctrine of res judicata . . . for the plaintiff in the New Jersey action was not the same as in the New York proceeding."[6] Here the New York plaintiffs brought suit for personal injuries in an automobile accident in New Jersey; subsequently, the plaintiffs' insurer, by way of subrogation, commenced suit against the defendant in New Jersey for property damages, but defendant obtained the judgment against the plaintiff who apparently was more negligent than the defendant. Defendant's effort to hold on to the successful New Jersey litigation went for naught, as the New York court denied defendant's motion for summary judgment under the doctrine of res judicata.[7] According to the New York court,

> the real party in interest was plaintiff's insurance company, who upon paying plaintiff was subrogated to plaintiff's claim and brought the action (in New Jersey) in plaintiff's name; that plaintiff had no interest in testifying other than being required to under his policy, for he had been reimbursed for the damages to the insured automobile. Hence, plaintiff was merely the nominal party. Having commenced a suit in this (New York) jurisdiction for personal injuries prior to the commencement of the New Jersey action, it would be grossly unfair for plaintiff and his wife to abandon their action and litigate it in New Jersey. . . . Plaintiff had little or no true legal or equitable interest in the New Jersey subrogation action; and by reason of his obligation under the insurance policy, he had no control over the litigation.

An individual proposing to build a discotheque sued the town board, a bank, and the manager of the skating rink, alleging a conspiracy to deny him a license to operate the disco, in violation of various federal and Massachusetts racial discrimination laws. The federal district court in Massachusetts dismissed the action for a failure to state a cause of action, but subsequently the plaintiff filed another lawsuit against the bank and the same defendants this time alleging violation of Section 1 of the Sherman Act in that defendants had barred him from competing with the skating rink. The federal district court held that this action was barred with respect to the bank and its officers on the grounds of res judicata. The First U.S. Court of Appeals affirmed, holding that under res judicata a final judgment on the merits of an action precludes the parties or their privies from relitigating issues that were or could have been raised in that first action, but that this bar is limited to cases arising out of the same cause of action or claim. Noting that the federal district court had determined that the facts forming the basis of the subsequent antitrust lawsuit could have been uncovered if the plaintiff had been diligent in his discovery efforts, the federal appellate court held that once the reasonable discovery issue is resolved, the focus of a "transactional analysis" is not on whether a second claim could have been brought in a prior suit, but whether the underlying facts of both transactions were the same or substantially similar.[8] In short, res judicata prevails where there is an identity of parties, identity of claim or cause of action, a valid and final judgment, and a full and fair opportunity to be heard.[9] In 1980 the U.S. Supreme Court in *Allen v. McCurry* had defined the doctrine of res judicata as "a final judgment on the merits of an action that precludes the parties or their privies from relitigating issues that were or could have been raised in that action."[10] Here the highest court ruled that the doctrine of collateral estoppel operated to preclude relitigation in federal court of civil rights issues under 28 USC 1983 that were previously decided by a state court. In *Migra v. Warren City School District Board of Education*,[11] the highest court concluded that prior state court judgments could prevent the federal courts from taking 28 USC 1983 claims that never had been litigated or that had been precluded by state preclusion laws.[12] Res judicata can halt a state court action that is similar to a federal court action, as illustrated in *Opeila v. Scherer*.[13] Here the plaintiff sued the defendant police officer, alleging that the officer used excessive force in arresting him for burglary, an offense to which the defendant pleaded guilty. After the federal court dismissed most of plaintiff's civil rights claims, the defendant moved in state court to do likewise, and the New York court agreed: "What is controlling is the identity of the issue which has necessarily been decided in the prior action or proceeding. The issue, of course, must have been material to the first action or proceeding and essential to the decision rendered therein, and it must be the point actually to be determined in the second action or proceeding. . . . Plaintiff's claims against defendants Scherer and the City are also barred by the doctrine of res judicata. . . ."[14]

In the field of bankruptcy law, the U.S. Supreme Court in *Brown v. Felsen* addressed the res judicata question when it considered whether a prior state court judgment that did not include a finding of fraud was res judicata in the subsequent federal bankruptcy debt dischargeability litigation.[15] The court held that the prior state court judgment was not binding on the federal bankruptcy court unless the state court had concurrent jurisdiction and if the debt dischargeability issue was or could have been raised in the prior state action. To the same issue is *University of Tennessee v. Elliott*, where the highest court ruled that administrative res judicata applies to civil rights claims under 28 USC 1983.[16]

The variety of res judicata claims can be illustrated by the following recent decisions:

1. *City of New York v. Associated Ambulance Service, Inc.*, decided by the New York Supreme Court, New York County, on March 15, 1988. Here, defendant's motion to dismiss the action for forfeiture of a vehicle seized in connection with unlawfully dumping oil onto a street was denied. An administrative hearing resulted in fines paid by the defendant but the city failed to show that oil was a hazardous waste or was toxic, as statutorily defined for forfeiture purposes. Nevertheless, the court ruled that res judicata attached to the administrative finding and precluded relitigating the issue of hazardous waste. The

court was confused about the distinction between res judicata and collateral estoppel, as illustrated in the following excerpt from its opinion:

> "The doctrine of res judicata and collateral estoppel are applicable to give conclusive effect to the quasi-judicial determinations of administrative agencies" (Ryan v. New York Telephone Company, 62 NY2d 494, 499). In that case the court ruled that (p. 504) "having been afforded a full opportunity at the administrative hearing to present" certain proofs, "the failure to do so . . . is certainly not a basis for defeating the application of collateral estoppel."
>
> CONCLUSION
>
> Having had the opportunity to present proof in the administrative proceeding as to the nature of the oil, and having failed to do so, the City should now be estopped from litigating in this court a claim that the substance was hazardous. Therefore, the motion to dismiss is granted, and the clerk may enter judgment accordingly.

2. *North Star Electrical Contracting v. Westinghouse Electric Corp.*, decided December 7, 1987, by the New York Supreme Court, New York County. Here, plaintiff moved to discontinue its action against the defendant and third-party defendants, but the third-party defendants objected, claiming that, since the court already had granted them partial summary judgment, a discontinuation would nullify that holding and its res judicata effects. But the court discounted that argument, holding that if a plaintiff should be forced to sue, the court would find the summary judgment disposition persuasive, regardless of res judicata. According to the court,

> This court fails to see how this would result in legal prejudice to the third-party defendants. Although this court's prior decision would become a legal nullity upon the discontinuance of this action and although it would no longer be res judicata in any subsequent lawsuit among the parties, presumably it would carry some persuasive weight. . . .
>
> Accordingly, the motion for leave to discontinue this action and the third-party action is granted. This is conditional upon payment by plaintiff to the third-party defendants of $100 costs plus disbursements within 30 days after service upon plaintiff's attorneys of an itemized bill of costs actually incurred by the third-party defendants (exclusive of counsel fees) (see Ruderman v. Brunn, 65 AD2d 771 [2d Dept. 1978]).

3. *Evans v. L. F. Rothschild, Unterberg, Towbin, Inc.*, decided November 19, 1987, by the New York Appellate Division, First Dept. Here, plaintiff had conferred discretionary authority on defendants to trade in securities on her behalf. She sued seeking to recover damages allegedly sustained as a result of defendant's breach of fiduciary duties, violation of contractual responsibilities, and negligence. Defendants appealed from a trial court order denying their motion to dismiss the complaint on grounds of res judicata because a federal

court had previously dismissed the complaint for failure to state a cause of action with respect to the same claim. The court affirmed, pointing out that the federal district court opinion "quite clearly recognized that the most substantial claim set forth was a State common law claim that the court did not address the merits . . . and had dismissed the claim solely on the basis that fraud had not been alleged with particularity required by Rule 9(b) of the Federal Rules of Civil Procedure. . . ."

4. *Taylor v. Ashby*, decided November 6, 1987, by the New York Appellate Division, Second Dept.[17] Here, in a negligence action to recover damages for personal injuries, the court opined:

> The doctrines of collateral estoppel and res judicata are applicable to give conclusive effect to quasi-judicial determinations of arbitrators and administrative agencies when rendered pursuant to their adjudicatory authority and employing procedures substantially similar to those used in a court of law (see, Ryan v. New York Tel. Co., 62 NY2d 494, 499; Matter of Ranni [Ross], 58 NY2d 715).
>
> The doctrine of collateral estoppel precludes a party from relitigating "an issue which has previously been decided against him in a proceeding in which he had a [full and] fair opportunity to litigate the point" (Gilberg v. Barbieri, 53 NY2d 285, 291). Two requirements must be satisfied before the doctrine may be invoked. First, the identical issue must necessarily have been decided in the prior action and be decisive of the present action, and second, the party to be precluded from relitigating the issue must have had a full and fair opportunity to contest the prior determination (see Kaufman v. Lilly & Co., 65 NY2d 449, 455).
>
> A review of the record herein indicates that the aforementioned criteria have been satisfied, and therefore summary judgment must be granted on the cross claims asserted against the defendant Lakshmi Paty. It should be noted, however, that this determination does not bar the plaintiffs from litigating their claims against any and all of the named defendants.

5. *Reardon v. Siegel*, decided January 13, 1988, by the New York Supreme Court, New York County. Here, defendant obtained an order to show cause and without giving adequate notice to the plaintiff and with the assistance of a police officer, gained possession of his former apartment. In a subsequent trial, plaintiff was awarded a judgment of possession, and plaintiff thereupon brought an action in the federal court alleging that defendants had violated her constitutional rights in depriving her of her right to property without due process of law. The federal court dismissed the action on the ground that there was no state action. Plaintiff then commenced this New York state action, but the court dismissed on res judicata grounds:

> The constitutional claims in the first cause of action are virtually identical to those dismissed in the federal action. Plaintiff, because she relies now on the New York State, rather than the United States, Constitution, claims that Judge Sprizzo's decision is not res judicata. However, our Court of Appeals has also expressly held—in Montalvo v.

Con Edison (92 AD2d 389 aff'd 61 NY2d 810 [1984]) and Sharrock v. Dell Buick–Cadillac, Inc. (45 NY2d 152 [1978])—that a claim of deprivation of protected constitutional right can only arise out of state action, and not from private action.

Here, the alleged corruption of the state process of litigation housing disputes by misuse of procedures—even if demonstrated to have been committed by defendants, and even affording plaintiff the benefit of every possible inference—cannot be said to be state action. To permit the cause of action to proceed to trial would clearly be a relitigation of that issue, and res judicata is therefore applicable.

6. *Green v. Santa Fe Industries.*[18] Here, plaintiffs-stockholders challenged a corporate merger alleging the merger was a violation of the Securities and Exchange Act of 1934. The case went up to the U.S. Supreme Court (430 US 462, 1977), which held against the plaintiffs. Then the plaintiffs filed in the federal district court claiming that the merger violated Section 352(c) of New York's Martin Act, but the court granted summary judgment to the defendant (576 F Supp 269, SDNY, 1983). Then, for the third time, plaintiffs filed in New York, joined this time by other stockholders, and again the New York court ruled that there was no claim under the Martin Act because that act did not provide for a private cause of action for fraudulent acts. In the 1987 litigation the defendant argued that simply adding new plaintiffs did not alter the case for res judicata; the new plaintiffs were not in privity with the other plaintiffs. But the New York Court of Appeals decided to give the plaintiffs another bite of the apple: "In addition to the conventional privity found in the foregoing cases, courts have also precluded parties from raising claims previously litigated when the party to be precluded can be said to have controlled the conduct of the prior action to further his own interests. . . . " The court found that there was no evidence that the prior actions had been "managed" by the same attorney, and the new plaintiff had, at most, only "monitored" the previous actions, so that the new plaintiff was not precluded!

7. In *Commissioner of Internal Revenue v. Sunnen* the U.S. Supreme Court declared:

> It is first necessary to understand something of the recognized meaning and scope of *res judicata*, a doctrine judicial in origin. The general rule of *res judicata* applies to repetitious suits involving the same cause of action. It rests upon considerations of economy of judicial time and public policy favoring the establishment of certainty in legal relations. The rule provides that when a court of competent jurisdiction has entered a final judgment on the merits of a cause of action, the parties to the suit and their privies are thereafter bound "not only as to every matter which was offered and received to sustain or defeat the claim or demand, but as to any other admissible matter which might have been offered for that purpose." Cromwell v. County of Sac. 94 U.S. 351, 352, 24 L.Ed. 195. The judgment puts an end to the cause of action, which cannot again be brought. . . . [19]

8. In *Country Mutual Insurance Co. v. Duncan*, 794 F2d 1211 (7th Cir., 1986), the federal appellate court declined to accept the insurer's argument that

a plea of guilty to voluntary manslaughter on the part of the insured estopped the insured from denying the intentionality of his actions. The insured here fatally shot a man he found asleep in bed with the insured's wife. Although the insured was charged with murder, he pleaded guilty to the lesser charge. A jury found that the insured had not acted intentionally and therefore the insurer had an obligation to defend: "A guilty plea, like any other admission, is not necessarily conclusive as to the facts underlying the plea but is subject to explanation." The court opined that the shooting could have been caused by an "irrestistible impulse" and therefore was not intentional! To the contrary was the Michigan case of *Group Insurance Co. v. Morelli*, 314 NW2d 672 (Mich. App., 1981), where the court ruled that the plea of guilty to second degree murder established that the insured performed a willful and wanton act tending to cause death or great bodily harm.

In the case of arbitration awards, the doctrine of res judicata has also played an important role as evidenced by *Gemco Latinoamerica, Inc. v. Seiko Time Corp.*[20] Here the federal district court for the Southern District of New York ruled that the doctrine of res judicata not only bars a second suit involving the same parties based upon the same cause of action, but even "precludes the parties and their privies from relitigating issues that were or could have been raised in the prior proceeding."[21] The arbitration award clearly barred the distributor's claims against the supplier for breach of contract, breach of duty to deal in good faith, and violation of Puerto Rican law on unfair competition. The New York Court of Appeals in *Claim of Guimarales*[22] ruled that the lower courts "erred in not giving collateral estoppel effect to the arbitrator's factual findings regarding claimant's conduct and to his conclusion of insubordination. . . . The Appeal Board and the administrative law judge, although bound by the arbitrator's factual findings regarding claimant's conduct and his conclusion of insubordination, were free to make their independent additional factual findings and form their own independent conclusion as to whether such conduct constituted misconduct for purposes of unemployment insurance."[23] It would appear that New York's highest court may have blurred the distinction between res judicata and collateral estoppel for the purposes of this case! However, the fact remains that arbitration can play a strong role in avoiding needless relitigation of claims raised or claims that could have been raised between parties and those privy to them arising out of the same facts.[24]

COLLATERAL ESTOPPEL

The doctrine of collateral estoppel is but a part of the preclusive device of res judicata, for collateral estoppel addresses issue preclusion, not claim or case preclusion.[25] In *People v. Acevedo* the New York Court of Appeals ruled that collateral estoppel can apply to "evidentiary facts" as well as "ultimate facts"; here the defendant was charged with robbery for two separate incidents and was acquitted on the first charge; during the trial on the second charge, the trial court permitted the alleged victim of the first robbery to testify to having seen the defendant the night of both robberies.[26] Accordingly, collateral estoppel applied to bar relitigation of these "evidentiary facts." In *Gerney v. Tishman Construction Corp.* the New York court ruled that criminal proceedings resulting in conviction of defendants collaterally estopped the defendants from defending their liability in a civil case.[27] The court stated that the first of the two requirements of collateral estoppel, that is, identity of issues, was satisfied because the elements of negligence in the civil suit were included in the criminal assault charges: "Although there is a difference in terms of negligent and intentional conduct, the elements of negligence are clearly subsumed into the element of assault." On the second requirement of collateral estoppel, the court ruled that both parties had a "full and fair" opportunity to litigate the question of their guilt in the criminal proceedings. But in *Country Mutual Insurance Co. v. Duncan*, the federal appellate court declined to accept the insurer's contention that a plea of guilty to voluntary manslaughter collaterally estopped the defendant from denying the intentionality of his criminal act.[28]

The U.S. Supreme Court in *Parklane Hosiery Co. v. Shore* sanctioned collateral estoppel in favor of a plaintiff who was *not* a party to the first action so as to bar the defendant from relitigating the issues that had been decided against the defendant in the first suit.[29] But "offensive" collateral estoppel could not be used if (a) the plaintiff could easily have joined in the first suit; (b) the defendant in the first action was sued for small or nominal damages and therefore did not have an adequate incentive to litigate; (c) the judgment relied upon for its collateral estoppel effects "is itself inconsistent with one or more previous judgments in favor of the defendant"; or (d) "the second action affords the defendant procedural opportunities unavailable in the first action that could readily cause a different result." This procedural gimmick is important in view of Section 5(a) of the Clayton Act, as amended, which provides that a final judgment obtained in a civil or criminal proceeding brought by the United States will be "prima facie evidence against such defendant in any action . . . brought by any other party against such defendant under said laws as to all matters respecting which such judgment or decree would be an estoppel as between the parties thereto. . . . " This statute means that once the government has successfully brought an antitrust suit against a defendant, all private parties injured by the same violations of the antitrust law may file suit against the defendant and have the benefit of a rebuttable presumption that the defendant violated the antitrust laws.

"The determination of whether to accord collateral estoppel effect to the quasi-judicial determination of an administrative agency must focus upon the realities of the prior litigation," according to the New York Court of Appeals in *Clemens v. Apple*.[30] The court observed that once the issue of identity between the prior and pending actions is established, "certain factors should be considered to determine whether a full and fair opportunity to litigate the issue at the bar existed including 'the nature of the forum and the importance of the claim in the prior litigation, the incentive and initiative to litigate and the actual extent of litigation, the competence and expertise of counsel, the availability of new evidence, the differences in the applicable law and the foreseeability of future litigation.' "[31] In *People v. Vera* the New York court proclaimed that collateral estoppel roams where double jeopardy fears to tread; here defendant was found not guilty of attempted arson but guilty of arson; the court then vacated the guilty verdict because new testimonial evidence was available; but before the second trial could begin, the prosecutor informed the court that he intended to elicit testimony concerning the attempted arson charge to demonstrate "identity."[32] The court concluded that the use of this testimony would not violate the double jeopardy provision of the state or federal Constitution, but that such testimony would be barred at trial under common law doctrine of collateral estoppel.[33]

The following recent cases illustrate collateral estoppel in action:

1. *People v. Kurshan*, decided March 10, 1988, by the New York Criminal Court, New York County. Here, in a prior case, defendant was charged with aggravated harassment stemming from a dispute between defendant and his upstairs neighbor. At the arraignment defendant was ordered to stop harassment but allegedly continued to do so, and the present case was brought against defendant for criminal contempt. Although defendant was acquitted of the underlying aggravated harassment, the court ruled that the state of New York was not barred from relitigating the crucial evidentiary issue since the intent requirement for conviction of aggravated harassment is separate and distinct from that required for conviction of criminal contempt. The court opined:

> The doctrine of collateral estoppel, although having its genesis in civil litigation, is recognized as having application to criminal proceedings as well. People v. Goodman, 69 N.Y.2d 32 (1986); see People v. Sailor, 65 N.Y.2d 224, 228 (1985); People v. Plevy, 52 N.Y.2d 58, 64–65 (1980); People v. Berkowitz, 50 N.Y.2d 333, 344 (1980); Matter of McGrath v. Gold, 36 N.Y.2d 406, 411 (1975); United States v. Oppenheimer, 242 U.S. 85 (1916). The doctrine, however, is not applied in a criminal setting in a fashion identical to that in a civil forum because the overriding concern in a criminal proceeding is to reach a correct result, as distinguished from the goal of economy of time and resources which is the objective in its civil application. (People v. Plevy, supra, at pp. 64–65).
>
> The doctrine acts to bar, in a new proceeding, relitigation of matters already decided with finality in a prior proceeding. Such a "final judgment" precludes the same parties from relitigating such a matter in a future suit. Matter of McGrath v. Gold, supra, at p. 411. Although the doctrine traditionally precluded the relitigation of matters of "ultimate fact" involved in the prior proceeding, the doctrine has been utilized to bar the relitigation of evidentiary issues as well. People v. Acevedo, 69 N.Y.2d 478 (1987); see Ashe v. Swenson, 397 U.S. 436 (1970).
>
> The application of the doctrine requires the satisfaction of a three-prong standard in order to preclude relitigation of either an ultimate or evidentiary issue. First, there must be an identity of parties [People v. Berkowitz, supra, at p. 345; People v. Reisman, 29 N.Y.2d 278, 285 (1971); People v. LoCicero, 14 N.Y.2d 374, 386 (1964)]. Next, there

must also be an identity of the issue involved [see People ex rel. Dowdy v. Smith, 48 N.Y.2d 477, 482–483 (1979); People v. Reisman, supra, 29 N.Y.2d 278, 285] and third, a final judgment on the merits must have resolved the particular issue in question, with the parties having been afforded a full and fair opportunity to litigate such issue. [See People v. Sailor, supra, at p. 229; People v. Berkowitz, supra, at p. 347; Schwartz v. Public Administrator, 24 N.Y.2d 65 (1969).]

The People are not estopped from pursuing prosecution of the criminal contempt charge. The evidentiary issue of verbal abuse litigated at the defendant's harassment trial is not the same issue sought to be litigated at his impending criminal contempt trial. The alleged verbal abuse of the complainant was not necessarily an integral part of the harassment by letter determination nor a necessary issue in the defendant's acquittal. The charges now leveled against the defendant, although apparently arising from one dispute, are distinct from the prior criminal proceeding. This branch of the defendant's motion is therefore denied.

The doctrine enjoys constitutional status in that it is embodied in the Fifth Amendment guarantee against double jeopardy. The doctrine guides the several states by virtue of the Fifth Amendment's incorporation into the Due Process clause of the Fourteenth Amendment to the United States Constitution. Ashe v. Swenson, supra; Benton v. Maryland, 395 U.S. 784 (1969). Such incorporation guarantees "that the state with all its resources and power [shall] not be allowed to make repeated attempts to convict an individual for an alleged offense, thereby subjecting him to embarrassment, expense and ordeal and compelling him to live in a continuing state of anxiety and insecurity. . . . " Green v. United States, 355 U.S. 184, 187 (1957). Indeed, New York statutory law presents a "generous version" of the double jeopardy defense. See Bellacosa, Practice Commentary, McKinney's Cons. Laws of N.Y., Book 11A CPL §40.10, pp. 243–244.

Applicability of the doctrine requires that the court determine what was actually resolved in the first trial and the relationship between that resolution and the issue sought to be litigated in the second trial. [United States v. Mespoulede, 597 F.2d 329, 333 (1979); United States v. Kramer, 289 F.2d 909, 913 (1961). Initially, the court must assume that the jury reached a rational verdict. See Ashe v. Swenson, supra, at p. 444]. The onus is then upon the defendant first to identify the issue on which he seeks to foreclose evidence and then demonstrate that the very same issue was resolved in his favor by verdict at the first trial. People v. Goodman, supra, at p. 40; United States v. Mespoulede, supra, at p. 333. . . .

Accordingly, upon application of the three-prong standard necessary to be satisfied to establish collateral estoppel in the instant case, it becomes apparent that only the parties are identical—that the issue of intent involved in the instant case is not the *same* issue as was involved in the prior proceeding. Thus there was not necessarily, in the prior proceeding, a full hearing and final judgment on the merits on the issue of intent in the instant case.

2. *Goodman v. Temco Service Industries, Inc.*, decided December 22, 1987, by the New York Supreme Court, New York County. Here, a plaintiff, while exiting an elevator in a building owned by his employer, slipped and fell on the lobby floor injuring his back. He filed a claim for workers' compensation benefits, which were denied since the accident did not arise out of the course

of his employment. Plaintiff then commenced action against the building owner alleging negligence, and defendants argued that he was collaterally estopped from bringing the action. But the court rejected defendant's argument because there was not an identity of issues in the two actions. According to the court:

> Before invoking collateral estoppel to bar relitigation of an issue, '[t]here must be an identity of issue which has necessarily been decided in the prior action and is decisive of the present action, and, second, there must have been a full and fair opportunity to contest the decision now said to be controlling.' (Schwartz v. Public Administrator, 24 NY2d 65, 71 [1969]). Because the issues to be determined on the negligence cause of action are not identical to those decided by the Board, Goodman is not collaterally estopped by the Board's dismissal of his claim from bringing the first cause of action. In view of this holding, that branch of Universal's motion seeking summary judgment on the first cause of action is denied.
>
> Where Workers' Compensation benefits are denied on the ground that an accident did not arise out of or in the course of a claimant's employment, a claimant may avail him/herself of any common law remedies that may exist, and the employer may not assert as a defense, the exclusivity of the Workers' Compensation Law (Weber v. State of New York, 111 Misc 2d 809 [Ct. of Claims 1981]; see also Milshouskas v. Mercy Hospital, 64 AD2d 978 [2d Dept. 1978]).

3. *Courtney v. Nuding*.[34] Here, the decision of the administrative law judge at a driver's license revocation hearing was not given collateral estoppel effect in a subsequent civil action because the quantum of proof in the prior administrative proceeding fell far short of the level required in civil actions. Furthermore, for collateral estoppel to apply, the original action must be a final judgment or order.

4. *Costa v. State of New York*, decided February 11, 1987, by the New York Court of Claims. Here, the state of New York was sued for the wrongful death of plaintiff's husband who apparently committed suicide by taking an overdose of a prescribed medication shortly after his release from involuntary commitment at a mental institution. Plaintiff argued that the physician who prescribed the medication should have realized that her husband was suicidal and should have prescribed a smaller amount that could not cause death if taken at once. The court rejected her argument on the grounds that a court had ordered the patient's release after his family had contended that he was not a danger to himself or to others, and that determination constituted a collateral estoppel, precluding plaintiff from taking the opposite position that her husband was suicidal when released from the mental institution. According to the court: "The doctrine of collateral estoppel applies here as there was an identity of issue which was necessarily decided in the prior action and there was a full opportunity to contest the issue (Schwartz v. Public Administrator, 24 NY2d 65). The decedent, or in this instance, his representative, may not now repudiate or impeach the conclusion which they previously advanced and upon which the prior Court order was premised (50 CJS, Judgments, §727). Implicit in that

order was a finding that he was not a danger to himself or others (Mental Hygiene Law §9.33; In the Matter of Carl C., 126 AD2d 640).''

5. *Matter of Ettore v. Angela D.*, decided by the New York Appellate Division, Second Dept., on March 30, 1987. Here, the petitioner instituted a paternity proceeding claiming to be the father of a three-year-old child, and blood tests indicated that he could be the father of the child. Both the mother and her husband opposed the late application as did the child's guardian. But the family court judge asserted that collateral estoppel was not available in a paternity proceeding, and declared that petitioner was the child's father. But the appellate court reversed: ''The excuse offered by petitioner, in an attempt to justify his delay (in claiming paternity) is patently insufficient to defeat the defense of estoppel, for any party against whom the doctrine is invoked could claim inaction out of a desire to protect existing relationships. Acceptance of such a self-serving excuse (that he did not want to interrupt the relationship which subsequently resulted in a separation of the wife and her husband) would be fundamentally inconsistent with the purpose of estoppel which is to protect innocent children from an irreparable loss of legal rights and status, and to protect the right of unsuspecting persons who have developed strong bonds with the child during the period of inaction.'' The court concluded:

> The efficacy of the doctrine of estoppel, as it applies to paternity proceedings, achieved full recognition in *Matter of Sharon GG. v. Duane HH.* (95 AD2d 466, *affd* 63 NY2d 859). In the *Sharon GG.* case, the petitioner, the mother of the child, commenced a paternity proceeding, naming her boyfriend as the child's biological father. She thereafter sought to compel her estranged husband to submit to an HLA test. The Appellate Division, Third Department, upon an appeal by the mother and boyfriend, affirmed the Family Court's order denying the application for the HLA test and its dismissal of the petition on estoppel grounds. Significantly, the court stated:
>
>> Estoppel is equally as applicable to a paternity proceeding in Family Court as it was to the divorce actions in the cited cases. In each instance, the purpose of the challenge to the paternity of the mother's husband was to deprive him of his parental rights and status, with a concomitant loss of rights and status for the child. . . . [T]he desirability that the child know its true father . . . is not sufficient to overcome the undisputed equities in the husband's favor nor the benefits to the child accruing by preserving its legitimacy. (*Matter of Sharon GG. v. Duane HH., supra,* at pp. 468–469)

We note that, in general, the doctrine of equitable estoppel may successfully be invoked, in the interest of fairness, to prevent the enforcement of rights which would ultimately work fraud or injustice upon the person against whom enforcement is sought (*see, Nassau Trust Co. v. Montrose Concrete Prods. Corp.*, 56 NY2d 175, 184). An estoppel defense may also be invoked where the failure to promptly assert a right has given rise to circumstances rendering it inequitable to permit the exercise of the right after a lapse of time (*see*, 57 NY Jur. 2d, Estoppel, Ratification & Waiver, §27). Because of the same qualitative considerations which support the invocation of estoppel in other areas of law, the courts, in more recent years, have recognized the availability of this doctrine as a viable defense in various forms of proceedings involving domestic disputes.

In *Hill v. Hill* (20 AD2d 923), for example, the defense of estoppel was successfully invoked against a mother, who, in the context of a divorce action, attempted to secure custody of her nine-year-old son, by claiming that her husband was not the child's father. Cognizant of the adverse social, legal and psychological ramifications of illegitimatizing children, this court rejected the mother's assertions, noting:

> Common sense, public policy, reason and the overriding consideration for the welfare of the child will bar a wife from bastardizing her child where, as here, she lived with her husband as his wife during the period of conception and birth of the child and for six years thereafter all the while concealing from him the adultery to which she now confesses for the sole purpose of securing the child's custody. (*Hill v. Hill, supra*, at p. 924)

The Court of Appeals' uanimous adoption of the foregoing analysis (*see, Matter of Sharon GG. v. Duane HH.*, 63 NY2d 859, *supra*) reinforces our decision to apply the doctrine of estoppel in this case. Unlike the Family Court, we are not moved to any different determination in this case simply because we are confronted with a putative father who affirmatively seeks to establish his paternity, rather than a spouse who seeks to contest it, as was the situation in each of the cited cases. It would be incongruous, illogical and unrealistic to conclude that a child would be any less devastated by being forced to accept a stranger as her father merely because the stranger initiated the legal proceeding. . . . "

It is of more than passing interest to note that a criminal conviction will collaterally estop the defendant's later assertion of a civil claim arising from the same transaction.[35] In the *S. T. Grand* case plaintiff had sued the City of New York on a contract for the cleaning of a reservoir, and the City had moved for a summary judgment on the ground that plaintiff had been convicted in federal court for bribery in obtaining that very contract with the City.[36] The New York Court of Appeals affirmed the summary judgment for the City because the criminal conviction was conclusive on the question of the legality of the contract.[37]

6. *Brieant v. Buettner-Janush*, decided April 15, 1988, by the New York Supreme Court, Westchester County. Here, the former chairman of the anthropology department of New York University, serving a 40-year prison term for mailing poisoned boxes of chocolates to a federal judge and former colleague, was found liable for injuries suffered by the judge's wife after she ate the poisoned candy. The defendant had argued that his liability on the civil claims should not be established by operation of the doctrine of collateral estoppel because, even though he admitted mailing a box of poisoned chocolates, he had not conceded that he was involved in plaintiff's injuries. According to the court that ordered a partial summary judgment in favor of the plaintiff:

> The plaintiff's motion is based on the principle of collateral estoppel. Defendant's criminal conviction, plaintiff argues, is conclusive in subsequent civil litigation as to issues litigated and adjudicated previously (S. T. Grand v. City of New York, 32 NY2d 300; Schwartz v. Public Administrator of County of the Bronx, 24 NY2d 95). Collateral estoppel or issue preclusion as it is termed, prevents the relitigation of identical issues

previously decided—so long as a full and fair opportunity to contest the accusation was had.

Defendant argues that the Judgment of Conviction submitted by plaintiff is not conclusive proof of the identity of issues between the criminal and civil actions, because the judgment states only that defendant mailed a box of poisoned chocolates and does not state defendant mailed the chocolates specifically to plaintiff.

The issue before this court is whether the submitted proofs conclusively establish identical issues between the criminal and civil actions so as to prevent defendant from relitigating the issue that he mailed poisoned chocolates to plaintiff.

CPLR 3212(b) requires on a motion for summary judgment that the opposing party "come forward and lay bare his proofs of evidentiary facts showing there is bona fide issue requiring a trial" (McKinneys Consolid. Laws CPLR 3212, Commentary by David Siegel C 3212:16 citing Hanson v. Ontario Milk Producer's Coop., Inc., 58 M 2d 138). "If a key fact appears in the movant's papers and the opposing party makes no reference to it, he is deemed to have admitted it" (Commentary by Siegel, supra, citing Laye v. Shepard, 58 M 2d 478. affd 25 AD 2d 4 98 [1st D. 1966]). "Evasiveness in an opposing affidavit—indirect reference to the key facts, undue accents on immaterial points and any other mode of behavior which suggests that the opposing party really cannot deny the movant's evidence—will give it an aura of sham and increase the prospects for a grant of the motion" (Commentary by Siegel, supra).

Since defendant has failed to deny that he mailed the poisoned candy to plaintiff, and that he pleaded guilty to mailing the poisoned package to plaintiff at her home he is deemed to have admitted these crucial facts. The facts cannot now be raised as an issue to be tried, so as to defeat plaintiff's motion for summary judgment. CPLR 3212(b).

Nor has the defendant's claim that causation is an issue of fact to be determined at trial, which would serve to defeat plaintiff's summary judgment motion, any greater merit. It is basic handbook law that one is held responsible for the consequences which reasonably flow from his acts (Prosser Law of Torts, sec. 9, 43 [4th ed.]). The sole and inescapable inference arising from the facts in this case is that harmful consequences were reasonably foreseeable and that defendant's act was the proximate cause of damages sustained by the plaintiff who ate the poisoned chocolates which defendant mailed. The extent of plaintiff's injuries has yet to be determined.

7. Collateral estoppel was applied to administrative rulings by the New York Court of Appeals on July 7, 1988, in *Allied Chemical v. Niagara Power Corp.* The court summarized the problem:

The elements necessary in all cases for issue preclusion are well known. It is required that an issue in the present proceeding be identical to that necessarily decided in a prior proceeding, and that in the prior proceeding the party against whom preclusion is sought was accorded a full and fair opportunity to contest the issue (*Schwartz v. Public Administrator*, 24 NY2d 65, 71; *Ryan v. New York Telephone Co.*, 62 NY2d 494, 500–502). While issue preclusion may arise from the determinations of administrative agencies, in that context the doctrine is applied more flexibly, and additional factors must be considered by the court (cf. *Staatsburg Water Co. v. Staatsburg Fire District*, NY2d [decided today]). These additional requirements are often summed up in the beguilingly simple prerequisite that the administrative decision be "quasi-judicial" in character (*see, e.g. Ryan v. New York Telephone Co., supra*, at 500; *Bernstein v. Birch Walthan School*, 71 AD2d 129, 132, *aff'd* 51 NY2d 932 . However, the determination of whether an agency proceeding was quasi-judicial actually involves a multifaceted inquiry.

First, the court must make the threshold determination that the agency has the statutory authority to act adjudicatively. If the agency has such authority, the court must then ascertain whether the procedures used in the administrative proceeding assured that the information presented to the agency were sufficient both quantitatively and qualitatively, so as to permit confidence that the facts asserted were adequately tested, and the issue was fully aired (*see, Brugman v. City of New York*, 64 NY2d 1011, 1012; *Ryan v. New York Telephone Co., supra*, 498; 4 Davis, Administrative Law Treatise, §21:3 [2d ed. 1983]; Restatement [Second] of Judgments §83). Additionally, the expectation of the parties is important in determining the fairness of applying issue preclusion in a particular case; thus, a party explicitly soliciting resolution of an issue from an agency, who fully participates in the administrative proceeding which follows with the expectation that all will be bound by the result reached there, may be fairly precluded from relitigating the issue in a subsequent proceeding (*see, Staatsburg Water Co. v. Staatsburg Fire Dist., supra*). The court must look at the overall context of the agency's decision to assess whether according a preclusive effect to a particular agency determination is consistent with the agency's scheme of administration; for example, the agency's need for flexibility, and its need to modify prior determinations in order to adapt its policy to changing contitions, may counsel against applying issue preclusion to a particular administrative decision (*see, Matter of Venes v. Community School Bd.*, 43 NY2d 520, 525; *Second Taxing District of City of Norwalk v. Federal Energy Regulatory Commn.*, 683 F2d 477, 484).

Applying these factors and considerations to the case now before us, we conclude that a preclusive effect is properly accorded to the PSC's determination that the new tariff was not an "applicable rate" under the contract. First, there can be no doubt that it is within the PSC's statutory mandate to act adjudicatively (see, *Long Island Lighting Co. v. Transamerica Delaval*, 646 F Supp 1442).

8. The same day of July 7, 1988, the New York Court of Appeals also issued its opinion in *Staatsburg Water Co. v. Staatsburg Fire District*. Chief Judge Wachtler stated at the outset that, unlike the determination in the *Allied Chemical* case above, the principle of issue preclusion was not applicable:

This convoluted procedural background gives rise to a straight-forward question: Should the PSC's determination that plaintiff's service to defendant was adequate be binding on defendant in this litigation? Plaintiff's primary contention is that the doctrine of collateral estoppel precludes relitigation of the issue.

The relevant principles may be quickly restated. Collateral estoppel, or issue preclusion, may be invoked in a subsequent action or proceeding to prevent a party from relitigating an issue decided against that party in a prior adjudication (Ryan v. New York Tel Co., supra at 500; Schwartz v. Public Administrator of County of Bronx, 24 NY2d 65, 70). It is now familiar law that "the doctrines of res judicata and collateral estoppel are applicable to give conclusive effect to the quasi-judicial determinations of administrative agencies . . . when rendered pursuant to the adjudicatory authority of an agency to decide cases brought before its tribunal employing procedures substantially similar to those used in a court of law'' (*Ryan v. New York Tel Co.*, supra, at 499 [citations omitted]). Whether the prior adjudication occurred in the context of an administrative determination, an arbitration or a full-fledged judicial proceeding, issue preclusion is applicable only if there is ''an identity of issue which has necessarily been decided in the prior action and is decisive of the present action and [there was] a full and fair opportunity to contest the decision now said to be controlling'' (*Schwartz v. Public Administrator of County of Bronx*, supra, at 71).

In addition, we have consistently emphasized that these principles are not to be mechanically applied as a mere checklist. Collateral estoppel is an elastic doctrine and the enumeration of these elements is intended as a framework, rather than a substitute, for analysis. For example, the question whether a party had a full and fair opportunity to contest the prior decision is not answered simply by reference to the procedural benefits available in the first forum or by a conclusion that the requirements of due process were satisfied (see, *Gilberg v. Barbieri*, 53 NY2d 285, 292). Instead, the analysis requires consideratiton of ''the realities of litigation,'' such as recognition that if the first proceeding involved trivial stakes, it may not have been litigated vigorously (*see id.* at 292–293; *Schwartz v. Public Administrator of County of Bronx*, supra, at 72).

In the end, the fundamental inquiry is whether relitigation should be permitted in a particular case in light of what are often competing policy considerations, including fairness to the parties, conservation of the resources of the court and the litigants, and the societal interests in consistent and accurate results. No rigid rules are possible, because even these factors may vary in relative importance depending on the nature of the proceedings (*see, Gilberg v. Barbieri*, supra, at 291–292; *People v. Berkowitz*, 50 NY2d 333, 344; *Matter of Venes v. Community School Bd.*, 43 NY2d 520, 524).

With these principles in mind, we conclude that the proceeding which led to the PSC's determination suffers from a number of defects which in combination, deprive it of preclusive effect. These defects all spring from the fact that the PSC's finding was, in essence, an unsolicited advisory opinion made outside the context of any complaint pending before the agency and without any direct consequences for defendant.

As a result, defendant was not, in the true sense of the word, a party to the PSC proceeding—a basic prerequisite for application of the doctrine (see, *Liss v. Trans Auto Sys.*, 68 NY2d 15; *Gilberg v. Barbieri*, supra, at 291). Significantly, defendant did not choose to litigate the parties' dispute before the PSC (*cf. Clemens v. Apple*, 65 NY2d 746; *Ryan v. New York Tel Co.*, 62 NY2d 494, supra). Had defendant filed a complaint with the PSC concerning the adequacy of the fire protection service (see, Public Service Law §§ 89-i, 89-j; 16 NYCRR 12.1), and thereby submitted to the PSC's jurisdiction over the matter, we might take a different view (*cf. Allied Chemical v. Niagara Mohawk Power Corp.*, NY2d [decided today]). . . . The doctrine of primary jurisdiction ''applies where a claim is originally cognizable in the courts, and comes into play whenever enforcement of the claim requires the resolution of issues which, under a regulatory scheme, have been placed within the special competence of an administrative body; in such a case the judicial process is suspended pending referral of such issues to the administrative body for its views'' (*United States v. Western Pacific R. Co.*, 352 US 59, 64; *see, Flacke v. Onondaga Landfill Systems*, 69 NY2d 355, 362; *Capital Tel. Co. v. Pattersonville Tel Co.*, 56 NY2d 11, 22; *see generally*, Jaffe, Primary Jurisdiction, 77 Harv L Rev 1037). It is apparent from this definition that the doctrine is not a license for an agency to interject itself into a pending court action, as the PSC attempted to do here. It is for the court to determine whether the doctrine is triggered by issues presented in a lawsuit and, if so, to refer such issues for the agency's resolution (*see, Nader v. Allegheny Airlines*, 426 US 290, 303–304; *Capital Tel. Co. v.'Pattersonville Tel Co.*, supra, at 22–23).

Notably, however, neither plaintiff nor defendant requested the court to refer any issues in this case to the PSC for resolution. Thus, this appeal does not require us to decide whether such an application should have been granted and we express no view on that question. Nor does the doctrine bolster plaintiff's collateral estoppel argument. Even assuming that the doctrine of primary jurisdiction is applicable because the PSC has special competence to decide the question, the barriers to application of issue preclusion remain. The competence or expertness of the tribunal does not neutralize the defects that we have identified and, in the absence of a reference of the issue to the agency to the court, the doctrine of primary jurisdiction does not provide an independent basis for giving the determination binding effect in this litigation. . . . For all of these reasons, we conclude that the PSC's determination is not entitled to preclusive effect and that, therefore, plaintiff's motion for summary judgment should not have been granted. However, the Appellate Division did not abuse its discretion in allowing plaintiff to amend the ad damnum clause of its complaint (*see, Loomis v. Civetta Corinno Constr. Corp.*, 54 NY2d 18).

9. And the third case decided by the New York Court of Appeals on July 7, 1988, was *In Matter of Halyalker v. Board of Regents*, dealing with the need for issue determination. The highest New York court opined that:

> the issue of petitioner's guilt of knowing and wilful misconduct cannot be said to have been actually litigated in the New Jersey proceeding or determined in the consent order and that, therefore, the necessary identicality of issue was not established (see, *Schwartz v. Public Administrator*, supra, at 71). A contrary holding would contravene precedent (see, *Kaufman v. Lilly & Co.*, supra, at pp. 456, 457) and the concept of fairness underlying the doctrine of collateral estoppel (see, *Gilberg v. Barbieri*, supra, at p. 291; Rosenberg, *Collateral Estoppel in New York*, 44 St. John's L Rev 173–182; Carlisle, *Getting a Full Bite of the Apple*: When Should the Doctrine of Issue Preclusion Make an Administrative or Arbitral Determination Binding in a Court of Law, 55 Fordham L Rev 63, 84–94, 99).[38]

10. In *Blake v. State of New York*, decided by the New York Court of Claims on December 15, 1988, res judicata was held to preclude a second suit against the same employee of the state who had allegedly injured the plaintiff, because "the issues raised in this second claim are the same as those previously resolved by the trial of the first action. They may not now be relitigated in another . . . court." (N.B. Issue-preclusion here is truly estoppel, not res judicata).

NOTES

1. See generally Warren Freedman, Res Judicata and Collateral Estoppel (1988).
2. Id. at Chapters 3 and 4.
3. Unreported (NY County, March 2, 1988).

4. 516 NYS2d 22 (July 1, 1987).

5. The court continued: "This is especially significant when the order made on motion is dispositive rather than interlocutory or intermediate. An order granting a motion for summary judgment, for example, should get res judicata treatment in an attempted second action, but here questions are usually avoided by getting a formal 'judgment' entered on the order. *Failure to do so, however, should not be controlling* [emphasis added]. Even in the appeal process today New York plays down the significance between judgments and orders: if one is appealed when the order should have been, the omission is disregarded as long as a copy of the proper paper is ultimately furnished to the appellate court."

6. Unreported (Dec. 17, 1986).

7. Manego v. Orleans Board of Trade, 773 F2d 1 (1st Cir., 1985), cert. den. 106 S. Ct. 1466 (1886).

8. See generally 82 ALR Fed. 829 (1985).

9. Supra note 1 at Chapter 3 therein.

10. 449 US 90 (1980).

11. 465 US 75 (1984).

12. See Minneapolis Auto Parts Co. v. City of Minneapolis, 739 F2d 408 (8th Cir., 1984). Note also Tomkins v. Gargiul 104 S. Ct. 1263 (1984).

13. Unreported (1987).

14. According to the court, "The Federal court, in its judgment dated Nov. 2, 1984, declined to exercise pendent jurisdiction, and dismissed without prejudice to renew in the State court plaintiff's pendent State claims as to the negligence of the defendants. According to the Federal court, this did not preserve the remainder of plaintiff's pendent State claims, and there is no basis for this court to expand the Federal court's judgment in order to permit plaintiff to renew all of his State claims. Any disagreement plaintiff has with the interpretation of the Federal court judgment should have been brought to the attention of that court, and it is not for this court to resolve such a disagreement.

Furthermore, it is apparent that plaintiff is relying upon the same evidence to make his case against the defendants herein as was adduced in the Federal court. However, where the elements of proof required for Federal and State actions are nearly identical, a prior federal determination may effectively bar a subsequent State action (Zarcone v. Perry, 55 NY2d 782, affg 78 AD2d 70; Hines v. City of Buffalo, 79 AD2d 218). In the case at bar, plaintiff's causes of action for false arrest, false imprisonment, malicious prosecution, and the intentional infliction of emotional distress require virtually the same proof, both as to the prima facie elements and damages, which the federal causes of action pursuant to section 1983 of title 42 of the United States Code comprehends. Therefore, as plaintiff's prior federal action resulted in a verdict and judgment dismissing the section 1983 claims against defendants Scherer and the City, these causes of action are barred by the principles of res judicata (Perry v. Zarcone, 55 NY2d 782 affg 78 AD2d 70, 77).

In addition, plaintiff concedes that the within cause of action for false arrest is barred by the doctrine of res judicata. The Federal court during the course of the trial dismissed the false arrest claim, without objection, on the basis of defendant Scherer's testimony. Thus, as the Federal court necessarily determined that there was probable cause for the arrest, and as false arrest is merely another name for the tort of false imprisonment, plaintiff is barred from relitigating these claims (see Broughton v. State of New York, 37 NY2d 451). Moreover, as plaintiff previously pled guilty to a count of attempted burglary in the second degree based on this incident, he may not maintain an action for false arrest or malicious prosecution (Jones v. Foster, 43 App Div 33; see, also, Bradford v. Lefkowitz, 240 F Supp 969).''

15. 442 US 127 (1979).
16. 54 USLW 5084 (1986).
17. 520 NYS2d 587 (1987).
18. 519 NYS2d 793 (1987).
19. 333 US 591 (1948).
20. 671 F. Supp. 972 (SDNY, 1987).
21. Id. at 978.
22. 68 NY2d 989, 510 NYS2d 558 (1986).
23. Id.
24. See, for example, Schwartz v. Public Administrator, 298 NYS2d 995, 246 NE2d 725 (1969), Federated Department Stores, Inc. v. Moltie, 452 US 394 (1981), and Shearson/American Express v. McMahon, 107 S. Ct. 2332 (1987).
25. Supra note 1 in Chapter 4.
26. 68 NY2d 665, 496 NE2d 688 (1987).
27. 518 NYS2d 564 (1987).
28. 794 F2d 1211 (7th Cir., 1986) Cf. Hopps v. Utica Mutual Insurance Co., 106 A2d 294 (N.H., 1985) where the New Hampshire Supreme Court applied the doctrine of collateral estoppel to preclude the insured, who was convicted of arson, from collecting on the fire insurance policy.
29. 439 US 322 (1979).
30. 65 NY2d 746 (1986).
31. See Dusovic v. New Jersey Transit Bus Operations, Inc., 124 AD2d 634, 508 NYS2d 26 (2d Dept., Nov. 14, 1986): ''At the outset, it should be made clear that the doctrines of res judicata and collateral estoppel are applicable to give conclusive effect to the quasi-judicial determinations of administrative agencies (Matter of Evans v. Monaghan, 306 N.Y. 312, 323–324; Parklane Hosiery Co. v. Shore, 439 US 322; see, also, Restatement Judgments 2d §83) when rendered pursuant to the adjudicatory authority of an agency to decide cases brought before its tribunals employing procedures substantially similar to those used in a court of law (Matter of Venes v. Community School Bd., 43 N.Y. 2d 520, 524; United States v. Utah Constr. Co., 384 US 394, 422; see, also, 2 Davis, Administrative Law, 3d ed., §§18.03, 18.08, 18.10; Restatement, Judgments 2d, §83, subd. [2], and Comment b). '[S]uch determinations, when final, become conclusive and binding on the courts' (Bernstein v. Birch Wathen School, 71 A.D. 2d 129, 132, aff'd 51 N.Y. 2d 932; see, also, Matter of Newsday Inc. v. Ross, 80 A.D. 2d 1, 5). . . .

In the application of collateral estoppel with respect to administrative determinations, the burden rests upon the proponent of collateral estoppel to demonstrate the identicality and decisiveness of the issue, while the burden rests upon the opponent to establish the absence of a full and fair opportunity to litigate the issue in prior action or proceeding (cf. Schwartz v. Public Administrator, [24 N.Y. 2d 65] supra, at p. 73; see, also B. R. Dewitt, Inc. v. Hall, 19 N.Y. 2d 141; compare Gramatan Home Investors Corp. v. Lopez [46 N.Y. 2d 481] supra, at p. 485). As we said in Schwartz, '[t]his apportionment of the burdens is both fair and necessary. Otherwise much of the value of collateral estoppel will be lost' (Id., at p. 73). Indeed, this apportionment accords, on the one hand, with the burden generally imposed on the moving party to make a prima facie demonstration of entitlement to summary judgment (see, e.g. Friends of Animals v. Associated Fur Mfrs., 46 N.Y. 2d 1965, 1067), and, on the other hand, with the burden placed on the opposing party to establish the necessity for a trial (Zuckerman v. City of New York, 49 N.Y. 2d 557, 562) or on any party attempting to rebut the presumptive regularity of prior judicial and administrative proceedings (see 21 NY Jur., Evidence, §§106, 108; 10 Carmody-Wait 2d, NY Prac., §§70:347; cf. People v. Harris, 61 N.Y. 2d 9, 16).

'Applying the foregoing rules of law to this case demonstrates clearly that collateral estoppel bars plaintiffs from litigating the subject claims. A comparison of the material issues raised in this action with those resolved by the prior administrative determination, and an examination of the prior proceeding itself show that both requisite criteria, the identicality and decisiveness of the issues and the opportunity for a full and fair hearing have been satisfied' (Ryan v. New York Tel Co., 62 N.Y. 2d 494, 499, 502, supra).

The holding of Ryan v. New York Tel Co. (supra) is clearly applicable to the case at bar.

The crucial issue in the prior administrative proceeding was whether the plaintiff was discharged by reason of certain specific misconduct arising out of the July 20, 1983, incident, as claimed by the defendant, and therefore not entitled to unemployment benefits. The administrative Law Judge specifically found, based on the credible evidence, that the plaintiff was not guilty of such misconduct as claimed by the defendant. That determination is conclusive between the parties to this action who appeared at the hearing before the Administrative Law Judge, and is dispositive of the defense of discharge for proper cause arising out of the July 20, 1983, incident, which the defendant now seeks to interpose in its late answer. Additionally, the record shows that the defendant had 'a full and fair opportunity at the prior administrative proceeding to litigate the question of [the plaintiff's] misconduct' and the defendant has 'failed to demonstrate otherwise' (Ryan v. New York Tel Co., supra, at p. 503). Therefore, defendant is precluded by the principle of collateral estoppel from defending the instant action based on the defense of discharge for proper cause arising out of the July 20, 1983, incident (see also, Samhammer v. Home Mut. Ins. Co. of Binghamton N.Y., A. D. 2d [33d Dept., Oct. 30, 1986])."

32. 514 NYS 2d 812 (Oct. 10, 1986).

33. Collateral estoppel as an aspect of the Fifth Amendment's double jeopardy prohibition, I find, is no more applicable to the case than is the prohibition itself. As noted previously, the allegations that were brought against Vera of arson and attempted arson are similar in certain respects. However, none of the factual elements that make up the charge of arson that is to be re-tried was decided by Vera's acquittal on the attempted arson charge. Unlike the situation in Ashe v. Swenson, the allegations against Vera have real differences, as opposed to mere logical ones. The testimony relating to Vera's identification as the perpetrator of the attempted arson on which he was acquitted is not determinative of the issue of his identification as the perpetrator of the earlier arson. Because collateral estoppel in its Fifth Amendment sense would not prevent prosecution of the arson charge nothing in the holding of Ashe v. Swenson would require the court to prohibit the prosecutor from introducing testimony relating to the attempted arson count at the re-trial of the arson charge.

The Common Law Doctrine of Collateral Estoppel

The doctrine of collateral estoppel is not restricted, of course, to the constitutional principle enunciated by the Supreme Court in Ashe v. Swenson. Collateral estoppel in its non-constitutional sense has its roots in common law. It has thus long been an important feature of the law of New York. It is often referred to as the doctrine of issue preclusion. (People ex rel. v. Dowdy v. Smith, 48 N.Y. 2d 477, 483 [1978]). Collateral estoppel prevents parties from repeatedly litigating issues of fact that already have been determined by a valid and final judgment that is binding upon them (Matter of McGrath v. Gold, 36 N.Y. 2d at 411). Although the common law doctrine of collateral estoppel originated in civil litigation, it is now 'well settled that [it] is applicable to criminal as well as civil matters' (People v. Berkowitz, 50 N.Y. 2d 333, 344 [1980]; see People v. Sailor, 65 N.Y. 2d 224, 228 [1985]).

A jury's verdict in a criminal case is incorporated in the court's judgment. It may, therefore, have a collateral estoppel effect in future cases between the same defendant and the state. A difficulty exists, however, in applying collateral estoppel on the basis of a jury's verdict in a criminal case due to the general nature of such verdicts. Often it is impossible to ascertain the exact import of an acquittal in a criminal trial (People v. Berkowitz, 50 N.Y. 2d at 346). In announcing a verdict, a jury typically states only that it has found the defendant guilty or not guilty. A jury in a criminal case in New York does not announce precisely what its specific finding may have been on any one of the several factual issues that it considered in the deliberative process.

Collateral estoppel may be properly invoked in a criminal case to preclude the relitigation of factual issues previously presented to a jury that returned a verdict of acquittal in favor of the defendant only if the record of the case firmly establishes that the jury must have based its verdict on that very issue (see People v. Rivera, 60 N.Y. 2d 110, 116 [1983]). Thus, a trial court in determining whether or not to apply collateral estoppel in a criminal case must review the entire record of the previous trial and decide whether a rational jury could have grounded its verdict upon an issue other than that which the defendant seeks to foreclose from consideration (see People v. Cornier, 42 Misc. 2d 963, 968; [Sup. Ct., 1984]). This is the procedure that the Supreme Court employed in Ashe v. Swenson when it ruled that collateral estoppel in its Fifth Amendment sense applied (397 U.S. at 444). The Supreme Court indicated that it had borrowed this procedure from criminal cases in which collateral estoppel was invoked as a doctrine of the common law. . . . "

34. 465 NYS2d 403 (1983).

35. 32 NY2d 300, 344 NYS2d 938 (1974).

36. Id.

37. See Gerney v. Tishman Realty Corp., supra note 26.

38. The court reasoned: "In *Kaufman v. Lilly & Co.*, supra, a civil action, we declined to apply issue preclusion based upon a liability determination made under the 'concerted action' theory against the defendant drug manufacturer in a prior action, because the applicability of the 'concerted action' theory had not been challenged and, thus, put in issue in the prior action. We held:

An issue is not actually litigated if, for example, there has been a default, a confession of liability, a failure to place a matter in issue by proper pleading or even because of a stipulation (*see*, Restatement [Second] of Judgments §27 comments d, e, at 255–257; *see also, Gilberg v. Barbieri*, 53 NY2d 285, supra. Because Lilly did not challenge the appropriateness of the concerted action theory in *Bichler*, it was not actually litigated and there is no identity between that issue in *Bichler* and here (*Kaufman v. Lilly & Co.*, 65 NY2d 449, 456, 457).' (Emphasis added.)

For a question to have been actually litigated so as to satisfy the identicality requirement under *Schwartz*, it must have been properly raised by the pleadings or otherwise placed in issue and actually determined in the prior proceeding. The rule is founded on considerations of fairness and recognizes that if preclusive effect were given to issues not truly adjudicated the result would be to discourage compromises and to accord them consequences which the parties neither intended nor foresaw (see, Restatement [Second] Judgments §27 comment d; *U.S. v. International Building Co.*, 345 US 502, 505; *Tutt v. Doby*, 459 F2d 1195, 1199; James, *Consent Judgments as Collateral Estoppel*, 108 U.Pa. L. Rev. 173–181; Rosenberg, supra, at 173). Application of the rule seems particularly appropriate in the circumstances here, where the judgment sought to be given preclusive effect is a consent order in an administrative proceeding which states, without elaboration, that the party being disciplined entered a plea of guilty. By signing the consent order in response to the 'Notice to Enter Plea,' the petitioner simply indicated that he did 'not wish to contest the charges stated, thus rendering unnecessary any hearing' and that he wanted to accept the minimal sanction that had been negotiated by counsel. Accordingly, the issue in question was neither argued, conceded nor even addressed in the New Jersey proceeding. It cannot fairly be said, therefore, that the issue was litigated or resolved in the prior action."

12

Bifurcation as a Preclusive Trial Technique

Bifurcation is the technique for simplifying and streamlining a trial when the trial court permits a separate trial of the issue of liability to be followed by a separate trial of the issue of damages. The multiplicity of parties, the complexity of scientific evidence, the novelty of some of the claims and defenses in cases—especially involving antitrust, securities, hazardous waste, and toxic torts—need for expedition, and economy of time have brought about the need for bifurcation.[1] Rule 42(b) of the Federal Rules of Civil Procedure provides that "the court, in furtherance of convenience or to avoid prejudice, or when separate trials will be conducive to expedition and economy, may order a separate trial of any claim, cross-claim, counterclaim, or third-party claim, or any separate issue or of any number of claims or issues, always preserving inviolate the right of trial by jury as declared by the Seventh Amendment to the Constitution or as given by statute of the United States."[2] Note that bifurcation did not exist as common law.[3]

Other grounds for granting a separate trial under Rule 42(b) include convenience, avoidance of prejudice,[4] or simply a class action where there are varying patterns of fact as to the issue of damages, for example, as shown in *Ellison v. Rock Hill Printing & Finishing Co.*[5] This was a class action for alleged deprivation of civil rights under 42 USC 1981 brought by black applicants, employees, and union members against an employer and certain unions.[6] Bifurcation was deemed necessary by the court in order to conserve judicial time! Although there were only 13 named representative plaintiffs, there were approximately 3,000 union members working at the employer's plant and this large number of employees was an indication that other claimants would soon come forward. The court observed that bifurcation would ease the caseload and require fewer judges: instead of spending ten weeks to hear the entire case, the court would hear the critical issue of liability in four weeks and refer the issue of damages, if necessary, to a special master for a second trial lasting less than six weeks!

In *Piva v. Xerox Corp.* the court ordered that the proceedings be bifurcated so that the court could first determine the issues of class liability and injunctive relief, and later determine the issue of back pay as to the class.[7] And in *EEOC v. Lucky Stores, Inc.*, the federal court in California pointed out that separating questions of liability from questions of individual relief, during the pretrial and trial phase, served to avoid unneccessary expenditure, not only of judicial time and labor, but more importantly, of attorney time and labor.[8] In *Love v. Pullman Co.* the defendant company, in opposing the bifurcation, argued that the question of damages was so intertwined with the question of liability that the two issues might not be tried separately without confusion and uncertainty amounting to a denial of a fair trial.[9] The court said that evidence relating to the fact of damage, as an element of liability for class-wide discrimination, and proof of individual claims did not overlap to any significant extent. The court explained that the essence of the claim was that maintenance of two job classifications—a porter-in-charge classification for black workers and a conductor classification for nonminority workers—had class-wide discriminatory effects, and thus, to establish liability, the employees had to prove that conductors, as a class, and porters-in-charge, as a class, received different compensation and benefits, and that such differences were not justified by functional differences between the two classifications. A racial disparity in compensation and benefits, the court said, might be characterized as the fact of damage, but, contrary to the company's contention, proof of this claim did not demand evidence of economic disparity as to each member of the plaintiff class; nor did it require evidence that accounted for all factual variations among the train ''runs'' that the company manned with porters-in-charge. The court stated that if it ordered bifurcation, and the employees failed to establish liability, lengthy discovery and complex evidentiary problems concerning individual membership in the class and individual damages would be unneccessary. The court disagreed with the company's contention that bifurcation would delay final disposition of the case, if liability were to be established. By limiting discovery to issues of liability, the court pointed out, the trial of those issues could be accelerated, and, then if liability was found, the parties could resume discovery on damages. The court also observed that separatiton for trial of the liability issues from the damages issues would cause no prejudice to the newspaper in its defense of the action.[10]

In *Lowe v. Philadelphia Newspapers, Inc.*, a black female employee alleged that she was denied promotion because of her race; the court stated that bifurcation would be inappropriate under Rule 24(b), and emphasized that the party seeking bifurcation has the burden of showing that bifurcation is proper in light of the general principle that a single trial tends to lessen the delay, expense, and inconvenience to all parties.[11] In opposing bifurcation the defendant newspaper pointed to the fact that bifurcation would cause numerous witnesses including physicians to be called twice to testify in both the liability and damages stages of the case. To the same effect was *In re Selcraig*, decided by the Fifth U.S. Court of Appeals; here a discharged school official sought to recover compensatory and punitive damages from a school district and two of its officers for publicizing false and stigmatizing charges against him.[12] The two officers disseminated the defamatory charges to a newspaper reporter. To protect the reporter's privilege was no ground for bifurcation, according to the court.

The decision to bifurcate rests in the sound discretion of the trial court, and bifurcation is permitted even over the objection of a party.[13] In *Gasoline Products Co., Inc. v. Champlin Refining Co.* the U.S. Supreme Court, more than 58 years ago, spelled out the standard for permissible bifurcation: "Where it clearly appears that the issue to be separately tried is so distinct and separable from the others that trial of it alone may be had without injustice."[14] In the instant case, bifurcation was not permitted because the question of damages was so intermeshed with the question of liability that the court experienced difficulty in achieving any bifurcation. It should be obvious that most plaintiffs oppose bifurcation because plaintiffs believe that trying liability and damages together will create sympathy for the injured plaintiff and sway a jury favorably.[15]

The Fifth U.S. Court of Appeals in the *Rosales* case took a bold step favoring bifurcation by holding the Rule 42(b) authorized bifurcation even in face of state law against bifurcation.[16] And in *Hannah v. Plumer* the U.S. Supreme Court ruled that federal procedural law controls over Texas procedural law that did not favor bifurcation.[17] However, in *Lowe v. Philadelphia Newspapers, Inc.*[18] the court refused to order bifurcation when the same witnesses were to testify on both issues of liability and of damages.[19]

When the issues of liability and of damages are bifurcated, the same jury may hear both phases of the trial, as was evident in *O'Donnell v. Watson Bros. Transporation Co.*[20] It is certainly less expensive than impaneling a new jury, but whether the same group of jurors can intelligently and fairly determine the complex issues of liability and of damages may be open to question. The same jury might well have tried the unbifurcated trial in the first place!

Opposition to bifurcation is seen in *Peasley v. Quinn*, were the Michigan Supreme Court noting the state rule based on Federal Rule 42(b) opined: "The showing of compelling necessity for separation under the circumstances, in the interest of convenience or the avoidance of prejudice, would have to be very strong to justify interference with a party's presentation of proofs in the customary fashion."[21] What the state court undoubtedly had in mind was the fact that in personal injury suits the issues of liability and damages may be so interwoven that it is difficult to separate the issues for purposes of bifurcation.[22]

The New York case of *Goldsmith v. Nightingale Restaurant Corp.* presented an unusual problem in bifurcated trials.[23] Here, in an action for personal injuries, the jury returned a verdict in favor of the plaintiff on the issue of liability.

During the damages portion of the bifurcated trial, one of the jurors became ill and was unable to continue her jury service. The court declared a mistrial on the issue of damages since no alternate jurors were available. But after the jury was discharged, one of the jurors informed the court that the jury had been split on the liability question and had formed an agreement to rule in plaintiff's favor as to liability but award only nominal damages. The court thereupon set aside the verdict in the liability portion of the bifurcated trial and restored the case to the calendar. The court found that the juror's testimony was credible and motivated solely by a desire to avoid an unjust result.

In general, a juror may not be heard to impeach the verdict of the jury on which he or she sat. The reasons for such a policy were stated by the United States Supreme Court in *McDonald v. Pless*, 238 U.S. 264 as follows (pp. 267–268):

> But let it once be established that verdicts solemnly made and publicly returned into court can be attacked and set aside on the testimony of those who took part in their publication and all verdicts could be, and many would be, followed by an inquiry in the hope of discovering something which might invalidate the finding. Jurors would be harassed and beset by the defeated party in an effort to secure from them evidence of facts which might establish misconduct sufficient to set aside a verdict. If evidence thus secured could be thus used, the result would be to make what was intended to be a private deliberation, the constant subject of public investigation; to the destruction of all frankness and freedom of discussion and conference.

Professors Wright and Miller, in their treatise, *Federal Practice and Procedure*, opined in 1971 that 79 percent of defendants win where liability is the sole issue for jury determination compared to a 42 percent defendant success rate when cases are tried considering both liability and damages issues.[24] It is argued that contemporaneous presentation of liability and damages evidence may prejudice a jury toward a finding of liability; second, separation of liability and damages issues precludes compromise verdicts, especially where proof of liability is weak but damages are extensive; and third, prejudicial evidence admissible for proof of one issue or claim but inadmissible to prove another, may come into evidence with limiting instructions if liability and damages are tried together. It is also contended that a separate trial for damages may decrease damage awards.[25]

A typical state statute might be New York CPL & R 603, which provides for severance and separate trials: "In furtherance of convenience or to avoid prejudice, the court may order a severance of claims, or may order a separate trial of any claim, or any separate issue. The court may order the trial of any claim or issue prior to the trial of others." In *Schwartz v. Binder*, the trial court had ordered a bifurcated trial, and the defendant received the verdict; upon appeal, the New York Appellate Division, 2d Dept., reversed and stated: "Separate trials on the issues of liability and damage should not be held where the nature of the injuries has an important bearing on the issue of liability (see *Culley v. City of New York*, 25 AD2d 519, 267 NYS2d 282). In order to establish liability under the circumstances of this case, it was necessary for the plaintiffs to offer medical evidence of the injuries and of the type of force necessary to cause those injuries. . . . ''[26]

NOTES

1. Note Allen v. United States, 588 F. Supp. 247 (Utah, 1984) which took 3 months and involved a 7000-page trial transcript and 54,000 pages of exhibits!
2. See Collins v. Metro-Goldwyn Pictures Corp., 106 F2d 83 (2d Cir., 1939) on background of Rule 42(b) of the Federal Rules of Civil Procedure (FRCP).
3. See Curry and Snider, ''Bifurcated Trials: How to Avoid Them and How to Win Them,'' Trial Mag. (March 1988) at 47 et seq. Also see 5 U. Ark. LR. L.J. 405 (1982).
4. Note In re Paris Air Crash, 69 FRD 310 (CD Cal., 1975).
5. 64 FRD 415 (S.C., 1974).
6. See 79 ALR Fed. 220.
7. 70 FRD 378 (ND Cal., 1975).
8. 37 FR Serv. 2d 333 (ED Cal., 1982).
9. 21 FR Serv. 2d 629 (Colo., 1975).
10. Supra note 6.
11. 594 F. Supp. 123 (ED Pa., 1984).
12. 705 F 2d 789 (5th Cir., 1983).
13. See Helminski v. Ayerst Laboratories, 765 F2d 208 (6th Cir., 1985) and Rosales v. Honda Motor Co., Ltd., 726 F2d 259 (5th Cir., 1984).
14. 283 US 494 (1930).
15. Supra note 3.
16. Supra note 3.
17. 85 S. Ct. 1136 (1965).
18. Supra note 11.
19. See Linder Steel Co. v. Wedemeyer, 585 F. Supp. 1530 (Md., 1984).
20. 183 F. Supp. 577 (ND Ill., 1960).
21. 128 NW2d 515 (Mich., 1964).
22. Note Brown v. General Motors Corp., 407 P2d 461 (Wash., 1965).
23. Unreported (New York County, April 19, 1988).
24. Section 2390 (1971).
25. Note 3A Personal Injury Evaluation Handbook No. 210 (1978) at 803.
26. 457 NYS2d 109 (1982).

13

The Summary Jury Trial

The summary jury trial, a brief and nonbinding trial by jury, is but one of several alternative dispute resolution methods that are now in active use.[1] The summary jury trial is designed to assist the courts and litigants who suffer delays from an overburdened judicial system.[2] The process seeks to reduce costs as a settlement tool, and at the same time seeks to give the parties a realistic perspective of the value of the case.[3] Rule 16(a)(5) of the Federal Rules of Civil Procedure permits a court to bring parties into court in order to facilitate "the settlement of the case," and Rule 16(d) permits a final pretrial conference, which presumably encompasses a summary and nonbinding advisory jury. The Third U.S. Court of Appeals in *Eash v. Riggins Trucking Co.* appears to have approved the summary jury trial process as an effort to reduce civil litigation and encourage settlements.[4]

The summary jury trial proceeds like an ordinary trial except for the lack of live witnesses; the presentation of evidence is given in narrative form so as to save the money and time of the court and the parties. It was Judge Thomas D. Lambros of the U.S. District Court for the Northern District of Ohio who developed the nonbinding technique in 1980.[5]

The tentative views favoring and rejecting the summary jury system can be summarized as follows:

PRO

- Parties must reveal more in a summary jury trial than in a pretrial conference.
- Parties who have done their homework are at a disadvantage where opponents are not prepared.
- Since the burden of proof is usually on a plaintiff and a defendant has only to sit back, the procedure gives a defendant two bites at the apple.

- The procedure gives parties "free" discovery that they might not otherwise receive.
- The procedure gives a cogent view of how a party will present a case, the techniques the opponent will use, and the style of presentation.
- A defendant is more likely to win than a plaintiff, and the verdict amount is likely to be smaller because a jury does not have to engage in the "leavening" process that is an inevitable part of a jury trial.

CON

- A defendant must prepare as much as the plaintiff for the summary jury trial, otherwise the plaintiff may receive a better verdict than he would at trial, thus forcing the defendant into a higher settlement position.
- Both sides must tip their hands so as not to come out with a bad result that would force a settlement on an unwilling party.
- Plaintiffs can get a good idea of how a defendant intends to defend the case and what points a defendant intends to stress.
- In the "tough" case, both plaintiff and defendant can weed out the unimportant or ineffective arguments and get a true feeling for the strongest aspect of the case.
- Both sides can try theories and arguments on the jury they would not be able to do as comfortably in a "real" trial.
- In limine rulings are quicker and more accurate, thus resolving issues that may assist in settlement.
- Clients feel they have had their day in court, which reduces the incentive to hold an unrealistic position.
- The court can get a better feel for the case and thus aid in further settlement negotiations.[6]

Advisory juries are authorized by many state statutes, like Section 4212 of New York Civil Practice Law & Rules,[7] but obviously such advisory juries do not allow for nonbinding verdicts and do not permit the totally abbreviated procedures inherent in summary jury trials.

NOTES

1. See generally Brand and Sogolow, "Summary Jury Trials—A Process Perspective," NYL (July 30, 1987) at 1 et seq.

2. Id. See *The Summary Jury Trial and Other Alternative Methods of Dispute Resolution: A Report to the Judicial Conference of the United States Committee on the Operation of the Jury System*, January 1984, Revised August 1986, by Judge Thomas D. Lambros, United States District Court, Northern District of Ohio, Cleveland, Ohio. See especially the section of selected articles, "The Untapped Resources of the Adversarial Process: How Summary Jury Trials Can Be Employed Most Effectively," by Thomas D. Lambros. Mary Gates, Clerk, Judge Lambros's Court, most kindly provided SJT reference materials. Also, she provided expert assistance and additional materials in response to our requests for information.

On the broader subject of ADR, see Peter S. Adler, "Is ADR a Social Movement," *Negotiation Journal* 3:1 (January 1987); Jonathan S. Marks, Earl Johnson, Jr., and Peter L. Stanton, *Dispute Resolution in America: Processes in Evolution*, National Institute for Dispute Resolution, 1984; and Michael F. Hoellering, "The Mini-Trial," *The Arbitration Journal*, 34:4 (December 1982). See also Judge Lambros' description of different ADR methods in the section of his *Report*, entitled "Alternative Dispute Resolution Techniques."

3. See generally Rieders, "Summary Jury Trials: A Settlement Technique," Trial Mag. (September 1987) at 93 et seq.

4. 757 F2d 557 (3d Cir., 1985).

5. Supra note 2.

6. Supra note 3.

7. *Rule 4212. Advisory jury; referee to report.*

Upon the motion of any party as provided in rule 4015 or on its initiative, the court may submit any issue of fact required to be decided by the court to an advisory jury or, upon a showing of some exceptional condition requiring it or in matters of account, to a referee to report. An order under this rule shall specify the issues to be submitted. The procedures to be followed in the use of an advisory jury shall be the same as those for a jury selected under article forty-one. Where no issues remain to be tried, the court shall render decision directing judgment in the action.

14

Court Sanctions for Nonpreclusion

TO ABBREVIATE OR SHORTEN THE TRIAL

It is abundantly clear that nonpreclusive actions by the parties to litigation, such as filing frivolous lawsuits or frivolous defenses, must be rigidly abated by the courts.[1] Sanctions imposed by courts for delaying tactics are indeed very popular today; in *Record Club of America, Inc. v. Credit Services, Inc.*,[2] the federal district court for the Southern District of New York imposed a $5,000 fine under Rule 11 of the Federal Rules of Civil Procedure against a lawyer who filed a fourth lawsuit on the same claim after three prior lawsuits had been dismissed.[3] Plaintiff's counsel, the wife of the president of plaintiff corporation, had argued that this fourth action was proper because the court's dismissal of the third action did not expressly provide that it was with prejudice. The court rebuked plaintiff's cousel in sharp language for making such an argument: the third action dismissal was based upon plaintiff's "affirmative misconduct in seeking to litigate a single claim against defendant simultaneously in several fora. . . . Plaintiff's counsel is either so ignorant of the Rules of this court or so deliberate in her disregard of the Rules that no useful purpose could be served in discussing her most recent conduct, which brings on defendant's motion to dismiss this latest duplicative action." The fine of $5,000 was accompanied by an order enjoining plaintiff corporation from instituting any further actions based upon the claim asserted in the complaint!

There can be no doubt that plaintiff's counsel's behavior simply did not help to abbreviate or shorten the trial. Sham litigation that both offends the judicial sense of fair play and obstructs the expedition of trial is delineated in the landmark case of *Western Railroad Presidents Conference v. Noerr Motor Freight, Inc.*[4] Here a group of railroad companies waged a successful publicity campaign aimed at influencing state legislators to adopt and retain laws detrimental to the trucking industry. The truckers retaliated by suing the railroads, alleging that railroads' activities violated Sections 1 and 2 of the Sherman Antitrust Act. But the highest court opined that a concerted effort to influence the passage or enforcement of laws is immune from the Sherman Act, regardless of any anticompetitive motive behind the effort. However, this antitrust immunity does not extend to sham activities, that is, activities that are designed "to interfere with the business relationships of a competitor."[5] More than 20 years later in *Grip-Pak, Inc. v. Illinois Tool Works* the Seventh U.S. Court of Appeals opined: "If all nonmalicious litigation were immunized from government regulation by the First Amendment, the tort of abuse of process would be unconstitutional—something that, so far as we know, no one believes. . . . If abuse of process is not constitutionally protected, no more should litigation that has an improper anticompetitive purpose be protected, even though the plaintiff has a colorable claim. . . . [I]t has long been thought that litigation could be used for improper purposes even where there is probable cause for litigation; and if the improper purpose is to use litigation as a tool for supressing competition in its antitrust sense, it becomes a matter of antitrust concern."[6] In short, meritorious claims might never be brought for their own sake if the stakes, discounted by the probability of winning, would be too low to repay the investment in litigation. Sham activities, however, must be curbed if the trial is to be abbreviated or shortened in the interests of justice and fair play.

In all these instances it is the lawyer who does the legal work that results in either the sham activity of the client or the improper legal activity. *In re Lawrence*, decided by the District of Columbia Court of Appeals, revealed that the proofs established that the respondent lawyer failed to file his client's federal employment discrimination claim in a timely manner.[7] The lawyer's defense was predicated upon Rule 11 of the Federal Rules of Civil Procedure, which prohibits a lawyer from signing and filing a complaint that is believed to be meritless. The lawyer asserted here that his client's case was not sufficiently grounded in law or fact, and that he was unable to file it. But the court disagreed with his view and suspended the lawyer for 90 days for his improper legal activity: if he honestly believed that filing his client's complaint violated Rule 11, he should have notified the client of his concerns, and the client would have hired another attorney or the lawyer could have withdrawn from the representation.[8]

This improper activity by a lawyer establishes the basis for legal malpractice in many instances. The American Bar Association's Committee on Lawyers' Professional Liability analyzed almost 30,000 insurance claims between 1981 and 1985 to profile legal malpractice claims, and found that 25.1% of these claims pertained to personal injury litigation, that almost 70% of those claims involved amounts less than $1,000, and that the lawyer with at least 10 years' experience was the most likely target of legal malpractice claims.[9]

SANCTIONS AGAINST ATTORNEYS

Sanctions by courts for nonpreclusive activities that result in prolonged and extensive litigation generally fall upon the shoulders of the attorneys. In *Zissu v. Bear, Stearns & Co.* the Second U.S. Court of Appeals affirmed a New York lawyer's liability for $550,000 in attorney's fees sustained by defendants in what was described by the court as a "frivolous" and "meritless" securities fraud.[10] It appears that the lawyer was also a principal in several corporations, that he had failed to produce evidence for many of his claims, that he testified contradictorily, and that the jury did not find his views credible. The court found expressly that "the record indicates that this lawsuit was both meritless and conducted in bad faith." He had invested $1.5 million in an oil and gas limited partnership after he realized that his taxable income was in excess of $600,000, and that he would need a tax shelter. When the investment soured, he brought suit alleging misstatements about the degree of risk in the drilling program. The case was "the prototype of a securities lawsuit brought in bad faith by a disappointed investor without an arguable right to relief."

Illustrative of the problem are the following recent cases:

1. *Unioil v. E. F. Hutton*, where the Ninth U.S. Court of Appeals upheld nearly $300,000 in sanctions against an attorney who failed to investigate adequately the truthfulness of allegations in a stockholder class action that he filed and who also ignored a potential conflict of interest in the case.[11] More specifically, the attorney failed to interview a named plaintiff in order to discover whether he was in fact representative of the class of shareholders. The court found that his arguments "were without basis and were made in bad faith."

2. *Eastway Construction Corp. v. City of New York*, where after considerable litigation over sanctions, attorneys' fees of $10,000 were assessed against the client and the lawyer, although the defendant had apparently expended more than $52,000 in defending the suit.[12] The plaintiffs had made civil rights and antitrust claims against the defendant City because of the City's policy of refusing to deal with plaintiffs on construction contracts. It was in June 1987 that the matter was finally settled, although the federal district court had first dismissed the baseless suit in 1984.

3. On the other hand, in *Photosound, Inc. v. Gourdine*, the New York Appellate Division, First Dept., determined that the trial court had exceeded its discretion by imposing a $2,000 sanction against a lawyer for "frivolous" motions to hold in contempt two assistant corporation counsels representing the City of New York.[13] The trial court had asserted that "the time has come for the bar to realize it cannot waste the time of the courts, fellow attorneys, and litigants with impunity."

4. In *International Shipping Co., S.A. v. Hydra Offshore, Inc.*, the court awarded defendant's counsel $10,000 in defending against a motion for a preliminary injunction because the court had concluded that plaintiff's counsel had

not conducted a most basic review of the applicable law, which would have compelled the conclusion that the federal court lacked subject-matter jurisdiction over the action: "It is elementary hornbook law that a contract for the sale of a vessel is not within the admiralty jurisdiction of the district courts."[14] Furthermore, diversity of citizenship did not exist where there are aliens on both sides. Here was "an egregious example of violation of the spirit and letter of Rule 11."

5. In *Nassau-Suffolk Ice Cream, Inc. v. Integrated Resources, Inc.*, the same federal district court refused to impose Rule 11 sanctions and criticized counsel who had brought the sanctions motion, suggesting that the movant had not fairly represented the record.[15] Previously, the court had sanctioned the plaintiffs for naming a corporation as a defendant without conducting a reasonable, prefiling investigation. According to the court,

> when the attorney can obtain the information necessary to certify the validity of the claim in public fashion and need not rely on the client, the lawyer is obligated to do so. To decide if the attorney may rely solely on the client, the lawyer should determine if knowledge thereof is direct or hearsay and check closely the plausibility of the clients' account. . . . When an attorney must rely on the client, the lawyer should question the client thoroughly, not accepting the client's version on faith alone. . . . However, if all the attorney has is the client's assurance that facts exist or do not exist, when a reasonable inquiry would reveal otherwise, the attorney has not satisfied the obligation of Rule 11. . . . [But] Rule 11 is a two-way instrument—it may not be employed for harassment of opponents on expurgated and questionable submissions based on deficiencies of disclosure or other impropriety.

6. In *Kamen v. American Telephone & Telegraph Co.*, the Second U.S. Court of Appeals reversed a $4,000 award to the defendant as a result of a sanction imposed for failure to make reasonable inquiry into the basis for a lawsuit.[16] Plaintiff had sued under the U.S. Rehabilitation Act and the New York Human Rights Law, claiming that she was covered as a person with a life-long history of severe tobacco smoke hypersensitivity and that the laws were violated when she was suspended from her job for insubordination because she sought medical aid from company doctors. The suit was dismissed because no federal funds had been received by defendant despite plaintiff's allegation to that effect. The appellate court found that plaintiff had provided information to her lawyers, who had sought relevant information within defendant's control but which information defendant refused to provide. The sanction by the trial court would stifle "the enthusiasm or chill the creativity that is the very lifeblood of the law."

7. In *Lopez v. Western Electric Co.* the federal district court in Denver, Colorado, called the employment discrimination suit involving a Hispanic "so totally lacking in merit as to be frivolous, groundless, and unreasonable," and ordered payment of attorneys' fees to the defendant.[17] In dismissing the suit

the court observed that "plaintiff's attorneys never contacted him to ask whether he was or was not an Anglo, even though the fact was critical to their prima facie case and had been represented to the court repeatedly. It seem inconceivable that the plaintiff's attorneys could have pursued this case for nearly two years without investigating and finding this out."

8. A $7,500 fine was imposed in *Four Keys v. Simithis* and unanimously upheld by the Second U.S. Court of Appeals: "A competent attorney, after reasonable inquiry into the applicable law and the facts and procedural history of this case, would have known that there was no justification whatever for removal of this action."[18]

9. In *Bannon v. Joyce Beverages, Inc.*,[19] alleging that defendant violated federal security laws and breached its fiduciary duty concerning the sale of plaintiff's shares of stock, plaintiff listed nine items of information that the defendant had allegedly misrepresented or had not disclosed to him when he made his decision to sell the stock.[20] In his deposition, however, plaintiff acknowledged only four misrepresentations and stated that he did not rely on them in deciding to sell his stock. Defendant moved for sanctions and the court granted the motion: "The most positive aspect of plaintiff's conduct is that counsel did not take action to amend the complaint long after the Bannon deposition occurred. . . . Attorneys who recognize (if belatedly) their duties under Rule 11 should not be penalized as harshly as those who never acknowledge the unreasonableness of their positions."

10. The case of *Fuji Photo Film, USA v. Aero Mayflower Transit* holds to the proposition that a lawyer filing an amended complaint but against the wrong defendant was subject to sanctions under Rule 11.[21] The attorney's "blind obstinacy in the face of overwhelming evidence that he was pursuing the wrong defendant is precisely the type of conduct that Rule 11 is designed to deter."

11. In *Dries & Krump Manufacturing Co. v. International Association of Machinists*,[22] the Seventh U.S. Court of Appeals emphasized the importance of imposing sanctions when Rule 11 violations occur: "Mounting federal caseloads and growing dissatisfaction with the costs and delays of litigation have made it imperative that the federal courts impose sanctions on persons and firms that abuse their right to access to these courts. The rules, whether statutory or judge-made, designed to discourage groundless litigation are being and will continue to be enforced in this circuit to the hilt—as a recital of opinions published by this court since the first of the year imposing sanctions for groundless litigation should make clear. . . . Lawyers practicing in the Seventh Circuit, take heed!"[23]

12. The federal district court in Colorado in *Wold v. Minerals Engineering Co.* imposed sanctions against counsel including the reasonable attorney's fees incurred by the plaintiffs in an effort to resist their disqualification: "No personal interviews of knowledgeable witnesses were conducted, and the limited telephone inquiries did not meaningfully address the relevant facts. MECO's attorney also received information which contradicted the assertions of their

motion and which, at the very least, should have put them on notice and given them reason to suspect the accuracy of their own factual assertions and cause them to be investigated further. [24]

13. On the other hand, "One reason for requiring the association of an attorney who is a member of the bar of this court . . . is to assure that standards of professional conduct will be met. . . . Accordingly, local counsel has an obligation to satisfy himself before signing a paper that it complies with applicable requirements. However, in the absence of an indication of active participation in the preparation or decision to file a paper by local counsel—of which there is none here—it does not seem appropriate to subject them to sanctions other than criticism for their apparent neglect," according to *Golden Eagle Distributing Co. v. Burroughs*.[25] Rule 11 sanctions were not imposed against local counsel, but sanctions were imposed against lead counsel who had accepted responsibility for the preparation of the motion.

14. In *Ford Piano Supply Co. v. Steinway & Sons*, plaintiff's counsel was sanctioned for failure to conduct a reasonable prefiling inquiry into the applicable antitrust law;[26] He failed to properly allege (a) relevant market, (b) joint conspiratorial activity concerning the alleged price-fixing, and (c) sufficient facts to show standing for a Robinson-Patman claim.[27]

There can be no doubt that imposing sanctions on lawyers in violation of Rule 11 does alter the balance between open access to courts and the efficient disposition of claims.[28] Open access to courts by simplified pleading is somewhat impeded by claims that would only waste the time and resources of courts and litigants.[29] To a great extent, courts have applied Rule 11 too broadly as a tool for docket management and have therefore somewhat undermined the value of open access to the courts. Of course, shotgun complaints or baseless pleadings should not be tolerated; the heat of battle provides no excuse for attorneys' unreasonable conduct. As the Seventh U.S. Court of Appeals in *Thornton v. Wahl* expressed it, "an empty head but a pure heart is no excuse."[30]

SANCTIONS AGAINST PLAINTIFFS AND PRO SE LITIGANTS

The pro se litigant (acting as an attorney) and the plaintiff have also been subjected to sanctions under Rule 11 of the Federal Rules of Civil Procedure, as is illustrated in *Bonheur v. Dresdner Bank A.B.* where the court assessed $500 in costs against the plaintiff for prosecuting a frivolous motion for partial summary judgment in a defamation suit.[31] The plaintiff bank officer was fired after he submitted false reimbursement vouchers, and he sued the bank claiming that the bank defamed him by disseminating a statement that he "tried to cheat"; he moved for partial summary judgment based upon a written decision in his state unemployment compensation hearing. But the court found that the motion was based upon a single sentence "taken totally out of context," and plaintiff's reliance on the phrase was "patently frivolous, and not well grounded in fact.'' In *Selbst v. Touche Ross & Co.* the court fined the plaintiff for continuing to claim that she was fired because of her pregnancy and not for cause; in her deposition she had conceded that the head of her department did not know of her pregnancy when he discharged her, but nevertheless plaintiff had ''resurrected'' the claim of pregnancy as a ''central theme'' of her case.[32] Plaintiff, according to the court, had ''no corroborating evidence and could point to no circumstances affording a guarantee of genuineness with regard to a claim of any damages for mental anguish. . . . Plaintiff's continued litigation of her claim was unreasonable and likely in bad faith.'' The Ninth U.S. Court of Appeals in *Hudson v. Moore Business Forms, Inc.* was irate over the ad damnum clause of $4.2 million punitive damages in a counterclaim, and the court ruled that the clause was frivolous and designed to harass the opposing party.[33]

The pro se litigant may be given ''one free bite,'' but sanctions under Rule 11 do apply to subsequent conduct.[34] In *Moss v. Air Products and Chemicals, Inc.*, the court imposed sanctions upon a pro se plaintiff for failing to conduct a reasonable inquiry as to whether his claim for age discrimination was well grounded in fact and warranted by existing law or was good faith argument for the extension, modification, or reversal of existing law.[35] The court pointed out that the New York State Divisison of Human Rights had previously issued a ''no probable cause'' determination clearly stating that the position plaintiff had applied for had been withdrawn by the employer. Nevertheless, plaintiff proceeded to bring this action ''apparently oblivious to the legal requirement that a plaintiff claiming age discrimination must be prepared to prove that a person outside the protective age group was awarded the position.'' According to the court, the pro se plaintiff ''considers himself a crusader, rather than a litigant seeking vindication for denial of his individual rights''; and that his submissions ''when not outrightly bombastic, take on the tone of political tracts, rather than of legal memoranda.'' And in *Rivera v. Simmons* the court warned a pro se plaintiff that if he failed to comply with the court's prior orders compelling him to answer defendant's interrogatories, the court would dismiss the complaint.[36] Plaintiff supplied answers to only 19 of 45 interrogatories (only 13 were full answers), and court responded: ''plaintiff's repeated failure to comply with defendants' discovery request of the Court's orders demonstrates manifest bad faith. . . . Plaintiff's conduct—such as his refusal to respond to questions seeking background information, references to medical records which he has never provided to defendants, evasive answers promising future responses, and his failure to respond to the instant motion—demonstrates not a lack of understanding, but a deliberate attempt to frustrate this litigation.''

A New York City businessman was assessed $44,017.20 in counsel fees for ''misconduct'' in interposing ''entirely baseless'' defenses to a contractor's suit to recover $40,000 for unpaid labor and materials. In *H & W Construction Co. v. Wetenhall* the court determined that the defense ''had not the slightest color of merit . . . it was interposed exclusively for purposes of delay and harassment. The presentation of this defense culminated in the opinion testimony at trial . . . [which] was based upon such a complete lack of knowledge of the facts as to be worthless in almost all respects. Lest there be any misunderstanding, this is not a situation in which a party is misled by an expert but a situation where a party contrives to introduce testimony which is patently baseless.''[37] On the other hand, the Second U.S. Court of Appeals in *Brown v. Capitol Air, Inc.* took a different view of the need for sanctions: here plaintiff was removed from an airplane for drinking alcohol other than that served by the airline in violation of FAA regulations and for shouting obscene language.[38] She filed suit in state courts alleging false imprisonment and slander, and after her second state suit was removed to the federal court where it was dismissed, the defendant appealed for failure of the court to impose sanctions against plaintiff for bringing superfluous suits. But the federal appellate court opined: ''It would be counterproductive to allow Capitol to recover sanctions from plaintiff for the largely superfluous proceedings in the federal court. One purpose of the Rule is to bring about economies in the use of judicial resources. Imposition of sanctions in these circumstances would reward one who caused diseconomies. Capitol had a legal right to remove the second case but no right to profit from that act under Rule 11.''[39] In sharp contrast thereto is *Perez v. Velez*, where the court readily permitted to engage with impunity to conduct of egregious professional irresponsibility simply because the frivolous lawsuits they sponsor are in this sensitive civil rights area. Our responsibility is to take needed punitive action against irresponsible and unprofessional conduct without doing damage to the underlying cause of equal rights which the attorney has ill-served.''[40]

FRIVOLOUS APPEALS

Frivolous appeals[41] are also subject to sanctions, although the U.S. Supreme Court's caveat in *Anders v. California*[42] must be heeded: there the court sought to ensure that indigent defendants have the same rights and opportunities on appeal as defendants who have the financial means to hire the lawyer of their choice; if the court-appointed lawyer wants to withdraw on the grounds that the client's appeal is frivolous, he or she must include ''a brief referring to everything in the record that might arguably support the appeal.''[43] In 1988 the highest court gave added support to that view in *McCoy v. Wisconsin Court of Appeals* by requiring the court-appointed counsel on the appeal issue to explain also why those issues lack merit: ''If an attorney can advise the court of his or her conclusion that an appeal is frivolous without impairment of the client's fundamental rights, it must follow that no constitutional deprivation occurs when the attorney explains the basis for that conclusion.''[44] The dissent of Mr. Justice Brennan observed that ''there is no more reason to command defense counsel to refute defense arguments they deem frivolous than there is to force them to refute their own arguments on the merits of nonfrivolous appeals. In either situation, the State has a corps of lawyers ready and able to perform that task.''

On the other hand, it should be noted that bankruptcy judges and federal district court judges cannot fine a party for a frivolous appeal, according to *In re Emergency Beacon Corp.*[45]

SANCTIONS AND THE STATE COURTS

State courts like federal courts have placed sanctions on nonpreclusion activities of attorneys and their clients. The New York Court of Appeals in *A.G. Ship Maintenance Corp. v. Lezak*[46] held that the state court system has the power to fashion a rule imposing costs and money sanctions, including attorneys' fees, for frivolous litigation practices upon the parties and upon their attorneys.[47] As the court declared:

> It is not necessary to determine whether the power of the courts to impose sanctions for frivolous proceedings is inherent to the judicial functions or is merely delegable by the Legislature under our Constitution. The fact is that the most practicable means for establishing appropriate standards and procedures which will provide an effective tool for dealing with this problem is by plenary rule rather than by ad hoc judicial decisions. Thus in the case now before us sanctions cannot be imposed because at the time the petitioner instituted the proceeding, there was neither a statute nor a court rule authorizing the imposition of sanctions for frivolous actions.

The implementation of that ''power'' is seen in the Proposed Rules,[48] which set forth financial sanctions in New York up to $10,000 against attorneys and/or litigants.[49]

The bold attitude of New York courts is seen in the recent case of *England v. Gradowitz Brothers Realty Corp.*, where the court demonstrated its growing impatience with frivolous motions.[50] Here the court imposed a penalty of $250 on the plaintiff for moving for summary judgment in a slip-and-fall case in which plaintiff had presented no evidence and had conducted no discovery to substantiate the claim. The court admonished that here was ''a wasteful misuse and a burden on judicial resources as well as clerical back-up support.''

In the Texas case of *Smith International Inc. v. Texas Commerce Bank National Assn.*, the federal district court assessed nearly $250,000 in penalties againist the plaintiffs and their lawyers.[51] It appears that plaintiffs had compounded the wrong by injecting a racketeering allegation in the lawsuit, which plaintiffs ''could never have established that they suffered any loss in view of the fact that they exchanged worthless debt for a worthless promissory note.''

In *United States v. Klubock* a federal judge in Massachusetts upheld a Commonwealth disciplinary rule that would make it ''unprofessional conduct'' for prosecutors to serve grand jury subpoenas on lawyers without prior court approval.[52] And in Illinois, in *Bernier v. Burris*, the court struck down as unconstitutional the use of pretrial screening panels to weed out allegedly frivolous medical malpractice suits.[53]

SANCTIONS AND ARBITRATION

Admittedly, one of the primary purposes of arbitration is to provide a prompt and economic means of dispute resolution, but on occasion arbitration may be subjected to frivolity. Such conduct delays and disrupts the arbitration process, as illustrated in *Glyfada Seafaring Corp. v. Fillmore Shipping, Ltd.*[54] Here plaintiff sought to confirm an arbitration award and the federal district court sanctioned counsel for violation of Rule 11 for the pursuit of frivolous defenses to the arbitratiton. In *First Investors Corp. v. American Capital Financial Services, Inc.* the Ninth U.S. Court of Appeals held that the trial court had properly ordered arbitration and rejected plaintiff's position that only the member that brings the claim may invoke the arbitration provisions.[55] The court held that the appeal therefrom was frivolous because it "ignores clear precedent and defies the strong federal policy favoring arbitration in challenging a duty to arbitrate. . . . In bringing this appeal, plaintiff has caused . . . needless expense and delay, thereby defeating the very purpose of the arbitration agreement. . . ."

And in *Pallante v. Paine Webber Jackson and Curtis*, in granting defendant's motion for costs pursuant to Rule 11, a federal district court opined: "[a]ny experienced attorney in securities law must have known that this case arose out of the same factual predicate as plaintiff's earlier arbitration proceeding and therefore was meritless. While the plaintiffs themselves may have been unable to judge the clear impropriety of this suit, their counsel, who has had years of experience in this field, must have known not to pursue this litigation."[56]

NOTES

1. See Warren Freedman, Frivolous Lawsuits and Frivolous Defenses (1987).
2. 117 FRD 359 (SDNY, 1987).
3. Note that the third lawsuit had resulted in a fine of $2,000.
4. 365 US 127 (1961).
5. Id. at 145.
6. 694 F2d 466 (7th Cir., 1982), cert. den. 461 US 958 (1983).
7. Unreported (DC App., 1987).
8. Note DR 2–110(C)(1)(a) of the Code of Professional Responsibilty.
9. See ABAJ (April 1, 1986) at 25.
10. 805 F2d 75 (2d Cir., 1986). See NLJ (Dec. 8, 1986) at 3, ad NYLJ (Nov. 14, 1986) at 1 and 2.
11. 802 F2d 1080 (9th Cir., 1986).

12. 821 F2d 121 (2d Cir., 1987). Previous cases are reported at 637 F. Supp. 559 (EDNY, 1986) and 762 F2d 243 (2d Cir., 1985).
13. 499 NYS2d 751 (AD 1st Dept., 1986).
14. 675 F. Supp. 146 (SDNY, 1987).
15. 662 F. Supp. 1499 (SDNY, 1987).
16. Unreported (2d Cir., 1987).
17. Unreported (Col., 1986).
18. Unreported (SDNY, 1988), aff'd (2d Cir., 1988).
19. 113 FRD 669 (ND Ill., 1987).
20. See Trial Mag. (July 1987) at 91 et seq.
21. 112 FRD 664 (SDNY, 1986).
22. 802 F2d 247 (7th Cir., 1986).
23. Id. at 255. Also note Larimore, "Judicial Sanctions Under Federal Rule 11," For the Defense (March 1987) at 17 et seq.
24. 575 F. Supp. 166 (Colo., 1983).
25. 103 FRD 124 (ND Cal., 1984), rev'd on other grounds 801 F2d 1531 (9th Cir., 1986).
26. 1988 U.S. Dist. LEXIS 523 (SDNY, 1988).
27. Plaintiff's counsel had stated: "I agree with your honor that the law in this would be of greater interest, and I believe that we would unfortunately have to do a review of cases, but I feel very confident that we would find many instances where a unique product market was found on those bases, design, competition, and workmanship."
28. See Warren Freedman, The Right to a Speedy and Fair Trial (1988).
29. See generally 100 Harv. L. Rev. 630 (1987).
30. 787 F2d 1151 (7th Cir., 1986).
31. Unreported (SDNY, 1988).
32. 116 FRD 665 (SDNY, 1987).
33. 827 F2d 450 (9th Cir., 1987).
34. Note Taylor v. Prudential-Bache Securities, Inc., 39 Fed. Serv. 2d 1309 (NDNY, 1984); also ABAJ (Aug. 1, 1987) at 87 et seq.
35. Unreported (SDNY, 1988).
36. 116 FRD 593 (SDNY, 1987).
37. No. 84 Civ 3690 (SDNY, 1986).
38. 797 F2d 106 (2d Cir., 1986).
39. According to the court, "Rule 11 of course, does not purport to authorize sanctions for actions taken in state courts. It does, however, apply to proceedings following removal, Fed. R. Civ. P. 81(c), see *Hanna v. Plumer*, 380 U.S. 460 (1956), and sanctions may be imposed in appropriate circumstances for post-removal proceedings in the federal court. Capitol thus also argues that it is entitled to sanctions for the actions it had to take to dispose of this matter after removal.

We may assume *arguendo* that plaintiff's defense of her claim in federal court would justify sanctions under Rule 11, as not based on a reasonable belief that it was 'well grounded in fact and [was] warranted by existing law or a good faith argument for the extension, modification, or reversal of existing law . . . ' Fed. R. Civ. P. 11. Even on that assumption, however, we do not believe that Capitol is entitled to sanctions under the unique circumstances of this case. The present action added only variations on legal themes to the action already pending in the state court, and, when consolidated with the latter, would not have required substantial additional resources to litigate. By failing to remove the first case and then removing the second, Capitol bifurcated this essentially unitary claim and effectively increased the costs of this litigation for itself, its adversary, and the courts."

40. 629 F. Supp. 734 (SDNY, 1986).
41. Supra note 1 at Section 1.3.
42. 386 US 739 (1967).
43. Note NLJ (June 20, 1988) at 5.
44. Unreported (June 6, 1988).
45. 790 F2d 285 (2d Cir., 1986); see 27 BR 757, 40 BR 113, 52 BR 979 and 71 BR 117.
46. 69 NY2d 1, 511 NYS2d 216 (1986).
47. See Note NYLJ (Sept. 28, 1987) at S23.
48. "Text of Proposed Rules

Part 37 Award of Costs and Imposition of Financial Sanctions for Frivolous Conduct in Civil Litigation.

Section 37.1 Rules of the Chief Administrator of the Courts.

(a) The Chief Administrator of the Courts, with the advice and consent of the Administrative Board of the Court, shall adopt rules, applicable to all civil actions and proceedings in any trial or appellate court in the Unified Court System, providing for the award of costs, including reasonable attorney's fees, or the imposition of financial sanctions, or both, for frivolous conduct in litigation by any party or attorney.
(b) The rules shall include:
   (1) a definition of frivolous conduct;
   (2) a provision that the awarding of costs and imposition of financial sanctions by a court may be upon motion by any party or upon the court's own initiative;
   (3) a maximum monetary limit on costs and sanctions in any action or proceeding;
   (4) the opportunity to be heard before costs or sanctions are awarded; and
   (5) a requirement that reasons for the award of costs or imposition of sanctions be set forth in writing.
(c) The rules also may provide that, as appropriate, financial sanctions may be made payable to the Client's Security Fund established pursuant to §97–t of the State Finance Law or payable to the court.

Part 130 Award of Costs and Imposition of Financial Sanctions for Frivolous Conduct in Civil Litigation.

Section 130.1 Costs; sanctions.

(a) The court, in its discretion, may award to any party or attorney in any civil action or proceeding before the court costs in the form of reimbursement for actual expenses reasonably incurred and reasonable attorney's fees, resulting from frivolous conduct as defined in this Part. In addition to or in lieu of awarding costs, the court, in its discretion, may impose financial sanctions upon any party or attorney in a civil action or proceeding who engages in frivolous conduct as defined in this Part, which shall be payable as provided in §130.3 of this Part.

(b) The court, as appropriate, may make such award of costs or impose such financial sanctions against either an attorney or a party to the litigation. The award or sanctions may be imposed upon any attorney appearing in the action or upon a partnership, firm or corporation with which the attorney is associated.

(c) For purposes of this Part, conduct is frivolous if: (i) it is completely without merit in law or fact and cannot be supported by a reasonable argument for an extension, modification or reversal of existing law; or (ii) it is undertaken primarily to delay or prolong the resolution of the litigation, or to harass or maliciously injure another.

In determining whether the conduct undertaken was frivolous, the court shall consider, among other issues, (1) the circumstances under which the conduct took place, including the time available for investigating the legal or factual basis of the conduct; and (2) whether or not the conduct was continued when its lack of legal or factual basis was apparent or should have been apparent to counsel.

(d) An award of costs or the imposition of sanctions may be made upon motion in compliance with CPLR 2214 or upon the court's own initiative, after a reasonable opportunity to be heard. The form of the hearing shall depend upon the nature of the conduct and the totality of circumstances of the case.

Section 130.2 Order awarding costs or imposing sanctions.

The court may make an award of costs or impose sanctions only upon a written memorandum decision setting forth the conduct on which the award or imposition is based and the reasons why the court found the conduct to be frivolous. An award of costs or the imposition of sanctions shall be entered as a judgment of the court. In no event shall the total amount of costs awarded and sanctions imposed exceed $10,000 in any action or proceeding.

Section 130.3 Payment of sanctions.

Payments of sanctions by an attorney shall be deposited with the Clients' Security Fund established pursuant to §97–t of the State Finance Law. Payments of sanctions by a party who is not an attorney shall be deposited with the clerk of the court for transmittal to the State Commissioner of Taxation and Finance, with respect to all courts other than town and village courts, and to the Bureau of Justice Court Fund in the Office of the State Comptroller, with respect to town and village courts, and to the Bureau of Justice Court Fund in the Office of the State Comptroller, with respect to town and village courts."

49. The Proposed Rules in 1987 became Part 37 of the Rules of the Chief Judge of the State of New York and Part 130 of the Rules of the Chief Administrator of the Courts of the State of New York.

50. 519 NYS2d 784 (Bronx County, 1987). Note New York Assembly Bill No. 8193–A dated June 11, 1987.

51. 643 F. Supp. 14 (WD Tex., 1987).

52. 639 F. Supp. 117 (Mass., 1986).

53. Unreported (Ill., 1986).

54. 1988 U.S. Dist. LEXIS 6808 (SDNY, 1987).

55. 823 F2d 307 (9th Cir., 1987).

56. No. 84 CIV. 5761 (SDNY, 1985).

15

Addenda

PART ONE

The U.S. Supreme Court's decisive 1986 opinion in *Matsushita Electric Industrial Co. v. Zenith Radio Corp.*[1] altered the standards for summary judgment as well as the nature and type of evidence that is required to prove an antitrust conspiracy.[2] The highest court required the nonmoving antitrust plaintiff to establish that there is "a genuine issue of material fact as to whether petitioners entered into an illegal conspiracy that caused plaintiff to suffer cognizable injury. . . . If the factual context renders respondents' claim implausible, if the claim is one that simply makes no economic sense, respondents must come forward with more persuasive evidence to support their claim than would otherwise be necessary." Subsequently on December 28, 1988, the federal district court in Texas required the feeders to produce evidence tending to exclude the possibility of independent action by the defendant packers, following the holding in the *Matsushita* case.[3] The court found an absence of a plausible motive for the scheme described by the plaintiff! Another recent example, *Turner v. Johnson & Johnson*, arose from the purchase by the defendant of the plaintiff's business of manufacturing electronic clinical thermometers.[4] The federal district court in Massachusetts applied the *Matsushita* standard that "if the factual context makes an inference of fraud economically implausible, then the plaintiffs must come forward with more persuasive evidence to support their claim than would otherwise be necessary."[5] Despite the economic implausibility of plaintiff's fraud theory, however, the court was unwilling to grant summary judgment on the issue of fraudulent intent primarily because "defendant's secretive behavior was very peculiar, all the more so because apparently contrary to its economic interest."[6]

In the recent New York case of *Raynes v. Pepitone*, the plaintiff real estate broker agreed to act as a marketing and sales agent to be paid on commission and subsequently sought summary judgment for the commission due.[7] Defendant employer argued that plaintiff did not fulfill his marketing obligations and was not entitled to any commission. The court denied the motion for summary judgment, holding that the plaintiff's marketing obligations surpassed those of a broker entitled to commissions merely for producing buyers; furthermore, factual issues existed as to whether the plaintiff breached those marketing obligations. A second motion for renewal of the motion for summary judgment was denied in *Weiss v. G & S Management Corp.* because the mover of the motion did not produce any newly discovered evidence: "Absent something new, the earlier motion ought to be held to preclude a second motion, at the behest of the same party, on a fact situation not shown to have materially changed. Any other conclusion would usually have the effect of frustrating the earlier disposition."[8]

In *Key International Manufacturing, Inc. v. Morse/Diesel, Inc.*,[9] the New York Appellate Division, Second Dept., ruled that factual issues precluded summary judgment: "The awarding of summary judgment to the respondents was unwarranted. . . . [T]riable issues of fact exist as to whether Key may sue to enforce the contracts between Key Land and the respondents based on its status as a third party beneficiary."[10]

(See Chapters 2 and 3).

PART TWO

On the appealability of the summary judgment motion, it would appear that New York courts deem an order granting a motion for summary judgment to be final and not reviewable on an appeal from the final judgment.[11]

In *Metz v. City of New York* the federal district court for the Southern District of New York opined that an order adjourning the motion for summary judgment to permit the continuance of discovery was simply not appropriate.[12]

(See Chapter 1).

PART THREE

In *Dodd Mead & Co. v. Metro Services, Inc.*, the respondent contracted to provide fulfillment services for petitioner publisher.[13] While a payment dispute stayed arbitration, petitioner sought a preliminary injunction barring the respondent from discontinuing services, claiming irreparable injury because the respondent controlled its inventory and accounts receivable. But the New York court denied the injunction, holding that, because the injunction was sought in aid of arbitration, the usual test was inapplicable; the key issue was whether the arbitration award could be "rendered ineffectual without such provisional relief." The court explained:

There is a factual issue whether the denial of relief would render an award ineffectual based upon the conflicting papers submitted. It has not been established that petitioner's business would cease to function if the respondent suspended work. More fundamental is the fact that part payment of the amount allegedly due would obviate any alleged harsh result. Injunctions are rarely granted in breach of contract actions particularly when it would amount to a mandatory injunction forcing the respondent to work. The movant is in a position to prevent any disruption of services by making part payment of $108,000. There is little difference between granting or denying the injunction since in either event the petitioner is essentially posting an undertaking which maintains the status quo.

Any application to expedite the arbitration process should be directed to the AAA which entertains this type of application upon good cause shown.

(See Chapter 6).

PART FOUR

The New York Court of Appeals in *Wells v. Shearson Lehman* gave a liberal construction to the wording of a release so that defendants (who were not parties to a previous lawsuit that produced the release) were nevertheless released by the terms of the document, which named the parties, their agents, and representatives "or anyone else."[14] The highest New York court opined as follows:

The plain meaning of the statute is that a release must expressly indicate that it discharges parties in addition to those who contracted for the release. The reading urged by the plaintiff would make it impossible for a claimant conclusively to release all tortfeasors, and have an end to a dispute, if any of them remained unknown. . . . This case . . . cannot be analogized to all-inclusive boilerplate language found in printed release forms terminating personal injury actions as to unknown third parties, where the result might be different. But where, as here, the parties sought to be included under "anyone else" are clearly connected to the events in issue, holding them not covered "would be tantamount to the adoption of an inflexible rule that every release must invariably specify every party to be discharged or the transaction will be at risk of later unraveling."

NOTES

1. 106 S. Ct. 1348 (1986).
2. See generally Stoll and Goldfein, "Summary-Judgment Summary," NYLJ (Jan. 18, 1989) at 3 and 7.
3. In re Beef Industry Antitrust Litigation, MDL Docket No. 248 (SD Texas, 1988).
4. 688 F. Supp. 806 (Mass., 1988).
5. Id. at 808.
6. Id. at 809.

7. Unreported (New York County, Jan. 20, 1989).

8. Unreported (Queens County, Aug. 3, 1988).

9. Unreported (App. Div., 2d Dept., Dec. 30, 1988).

10. "In light of controlling precedent . . . the owner of a construction project may not recover compensation for economic damages caused by the negligence of an architect or engineer with whom it is not in privity of contract. This rule is analogous to the well-settled rule that the manufacturer of a product may not be held liable to a party with whom it is not in privity for economic losses suffered as a result of a defect in the product.

In the area of products liability, the majority rule, as reflected in the seminal case of *Seely v. White Motor Co.* (63 Cal 2d 9, 403 P2d 145), has always been that a product owner has no tort remedy for economic losses, as distinguished from personal injury or property damage, against a product manufacturer. An owner of a product who suffers economic loss is limited to whatever remedy the owner may have in contract. This rule has recently been embraced by the Supreme Court of the United States as an aspect of general maritime law (see, *East River S.S. Corp. v. Transamerica Delaval*, 476 US 858). As discussed in these cases, the rationale for this rule is based upon the perception that to allow tort recovery in the absence of privity for economic losses would virtually negate the law of warranty, as codified in the provisions of the Uniform Commercial Code. Those courts which have adopted the majority rule have done so based on 'the need to keep products liability and contract law in separate spheres and to maintain a realistic limitation on damages' (*East River S.S. Corp. v. Transamerica Delaval*, supra, at 870–871; see also, *Moorman Mfg. Co. v. National Tank Co.*, 90 Ill 2d 69, 435 NE2d 443). It is thought that abandonment of the doctrine of privity in cases of economic loss would cause 'contract law [to] drown in a sea of tort' (*East River S.S. v. Transamerica Delaval*, supra, at 866)."

11. Crystal v. Manes, 516 NYS2d 823 (App. Div., 4th Dept., 1987). See generally Barker, "Summary Judgment and 'Release,' " NYLJ (Oct. 24, 1988) at 3 and 4.

12. Unreported (SDNY, July 25, 1988).

13. Unreported (New York County, Feb. 17, 1989).

14. 530 NYS2d 517 (1988).

Table of Cases

Index

About the Author

WARREN FREEDMAN was formerly Liability Counsel and Assistant Secretary for Bristol-Myers Co. Among his previous books are *Foreign Plaintiffs in Products Liability Actions*, *Frivolous Lawsuits and Frivolous Defenses*, *Federal Statutes on Environmental Protection*, *The Right of Privacy in the Computer Age*, *The Tort of Discovery Abuse,* and the *Constitutional Right to a Fair and Speedy Trial*, all published by Quorum Books.